D0778951

Lithuania Awakening

Lithuania Awakening

Alfred Erich Senn

UNIVERSITY OF CALIFORNIA PRESS
BERKELEY LOS ANGELES OXFORD

University of California Press
Berkeley and Los Angeles, California

University of California Press
Oxford, England

Copyright © 1990 by
The Regents of the University of California

Library of Congress Cataloging-in-Publication Data
Senn, Alfred Erich.
    Lithuania awakening
  Alfred Erich Senn.
        p.   cm.—(Society and Culture in East-Central Europe; 4)
      ISBN 0–520–07170–0 (alk. paper)
      1. Lithuania—History—1918–1945. 2. Lithuania—History—1945–
  3. Nationalism—Lithuania—History—20th century. I. Title.
  DK505.74.S46   1990
  947'.5084—dc20   90–32503
                                                                            CIP

Printed in the United States of America

1   2   3   4   5   6   7   8   9

The paper used in this publication meets the minimum requirements of
American National Standard for Information Sciences—Permanence of
Paper for Printed Library Materials, ANSI Z39.48–1984 ∞

Contents

Introduction

August 23, 1988. Streams of people were flowing into Vingis Park on the west side of Vilnius, the capital of the Lithuanian Soviet Socialist Republic, for a massive commemoration of the Non-Aggression Pact between Nazi Germany and the Soviet Union, signed on August 23, 1939. We all realized that this would be a momentous occasion, a memorial to the fate that the Nazi-Soviet pact had forced on Lithuania. A secret protocol to that pact had divided up Eastern Europe between the two parties "in the event of territorial and political rearrangement"; a week later, on September 1, 1939, German troops invaded Poland. In October 1939 the Soviet Union forced the three Baltic states of Lithuania, Latvia, and Estonia to accept Soviet troops within their frontiers. In the summer of 1940, under pressure from Moscow, the three republics installed new governments that quickly led them into the Soviet state as the fourteenth, fifteenth, and sixteenth members of the Union of Soviet Socialist Republics.

On this evening, August 23, 1988, an estimated 150,000 to 200,000 people, perhaps 4 to 5 percent of all the people in the world who speak Lithuanian, assembled in the park to discuss the unmentionable, to push the boundaries of their own consciousness; they came to reclaim their history. A week earlier it had not even been clear that this meeting would take place; now Lithuanians seemed incapable of thinking of anything else. In Klaipeda, the Lithuanian rock group Antis, known for its political themes, canceled its scheduled concert. Lithuanians wanted to discuss how their land had become a part of the Soviet Union.

The sponsor of the meeting, *Lietuvos persitvarkymo sajudis* (officially translated into English as: "Lithuanian Reform Movement 'Sajudis'"), had come onto the Lithuanian scene less than three months earlier. Made up mainly of intellectuals, the group had become a major force in contemporary Lithuania, and this evening it was challenging some of the fundamental concepts of Soviet Lithuania's past which the historical establishment had worked so assiduously to inculcate into the nation's memory. The demolition job proved to be remarkably easy.

The Soviet historian Mikhail Pokrovsky had spoken of history as politics projected on the past but, in the Lithuania of 1988, history constituted the essence of contemporary politics. The Lithuanians were rebelling, and history stood in the forefront of their thoughts. The commemoration of historical events released feelings long suppressed and almost forgotten but now revealed to be so strong that the Lithuanians surprised even themselves.

Discussions focused on the history of Lithuania from 1918 to 1940, the lifespan of the independent Lithuanian state. Between the two World Wars Lithuania had been a member of the League of Nations and had even participated in the Olympic Games. Since World War II, by contrast, Lithuania had been a part of the Soviet Union. The question was, where was one to find the "true Lithuania"? In the period of independence or in the period of Soviet rule? From this question arose the astonishing course of Lithuanian history in 1988.

In 1988 Soviet Lithuanian historians, the official caretakers of the people's collective memory, found themselves in an embarrassing position. In an era when the central authorities in Moscow, led by Mikhail Gorbachev, were talking of the dismantling of the "command-administrative system" that had dominated Soviet life since Stalin's time, the historical profession remained one of the most vivid examples of that system. Historians had long made their livings by producing on order and by repeating established truths. Gorbachev had demonstrated his own dissatisfaction with the state of historical writing by abolishing school examinations in the subject in the spring of 1988. In Lithuania the distrust of the establishment's history ran even deeper than it did in Moscow. Not only did the historians have to respond to criticisms from on high; they now suddenly learned that their readers had long distrusted them.

Since World War II, Soviet Lithuanian historians had formulated a comprehensive intepretation of the nation's history. In 1953 Romas Šarmaitis took the lead with his essay *Some Questions of the History of the Lithuanian National Liberation Movement in the Second Half of the Nineteenth Century,* in which he declared that the class struggle in Lithuania had always taken precedence over national questions and that the "bourgeoisie" had always chosen their class interests over any considerations of national liberation. The period of independence, 1918–1940, was notable only for the ruthless exploitation of the toiling masses and for the stagnation of Lithuanian culture. Antanas Smetona's authoritarian rule, 1926–1940, represented the triumph of fascism in Lithuania, and the collapse of the "Smetona regime" in 1940 opened the way for the liberation of the people. Once the Lithuanians had found their proper place in the Soviet system, "proletarian internationalism," following the lead of their Russian brothers, replaced the narrow "bourgeois nationalism" of the past.

Buttressed by strict governmental control of the printed word and the media, Šarmaitis's schema remained fundamentally intact into the 1980s. There had been, to be sure, some fraying around the edges; at the risk of "idealizing" the bourgeois order, literature specialists, for example, had rehabilitated some popular writers no longer among the living. In the turbulent days of 1988 Šarmaitis's simplistic pattern of interpretation faced open challenge. "It is always difficult for me to respond to students' questions as to why all Tsarist conquests were progressive and useful for the oppressed peoples," wrote the historian Liudas Truska in May.[1]

Most painful of all the questions in Lithuania's past were the ones that still lay in the living memory of many inhabitants of the republic, those surrounding the establishment of Soviet rule in Lithuania from 1940 to 1952. As one letter-writer put it, "We have to admit that most people under the age of 50 are poorly acquainted with Lithuanian history."[2] This indictment of the Soviet writing and teaching of history pointed at those who had begun their educational paths after 1945, but it also epitomized the role of popular memory as a control on official history—the older generation quietly kept trying to correct the historians.

According to the official historiography, in signing

the Non-Aggression Pact with Nazi Germany in 1939, Stalin had been defending peace. In 1940 "socialist revolution" had simultaneously brought Soviet rule to Lithuania and the other two Baltic republics of Latvia and Estonia. Lithuanian Communists had established a Lithuanian SSR in December 1918; as the Soviet Lithuanian constitution put it, "The working people of Lithuania, led by the Communist Party, stubbornly struggled against the dictatorship of the bourgeoisie and in 1940 restored Soviet rule." The "bourgeoisie" of Lithuania, however, resisted Soviet rule and thereby forced "civil war" on the land; in turn the government had to deport its foes. Lithuanians who had supported Soviet rule qualified as "defenders of the people," *liaudies gynejai*, while resisters were called first "enemies of the people" and subsequently just "bandits."

The older generation recalled those events in very different terms: Soviet troops had "occupied" Lithuania in 1940, and their return in 1944–1945 constituted a "second occupation." The mass deportations of Lithuanians, especially in 1941, 1948, and 1949, amounted to "genocide." In the late 1950s and early 1960s most of the deportees, those who were still living, were allowed to return to Lithuania, but only on the condition that they never publicly discuss their life in Siberia. These people knew the "defenders of the people" as "stribai" (from the Russian *istrebiteli*, "destroyers") and the resistance fighters as "forest brethren" and even "partisans."

The resistance of popular memory to official history long had to lie hidden, expressed publicly only in the form of guerrilla warfare over national symbols that the Soviet authorities tried to suppress. In the early 1950s Soviet authorities banned the singing of the *National Hymn* of the Lithuanians and the displaying of the tricolor yellow-green-red flag as well as the use of such national symbols as the knight on horseback or the schematicized representation of "the pillars of Gediminas." The standardized Soviet Lithuanian flag, virtually indistinguishable from the flags of the other republics, symbolized the process of assimilation of the nationalities of the USSR, of obliteration of Lithuanian culture. Using hit-and-run tactics, perhaps tearing down the Soviet flag and raising the tricolor, resisters sporadically struck back. One well-known journalist told me of his having waved the tricolor in a soccer demonstration in 1982, but the most widely told current story concerned the demonstrations of February 1988 when someone hung the national flag out of a window in that most private of public places, a toilet in the television building. The authorities used dogs in an unsuccessful effort to find the culprit.

As the throng gathered in Vingis Park, many recalled that a year earlier, August 23, 1987, only a few hundred people dared to commemorate this event. Now, this evening's organizers urged, "Let us remember. Just a year ago Lithuania and the entire Baltic awoke and rose to regain its true history and to advance to our real future. There were few of us then, since fear still ruled most souls."[3]

The people wanted to recover what they could of what Sajudis, the meeting's sponsor, called "the lost TRUTH and HISTORY" of their nation. Tricolor flags, adorned with black ribbons for the occasion, waved throughout the crowd. The evening opened with the mass singing of *Lithuania Beloved* (Lietuva Brangi), the "unofficial" national hymn of the last thirty-five years, and it closed three hours later with the singing of the *National Hymn* (Tautiška Giesme), which had been legalized less than a week before, on August 17. National symbols abounded, creating an intense, emotional atmosphere.[4]

The assembly in Vingis Park, moreover, occurred not in opposition to the local authorities, as had been the case in 1987, but with their participation. Among the speakers of the evening were Lionginas Šepetys, secretary of the Lithuanian Communist Party charged with ideological questions, and Vladislovas Mikučiauskas, the minister of foreign affairs of the Lithuanian SSR. Also on the stage were Algirdas Vileikis, chairman of the Vilnius city soviet's Executive Committee, and Justas Paleckis, the son of the former president of the Lithuanian SSR and now himself a cultural official within the Communist Party's Central Committee. The changes in the past year had forced the Communist leadership of the republic not only to abandon their opposition to memorializing the Nazi-Soviet pact but even to join in the observance.

This unprecedented gathering of Lithuanians wove themes of "the nation in danger" tightly into the fabric of its program. In the summer and fall of 1988, "history" meant not just the record of the past—which was controversial enough—but also even greater concern for the present and future condition of the nation and of the territory it inhabited. This meant questions of preserving national culture, national traditions, and even the environment.

On the question of preserving the national culture, concern about the status and future of the Lithuanian language stood in the forefront. The Soviet government's program of "bilingual education," teaching children both Russian and Lithuanian in elementary schools, meant in practice starting formal instruction in Russian before formal instruction in Lithuanian. In force for a decade by now, the policy had already resulted in a perceptible decline in the children's use and knowledge of Lithuanian. The authorities had gone on to require that all doctoral theses be presented in Russian, saying that Moscow had to be able to check their quality.

Both sides understood the potential of this linguistic policy. In the nineteenth century the language had barely escaped extinction between the pressures of Russification and Polonization; intellectuals now feared that they were on the verge of a similar crisis. For the authorities, bilingualism gave promise of being the "ultimate weapon" in the struggle with the national consciousness of Soviet minorities: "Bilingualism," wrote an approving commentator, "which is widespread in Lithuania, is a significant factor in the processes of ethnic assimilation."[5]

Lithuanian writers and linguists took the lead in challenging bilingualism. Writers naturally enough needed readers, but Vytautas Martinkus, the head of the Lithuanian Writers' Union, also told me of his concern that the requirement that dissertations be written in Russian could undermine the development of critical thought in the Lithuanian language, consigning it to an ever-diminishing role in public life. The meeting in Vingis Park was conducted entirely in Lithuanian; no one who could not speak the language had any business being there.

Throughout the years of Soviet rule, many Lithuanians had seen the Roman Catholic Church's struggle for survival in the land as a part of their own national consciousness; the church had provided an institutional alternative to the Soviet order. This evening a Catholic priest was scheduled to speak right after the ideological chief of the Lithuanian Communist Party. The intellectuals who had organized the meeting this August 23 were not necessarily religious themselves, but they were ready to recognize the church as having had a significant role in their history and as still deserving a legitimate place in their society.

Although many Lithuanian romantics spoke of the Lithuanians' love for nature, practical environmental questions, beginning with the enormous problem known simply as "Ignalina," also stood high on the Lithuanians' agenda for the future. Planned to consist of four units, the Ignalina nuclear energy plant, located in the eastern part of Lithuania, would eventually be the largest in the world. As of the summer of 1988, two units had been completed, the third was under construction. When finally forced to discuss the matter of safety, atomic energy officials from Moscow insisted that it was all perfectly safe; Lithuanians, to the contrary, understood that Ignalina's structure followed the model of the plant in Chernobyl, where an accident in 1986 had made the immediate locale uninhabitable for the near future. They remembered how the authorities had built the first unit in the years of Leonid Brezhnev, "the years of stagnation," and how they had boasted of saving time and money in the construction.

An accident in Ignalina could threaten the very existence of the Lithuanian nation. As it was, the Lithuanians could still not be sure what consequences Chernobyl had brought them. At the time the authorities had told them little; one friend wrote to me then, "From the newspapers you could conclude that this was good for us." Soon after my arrival in Vilnius in August 1988, however, friends advised me to be cautious about eat-ing mushrooms—mushrooms, they said, retained radio-activity longer than most other plants. Now even the Lithuanian Communist Party was challenging the central government in Moscow on the question of Ignalina's safety.[6]

The ferment in Lithuania in 1988 resulted directly from the waves of change arising in Moscow with Mikhail Gorbachev's message of *perestroika, glasnost, khozraschet* (economic accountability), and "democratization." Democratization called for more popular participation in decision making. Glasnost, openness, called for discussion of what was actually on the minds of the people, and this meant complaints, challenges to traditional authority. Khozraschet, economic accountability, meant learning how to balance books, to realize profits, and to pay taxes, and that demanded a significant reorganization of the republican economy.

Perestroika, "restructuring" (in Lithuanian *persitvarkymas*, or "reform"), actually produced much disorder and confusion in the republic; it disrupted the established ways of doing things. As the umbrella under which the other slogans functioned, "reform" called for more efficiency in labor, production, administration, and marketing; it demanded popular initiative as a corrective to the "command administrative system" that had brought the Soviet economy to its present difficulties. Local party and government officials, finding themselves the targets of complaints of bureaucracy, inertia, and "stagnation," supported the slogans publicly, but privately many insisted that since the slogans really called on people to do their jobs well, they referred only to others, not to them. Nevertheless, with the support of Moscow, the intellectuals of Vilnius had raised a storm to which the party establishment had had to respond.

By late summer 1988 the public discussions had even reached the seemingly ludicrous point that party and government officials, "functionaries" or "bureaucrats" in common parlance, were complaining about "bad press" and were demanding steps to improve their own image in the media. After decades of censorship, officials were complaining that the public did not understand that the rules of "democratic" discourse and of "socialist pluralism" required them to pay more attention and respect to the government's messages.

At the heart of the crisis in Lithuania lay some fundamental contradictions of Soviet society as a whole. The contradictions between ideal and reality, between form and substance, had escaped public discussion so long as censorship controlled access to the media. Under Gorbachev's glasnost, however, these contradictions were drawing new critical attention, and no one could know where the new thoughts would lead.

The constitution of the Soviet Union offered a vivid example of such contradictions. In proclaiming the advantages of Soviet rule in Lithuania, spokespersons for the establishment had repeatedly pointed to the constitution as proof of the rights of the people under this system. The people of Lithuania had the right to employment, to rest and leisure, to health protection, and to housing (Articles 40–44). They had the right "to attend a school where teaching is in the native language" (Article 45). They had the right to criticize officials (Article 49), and they enjoyed freedom of speech (Article 50) and an inviolable personal freedom (Article 55). The constitution guaranteed freedom of conscience "to pro-

fess or not to profess any religion, and to conduct religious worship or atheistic propaganda" (Article 52).
The Lithuanian constitution, moreover, declared, "All
power in the Lithuanian SSR belongs to the people"
(Article 2).

In a system that called itself "Soviet" but in which the
leadership itself was now talking of *restoring* the rule of
the soviets, or councils, what did the constitution really
mean? The leadership in Moscow was itself criticizing the constitution; the Lithuanians enthusiastically
joined in the discussion. Cynics both in Moscow and in
Lithuania might call the constitution more advertising
than fact, but in 1988 public discussion focused on the
"truth" in that advertising. Could the contradictions between constitutional form and the realities of Soviet
life be bridged? Such discussions, impossible in the
past, exploded in the heady atmosphere of 1988, re-
working long established ideological concepts and even
vocabulary.

One of the most heated topics of historical and political debate in Lithuania in 1988 was the question
of Lithuanian "sovereignty" or "statehood," *valstybingu-
mas* . The Soviet constitution called the Lithuanian SSR
"sovereign," and official historiography spoke of the
proclamation of the Lithuanian Soviet Socialist Republic on December 16, 1918, as the birth of Lithuanian
"sovereignty."[7] Lithuanian national historiography, established in the interwar period and nurtured in the
emigration, spoke instead of the Declaration of Independence issued by the Lithuanian National Council, the
Taryba, on February 16, 1918.[8] The year 1988, of course,
marked the seventieth anniversary of both those occasions, the one emphasizing Lithuania's existence inde-

pendent of Russia, the other asserting that Lithuania's fate had to be linked with Moscow.

In 1987 the Soviet Union had celebrated the seventieth anniversary of the "Great October Revolution," the Bolshevik seizure of power in 1917, and in 1988 the seventieth anniversary of the Lithuanian Soviet government was supposed to be a fitting echo. Historians had prepared appropriate studies and statements.[9] The events of 1988, however, disrupted the orderly celebration; the revisionists enjoyed the advantage of momentum simply by being able to raise objections after the many years of silence.

In considering the interpretations of the Soviet constitution, of course, one should also take note of the view, common in the past among emigres in the West, that Lithuania, like Latvia and Estonia, should not be called a Soviet Republic because the U.S. government has never recognized the incorporation of the three Baltic states into the USSR in 1940.[10] If consistently observed, this approach, insisting that Lithuania was an "occupied" territory, ruled by "collaborators," would put the constitution, indeed the events of 1988, in a totally different light, if it did not dismiss them altogether as irrelevant.

Conservative émigrés had long opposed contacts with Soviet institutions in Lithuania, with the "occupation regime," accepting only the thought of "personal" contacts between private individuals. When citizens of Madison, Wisconsin, "non-Lithuanians," for example, began to form "sister-city" relationships with Vilnius, the conservative emigration in the United States protested vigorously. Such action, they argued, recognized Soviet rule of Lithuania.[11]

By these standards, there was no room for considering reform in Lithuania, and Sajudis itself was suspect,
especially because half its leadership were members of
the Communist Party. Foreign observers spoke of Sajudis as "Gorbachev-supported" and "officially tolerated,"
as possibly a ruse to "coopt the mass movements and
blunt the move for independence." As late as March
1989 I heard Balys Gajauskas, a noted Lithuanian dissi-
dent, tell an audience in Chicago that Sajudis had been
"formed by the Central Committee."[12] This Manichean
view of occupation and independence tended to dismiss
the efforts of "reformers" as just diversionary maneu-
vers by the occupiers and their collaborators.

In Soviet Lithuania before 1988, only a few individuals, people without a position to protect, dared publicly
to utter the word *occupation*, and they understood its
connotations much in the sense that the conservative
émigrés did. But when the term entered the daily public vocabulary of the Lithuanians in the fall of 1988,
it became a psychological weapon and a negotiating
lever in the struggle with Moscow. The term became
a call for engagement rather than one for boycott and
quarantine; debate over possible constitutional reforms
provided a base for concrete negotiations toward the restructuring of the Soviet system. When the nationalist
Lithuanian Freedom League, moreover, called for a
boycott of the elections to the new Congress of People's
Deputies in March 1989, over 80 percent of the population of Lithuania turned out to vote and gave Sajudis
thirty-one of the thirty-nine seats for which it was cam-
paigning. The citizenry of Lithuania wanted to battle
the system from the inside.

Upon leaving Vingis Park that evening of August 23,
I recalled how I had seen the Poles reclaiming their own

history in 1957, and I resolved to record the changes and struggles I was witnessing. The study at hand purposes to explain the background and development of Lithuanian politics through the summer and fall of 1988, concentrating first of all on the Lithuanians' historical consciousness as a factor in the development of their national consciousness and of their political and cultural life. I was in Lithuania at this time as a guest of the Institute of History of the Lithuanian Academy of Sciences. The invitation had been several years in its realization, and the timing was the result of coincidence and luck.

The outstanding feature of the spiritual revolution that took place in Lithuania was the way in which the Lithuanians' self-consciousness and self-confidence grew. In the past, the people had tended to think in terms of what was permitted; speakers at the meeting of August 23 later admitted to having had butterflies—they could not be sure of the possible consequences of their bold words. After the meeting the Lithuanians gradually took over the initiative in their relations with Moscow; they thought more about what they wanted to do and physically could do than they did about Moscow's possible reaction. Using the principles of Gorbachev's perestroika, they began to take control of their own agenda.

The developing matrix of ideas, emotions, and symbols in any revolutionary situation does not translate easily into other cultures. Moscow did not understand what was happening in Lithuania in 1988, but then neither did the Lithuanians always understand the framework in which others understood them. In 1989 the *Washington Post* on one occasion compared Lithuania to the tiny fictional country in *The Mouse that*

Roared; a Lithuanian translation spoke of a fly frightening an elephant but, even when someone straightened out the bestiary, the Lithuanian commentators did not grasp the reference to the popular English movie of years back. The study at hand is meant to be a view of the unfolding situation in Lithuania from the inside.

I have used the upright pronoun in this study because for many of the details I have relied on my own observations and on interviews with participants and observers; for such details there exists no written documentation other than my own memory and notes. On occasion I have juxtaposed my observations against reports in the press as examples of problems in believing eyewitnesses. I can only hope for the toleration and understanding of the reader for the peculiarities of this account. As a help in dealing with the welter of events and personalities, I have added a brief chronology and a biographical index at the end of the work. I have deposited my copies of *Sajudžio žinios*, *Atgimimas*, and other rare publications and documents in the Department of Special Collections, Memorial Library, University of Wisconsin—Madison, as part of the Senn Lithuanian Collection.

I would like to express my deep gratitude for the help I have received in preparing this study. In particular I would like to mention Alfonsas Eidintas, Liutas Mockunas, Robert Otto, Ann Jablonski, Violeta Motulaite, and David McDonald, as well as the staffs of the Central Library of the Lithuanian Academy of Sciences and the Mažvydas Republican Library. I received financial assistance in my travel to Lithuania from IREX and the American Philosophical Society. All shortcomings in the work are of course my own.

I wish to dedicate this study to the men and women of Sajudis who risked their careers to change Lithuania in 1988.

AES
February 16, 1990

1

New Winds

The Lithuanian national rebirth of 1988 surprised many observers, but there had long been signs of trouble brewing, the most startling examples being the defection of the seaman Simas Kudirka in 1970 and the self-immolation of Romas Kalanta in 1972. Over the years western correspondents in Moscow had reported trouble within the republic, but there were few public signs of the development of any programmatic opposition. The *Chronicle of the Catholic Church in Lithuania,* which began publication in 1972, recorded the struggle for religious freedom, and the Lithuanians formed a "Helsinki group" to monitor observance of the terms of the Helsinki agreement of 1975, but Soviet authorities seemed able to prevent the establishment of any public rallying point that might focus and stimulate dissenting thought.[1]

The past and the future met in the demonstrations organized in Vilnius in August 1987 to mark the forty-eighth anniversary of the Nazi-Soviet pact of 1939. At the beginning of August 1987 a group of Lithuanian dissidents—Antanas Terleckas, Vytautas Bogušis, Petras Cidzikas, and Nijole Sadunaite—announced their intention to gather on the twenty-third, a Sunday, at the Adam Mickiewicz monument alongside St. Ann's Church in Vilnius's Old City. The demonstration would coincide with demonstrations in the other two Baltic capitals of Tallinn and Riga.

The actual demonstration was small. A year later more than one resident of Vilnius told me that people were afraid to attend the gathering, thinking that this was perhaps a provocation organized by the *Saugumas*, the security forces, with the aim of bringing potential dissidents out into the open. The Soviet press spoke of several hundred demonstrators; western sources raised the number to 5,000. The square where the demonstration took place is itself small, and a reliable observer estimated to me that there were about 300 people in St. Ann's Church, a core of about 500 demonstrators in the square, and some 2,000 passersby who manifested interest in varying degrees.[2]

In some ways the situation seemed routine. The organizers of the demonstration were well-known dissidents, and they had in their time experienced the repressive forces at the command of the regime. Terleckas and Sadunaite had spent time in prison, yet they persistently dared to challenge the regime.[3] The government's verbal counterattacks were also standard; it complained about "dupes" of Western "radio voices" as it had since the end of World War II. Despite all the seemingly standard behavior, this time things turned out differently.

On this occasion the demonstrators made no secret of their gratitude to the "voices." Lacking the means to publicize their meeting themselves, the organizers had to rely on Western media. The Lithuanian Information Center in Brooklyn, New York, announced the plans, attributing its news to "reliable sources" and identifying the organizers as "renowned human rights activists." Western radio broadcasts to the Baltic area repeated the news release from Brooklyn. Sadunaite later told a Japanese journalist, "I asked the Western radios [*sic*] to broadcast our call for the demonstration because we cannot use local newspapers or TV."[4] However it had been publicized, the demonstration stimulated public interest in the next demonstration, whatever, wherever, and whenever it might be.

Since authorities in Moscow pointed to the demonstrations in the Baltic as a sign of "democracy," an accomplishment of perestroika and proof of glasnost, the Lithuanian authorities stumbled in confusion. Security officers pursued and harassed the organizers, warning them against continuing their activity, but in the end the authorities could not enforce their displeasure. The dissidents proclaimed that their persecution proved that glasnost was a fraud, yet at the same time they realized that the authorities somehow did not have the administrative powers of old.

On September 10, in a particularly unsuccessful effort to assert traditional authority, the trade union of the Youth Theater in Vilnius met to condemn the activity of Vytautas Bogušis, a member of their collective. The director of the theater read an indictment indicating that the accused had repeatedly ignored warnings from the authorities to desist in his various activities. Bogušis should, said the director, "switch to some other collective so as not to ruin our theater's reputation." After a few people had uttered routine condemnations,

Bogušis attacked their "Stalinist" thinking, and others rose to his defense. The meeting broke up in disorder with Bogušis still a member of the collective.[5]

Over the succeeding months the Lithuanian authorities pursued the topic of Western interference in Lithuanian affairs with a vengeance, seeking to embarrass the American government, which had routinely accommodated the demands of Lithuanian emigres for support. President Ronald Reagan, for example, continuing an established practice, had proclaimed June 14, 1987, as Baltic Freedom Day, condemning the "totalitarian persecution of the Balts." The Soviet Lithuanian press published letters from readers protesting American "interference" in Lithuania's internal affairs, and the historian Bronius Vaitkevičius referred to the American government's support of demonstrations as "an insult to my people."[6]

The Americans remained unrepentant, albeit inconsistent. On the one hand, the U.S. ambassador in Moscow, Jack Matlock, reportedly refused to accept a protest from a "Lithuanian government delegation" on the grounds that the United States had not recognized Lithuanian incorporation into the USSR.[7] American congressmen and senators, on the other hand, sent Mikhail Gorbachev and other Soviet leaders a number of protests and requests concerning affairs in the Baltic in the course of 1987 and 1988. Although the legislators' protests to Gorbachev would seem to indicate a recognition of Soviet rule in the Baltic, the Americans apparently considered themselves justified in complaining but immune to counterattack.

Even as it denounced enemies abroad, however, the Lithuanian Communist leadership had internal problems. Petras Griškevičius, since 1973 the first secretary of the Lithuanian Communist Party, had already come under criticism for the party's shortcomings in responding to calls for perestroika.[8] Even Griškevičius's death on November 14, 1987, however, brought no significant change to the leadership; his successor, Ringaudas Songaila, showed no more enthusiasm for the strange ideas emanating from Moscow. In its personnel and policies the Lithuanian Communist Party appeared mired in the cultural and national policies of Brezhnev's "era of stagnation."

Typifying the party's dilemma and confusion was its second secretary, Nikolai Mitkin, a Russian. In origin from Karelia, Mitkin had studied to be a teacher of history but had then found his career in party administration, eventually working in Moscow as the Central Committee's specialist for the Baltic and Belorussia. He had come to Vilnius in 1986 to become second secretary, a position controlling organizational matters that traditionally belonged to a Russian. Enforcing Gorbachev's call for equal rights for Russians in all parts of the Soviet Union, Mitkin pressed first Griškevičius and then Songaila to increase the representation of non-Lithuanians in the administration of the republic and to pursue all manifestations of Lithuanian "nationalism." As one American observer put it, "While [Gorbachev] clearly is a master of bureaucratic politics, he not only does not understand ethnic feelings but acts in a way guaranteed to exacerbate them even if he does not intend to."[9] With Gorbachev's own appointee contributing to national unrest in Lithuania, the party leaders had no idea how to handle the new currents abroad in the republic.

The creative intelligentsia in Lithuania, especially artists and writers, responded more enthusiastically to

Gorbachev's calls for reform and local initiative. In 1986, condemning oil drilling in the Baltic as a threat to Lithuania's environment, the Writers' Union took the unprecedented step of circulating a petition of protest. Telephone calls rained in on the union as well as on the Saugumas, asking whether these petitions did not constitute an anti-Soviet act. Undaunted, the union went ahead, and it expanded its activity to other issues, including the use of chemical fertilizers and other factors of water pollution. The writers' debates and discussions reached the public through the pages of *Literatura ir menas* (Life and Art), the weekly organ of the Writers' Union, and although Griškevičius criticized the "nihilistic outlook" of some writers, the writers pushed other professionals, including the historians, to be more outspoken in defense of the nation and republic.

The artists carried out their own coup d'etat in November 1987, when a raucous meeting of the Artists' Union overthrew the group's old leadership and installed a new president and secretary. Conservatives complained of "unethical" behavior, but enthusiasts hailed the election as a victory for glasnost and perestroika. The legend soon grew that this meeting was the cause of Griškevičius's heart attack: the party secretary was present and he obviously did not enjoy the proceedings. He died that night in his sleep.[10]

The historians as a group were much slower to respond to the new currents, even though both public and government demanded that they speak. The Soviet press's denunciations of the August 23 demonstration stimulated discussion of Lithuanian history in the schools and in the press, and attention turned to the next controversial "anniversary date," February 16, 1988, the seventieth anniversary of the Lithuanian Taryba's declaration of independence in 1918. Dissatisfied with the answers that specialists had offered, the writers and other intellectuals leaped into the breach.

Prewar historical works, long consigned to *spetsfonds*, the collections of forbidden materials, now won new public attention. In Stalin's time it had been a crime for individuals even to own such works; in Khrushchev's time one could own them but not lend them out to friends; now they circulated in the black market and constituted a popular unofficial curriculum for the study of history. People, wrote one author, "are seeking historical truth in prewar literature"—shouldn't, he asked, some of this literature be legalized?[11]

One work in particular became the center of attention, Adolfas Šapoka's *History of Lithuania*, first published by the Lithuanian Ministry of Education in 1936 as a textbook and now exiled to the spetsfonds. Almost everyone, paradoxically, recognized the work's limitations. It had praised the authoritarian rule of Antanas Smetona; the basic historical research was long outdated. Šapoka, moreover, had written only part of the work, serving as the general editor, coordinating the work of four other historians. Nevertheless the book became a popular symbol, although no one dared mention it in print until Alfonsas Eidintas, in April 1987, spoke of its costing "several hundred rubles" in the black market. (Eidintas later specified "two hundred" to me, but a friend told me of having paid three hundred rubles for a copy.) In 1988 Šapoka's history became the embodiment of popular discontent with the official historiography.

A possible motive in criticizing contemporary Soviet historians lay in the fact that, in the forty-plus years since the end of World War II, a number of intellectuals who had considered studying history ultimately turned away from the field because of their dissatisfaction with the people and theories dominating it. This had been especially true in the first twenty years of Soviet rule, and in the latter 1980s such people, now in their fifties and probably well established in other professions, undoubtedly remembered having secretly read Šapoka in their youth. Now they had their own negative thoughts and feelings about the people who had chosen to become professional historians under the Soviet system.

Historians generally resented the public's idealization of older works. Historians all knew these prewar tomes, wrote Juozas Jurginis—the doyen of Soviet Lithuanian historians and a member of the Lithuanian Academy of Sciences—and the work of contemporary historians was far superior to what had been written in the 1930s. Jurginis pointed specifically to the new history of Lithuania by the Academy of Sciences' Institute of History, of which the first volume had appeared in 1985.[12]

Nevertheless for many Lithuanians Šapoka presented "the true history of Lithuania" (a term much in use in 1988). In July 1988, after *Komjaunimo tiesa*, the organ of the Communist Youth League, had polled its readers on their favorite books they would like to see reissued, the newspaper ruled Šapoka's work ineligible for inclusion since "this book until now has been almost inaccessible to readers, and therefore unread." Readers, the newspaper noted, were extremely interested in history, but the newspaper's list included no contemporary historians' works.[13]

Although artists and writers were already feeling considerably more freedom in choosing their topics and directing their efforts, the historians remained a part of the "command-administrative system," which posed demands from above and provided corresponding rewards. Some obeyed willingly, others explained that they had to go along in order to earn their keep and make some extra money. "The publishers dictate our activity," said one to me. Those who cherished their independence might choose to remain silent, but they forfeited considerable exposure and potential income.

The command-administrative system responded to the crisis of historical science by acknowledging the need to fill the "blank spots" of the people's history, but opinions differed as to what constituted "blank spots." "More personalities in history" was the code for paying more attention to Lithuanian national heroes of the past, but conservatives could respond with biographies of Lithuanian Communist Party heroes.[14] Calls for studies of "deportations" and "persecution" evoked countercalls for studies of executions in Smetona's Lithuania and of persecution of Lithuanian Communist revolutionaries both in Lithuania and in Stalin's Soviet Union.[15] The historians seemed as uncertain of what to do as the party was.

The Lithuanian historical establishment consisted of four major parts: the faculties of the Vilnius Pedagogical Institute and of Vilnius University, and the staffs of the Institute of Party History and of the Institute of History of the Lithuanian Academy of Sciences. In the ensuing debates, as in the past, the staff of the Institute of Party History constituted the core of the conservative approach to Lithuanian historical study, whereas the staff of the academy's institute provided much of the momentum for reform.

The Institute of Party History, an agency of the Central Committee of the Communist Party, usually laid

down the line for the others to follow. It rather naturally concentrated on "the history of socialism" in Lithuania. When party leaders needed historical documentation or justification, or perhaps just a speech, the
institute served as their first recourse. In turn the institute's library apparently had first call on all western
publications coming into the Lithuanian SSR, and institute members reputedly had excellent personal collections. In 1988, when the authorities began liquidating
the spetsfonds, into which almost any Western work
would be segregated, libraries discovered many unexpected gaps in the range of literature released to them;
many suspected that over the years members of the Institute of Party History had appropriated the items.

The dominant personality in the Institute of Party
History had long been Romas Šarmaitis. The director
of the institute until his retirement a few years earlier,
Šarmaitis had done much to shape the writing of Lithuanian history; now approaching eighty, he remained a
major force in Lithuanian historiography. As recently as
1986, together with Robertas Žiugžda, a historian at the
University of Vilnius, he had officially visited other institutions to investigate the reliability of their work and
their staffs.[16]

In 1987 the institute had appeared impregnable, but
soon it too came under attack. In June 1988, in a report
celebrating the fortieth anniversary of the institute's
founding, Vanda Kašauskiene, its director, noted that
"the one-sided orientation of the historians" had had "a
negative impact on the development of the science of
party history";[17] even conservative historians declared
that their work had wrongly assumed "that socialist society develops without conflicts, without any contradictions."[18] As the reform movement developed momentum

in the summer of 1988, the party institute became increasingly quiet.

For many years the Institute of History of the Academy of Sciences had also been a stronghold of orthodoxy. Juozas Žiugžda, Robertas Žiugžda's father, had directed the institute from its founding until his retirement in 1969.[19] Bronius Vaitkevičius had then taken over, being promoted from the position of an assistant in the Institute of Party History, and he followed a generally conservative line while tolerating some significant diversity within his staff.[20] In 1986 Vytautas Merkys, a specialist in nineteenth- and early twentieth-century history, replaced him as institute director.

Through 1987 the publication program of the institute remained conservative. As its contribution to the 600th anniversary of Lithuania's Christianization in 1387, it published a collection of papal bulls that had supported the efforts of the Teutonic Knights to bring Christianity at sword's point to the Baltic in the thirteenth and fourteenth centuries. Change came slowly. When it wanted to publish a symposium on the 80th anniversary of the Lithuanian newspaper *Auszra*, which first appeared in 1883, it had to wait several years to win the approval of the censorship. In the fall of 1987 it dared to use the phrase "Lithuanian national liberation" in a book title, but to critics that seemed a small step at best.[21]

At the end of 1987, the institute, which included three basic departments—history of feudalism, history of capitalism, and history of socialism—restructured its staff; the public's demands for filling the "blank spots" in Lithuania's history necessitated redirection of the institute's resources. Merkys assigned Alfonsas Eidintas to the task of studying and writing on the origins of the

Lithuanian "bourgeois" republic in 1917–1920, and the institute eventually took the lead among historians in revising the official memory of the past.

Eidintas, a specialist in emigration history, had already thrown himself into the public discussion, responding to the writer Vytautas Petkevičius's comments about historians "who fear everything, for whom one or another conception sent down from above is sacred." Eidintas answered that writers obviously had more freedom because they did not need documents to support their flights of fancy, and he had suggested that everyone would be better off if the authorities would publish needed documents such as the full text of the Nazi-Soviet agreements of 1939.[22] In the course of 1988 Eidintas strongly influenced public attitudes toward the history of Lithuania between the wars.

In December 1987, when *Literatura ir menas* concluded its discussion of history and literature by sponsoring a forum of writers and historians, the writers were still attacking, and the historians still seemed hesitant. Vaitkevičius complained about "nihilism"'s creeping into historical study but argued that even "the emigration recognizes, is forced to recognize," the high quality of the academy's recent textbook on Lithuanian history. Leonas Mulevičius, a specialist in the history of the Lithuanian peasantry in the nineteenth century, warned that history is an exact science that popularizers could corrupt.

The revisionists persisted. Petkevičius complained that the historians had done "enormous damage to our Lithuanian culture and literature." He took up the cudgel for more personalities in history, complaining about the Party History Institute's refusal to give him access to its archives and asking why the new history textbook, about which Vaitkevičius spoke so warmly, had refused to print a portrait of the Grand Duke Vytautas. When Vaitkevičius explained that no one really knew what Vytautas looked like, Petkevičius reiterated that the "depersonalization" of history limited its appeal for youth and therefore compromised its educational function.[23]

Writing in the January issue of *Komunistas*, the party's theoretical journal, Vytautas Merkys noted that the writers were justified in complaining about the state of historical writing, and he called the "blank spots" in history "a problem of historical truth." Historians have generally chosen, he charged, "themes that necessitated neither scientific nor civil daring." These shortcomings only benefited "hostilely inclined foreign historians and politicians." Merkys offered suggestions on how to improve the efficiency and productivity of the historians, but he made no predictions as to where the writing of history might go in the next year.[24]

With historical controversies still growing and February 16 fast approaching, the command-administrative structure mobilized a barrage of articles and books minimizing the significance of the upcoming date. Vaitkevičius and Žiugžda explained why the declaration of February 1918 had been meaningless, and party chief Songaila pointed out that the Soviet Union "is a union of sovereign states." ELTA, the government news agency, issued a communique denouncing Western "radio voices" and "clerical extremists," who "tendentiously, from nationalist positions," distort historical facts.[25]

Answering a schoolgirl's question in *Literatura ir menas*, Vaitkevičius pointed out that the study of history is a part of the ideological struggle between different societies and that Lithuanian historians had to recognize the class backgrounds of historical personages from Vytautas to Smetona. The preparation of good historical works took time, he explained, but when the historians will have had time to complete their work, people will recognize that although "forbidden fruit is the tastiest," it is not necessarily the most nutritious.[26]

In an effort to help its embattled Lithuanian comrades, Moscow sent Soviet President Andrei Gromyko to Vilnius to assure the people that the central authorities understood their concerns and problems. Gromyko spoke of the need to improve the production of consumer goods and to provide better housing; perestroika, he assured his listeners, was "irreversible." Soviet power, he added, was firmly established in Lithuania, and only lunatics "do not understand this."[27] Gromyko had no visible impact on the tension building for the upcoming anniversary.

In a remarkable example of quick publishing, editors put together an anthology entitled *Thoughts About Lithuanian Statehood*, with essays by authors ranging from Songaila to Eidintas, delivered it for typesetting on February 8, and approved it for printing the next day. Eidintas's contribution surveyed historical opinion on the significance of February 16, but the other articles argued heatedly that February 16 did not represent any turning point in Lithuanian history and that the Communist workers' and peasants' government constituted the real expression of Lithuanian statehood.[28]

Kostantinas Navickas, a professor of history at the University of Vilnius, published a mimeographed "Lecture Outline" on the subject "The Reestablishment and Consolidation of the Lithuanian People and Statehood." Warning that one could not allow "Lithuanian bourgeois nationalists and their protectors overseas to slander history and thereby to mislead our society," he quoted Lionginas Šepetys, the ideological chief of the Lithuanian Communist Party, as saying that historians must show the "reactionary significance" of the declaration of February 16. December 16, 1918, he insisted, was the real founding date of Lithuanian statehood.[29]

At the same time, contrary trends appeared even in official writings. In *Izvestiia* (Moscow) of February 9, Eidintas noted that critics were trying to cast doubt on the voluntary nature of Lithuania's joining the Soviet Union in 1940 and were calling Lithuanian Communists "traitors to the national interest of their own people." He welcomed the new interest in history being shown by the people of Lithuania, but he expressed regret that this interest seemed to be "a reaction to broadcasts by radio voices." It was time, he concluded, for "serious public examination" of the relations between the nationalities of the Soviet Union.

Finally, *the day*, February 16, came. In December 1987 the dissidents had announced their intentions to demonstrate on February 16, and they repeatedly insisted that the demonstrations would be peaceful. Sympathizers nevertheless predicted trouble: "Soviet officials allowed peaceful demonstrations in Lithuania, Latvia and Estonia, on August 23, 1987," announced the Lithuanian Information Center in Brooklyn, New York, but "since then Soviet officials have shown little tolerance for peaceful demonstrations." The militia, it was claimed, were preparing themselves with truncheons, or "bananas" as the Lithuanians called them, and Sadunaite reported that she had been beaten. Thirty-two U.S. senators appealed to Gorbachev to allow peaceful demonstrations in Lithuania and Estonia.[30] Authorities in Vilnius banned unofficial meetings and flooded the streets with *druzhenniki,* voluntary civilian enforcers of public order.

The occasion passed into Lithuanian history with two distinctly different forms of observation. Officially Lithuanians gathered several days earlier to protest the "crude interference" of the U.S. president and the Congress in the internal affairs of Lithuania. On February 12 Moscow's evening television news, "Vremia," reported protests throughout Lithuania against "the attempts of Western imperialist circles to interfere with Soviet Lithuania's internal affairs and to sow enmity between the peoples of our country." A picture in *Tiesa* showed a crowd, estimated at 15,000 people, carrying banners with slogans such as "'No' to Foreign Slander." Algirdas Vileikis, mayor of Vilnius, declared, "It is said that history is the teacher of life. Our nation's history teaches much. But some people want to distort both the history and the truth of today's life."[31]

The Soviet Foreign Ministry in Moscow arranged tours to Vilnius for foreign correspondents so that they might see how quiet things were. Antanas Terleckas had warned in advance, "The government wants to show that no one turned out. People are being intimidated in all kinds of ways. Students showing up will be expelled. Workers will be discharged." As Terleckas predicted, the correspondents saw little; Felicity Barringer of *The New York Times* wrote, "The 70th anniversary of Lithuania's independence passed over the Lithuanian capital like a shadow today, marked only by the police and security forces who kept a daylong vigil at the city's national and religious shrines." She reported "public nonchalance," and "not a feeling of hostility," as the most striking quality of the atmosphere in the city.[32]

Soviet spokespersons boasted that the Lithuanians

had rejected provocations. Lithuanian Minister of the Interior Stasys Lisauskas spoke of a "'fiasco' for Western propaganda, which failed to arouse the people to anti-Soviet actions." A Soviet Foreign Ministry spokesman pointed to the journalists' reports as proving that Western reports of trouble in Lithuania were false: "The ancient wisdom remains the same—eyewitnesses see better." Party Secretary Songaila later declared, "one can say" that nothing happened on the sixteenth.[33]

Unofficial demonstrations nevertheless took place in both Kaunas and Vilnius, despite the preemptive arrests of Sadunaite, Bogušis, Terleckas, and Cidzikas. At the Rasos cemetery in Vilnius, people placed flowers and candles at the grave of Jonas Basanavičius, the "patriarch of the Lithuanian national Renaissance"; worshippers filled St. Michael's Church in Vilnius's Old City to overflow for a special mass; and a crowd gathered in the evening at the monument to Adam Mickiewicz, the site of the demonstration of August 23, 1987.[34] Tricolor flags erupted throughout the city.

The authorities eventually admitted that there had been disturbances, but they dismissed them as insignificant. Moscow reported, "Militia detained 32 persons throughout Lithuania on those days for hooliganism and violations of public order, which, incidentally, had nothing to do with the extremists' calls. The number is even lower than usual. The intended ideological act of subversion against Soviet Lithuania has thus flopped." The Lithuanians, the dispatch concluded, "will celebrate the 70th anniversary of their true statehood on December 16 this year, on the day when Soviet power was proclaimed in Lithuania." For weeks thereafter, the media kept up a drumbeat of criticism aimed at Western "radio voices," including the Vatican.[35]

The dissidents complained angrily about how easily the foreign correspondents had allowed themselves to be deceived, and they sought to publicize their own stories. Sadunaite told contacts in the United States, "There were as many as 15,000 people. The militia urged everyone to go home. Then this mass of people started down Gediminas Avenue (a.k.a. Lenin Avenue). Since the crowd on the avenue was huge, the militia tried to break it up into small groups by sending people down side streets." The militia, she charged, used violence in breaking up various demonstrations around the city.[36]

Sadunaite's polemic exemplified the symbols of the day. Gediminas, whose spirit she invoked, was the legendary founder of Vilnius, and his name constituted a constant refrain in the events of 1988. Gediminas Square represented the emotional center of the city. The major building in the square had been until 1956 the cathedral of the Catholic Church, but since that year it had been an art gallery; in 1987 and 1988 calls for the restoration of the building to the church multiplied rapidly. On the hill overlooking the cathedral and the square stood Gediminas tower, the remaining ruin of Gediminas's castle built in the fourteenth century, where the rulers of Vilnius had always placed their flag. Many of the dramatic public confrontations of 1988 took place on this square, and demonstrators looked at the castle as a metaphor of their republic's sovereignty—what flag was flying above the tower?

The renaming of streets and public places, as exemplified by Sadunaite's reference to "Gediminas Avenue," constituted an important part of the revival of the Lithuanian national consciousness. In the early postwar years, the Soviet authorities had given a number of cities and streets new names. The Lithuanians could do nothing about it then, but in the Gorbachev era counter-initiatives became possible. At the urging of residents of Vilnius, the city authorities had given several streets back their old Lithuanian names. This meant, for example, dropping the Russian name "Gorky Street" in favor of Castle Street and Great Street. The thought of re-naming "Lenin Prospect" "Gediminas Street" now took a high place in the Lithuanians' agenda for restructuring the symbols of their daily life.

The Lithuanians understood that their history and their national self-consciousness were connected with every facet of life in the city; the demonstrative acts of laying flowers and candles, of singing, and of waving flags were only small tokens of the issues that had already arisen and of those that were yet to come in the course of the year. In *Literatura ir menas* of January 23, 1988, Alfredas Guščius had expressed pleasure that people were discussing history ever more boldly: "One after another we are destroying former tabus." The discussions among the intellectuals had yet to reach the demonstrators in the streets, but the day for that moment was approaching faster than most people realized.

2

The Debate Erupts

Beneath the placid surface that foreign correspondents saw on February 16, an explosive ferment was brewing. The yeast came from discussions within so-called informal associations, a relatively new phenomenon in the life of the Soviet Union as a whole. In the Caucasus, one such Armenian group, *Karabakh*, played an important role in the development of Armenian demands for Nagorno-Karabakh's detachment from the Azerbaidzhan SSR in the Caucasus. Lithuania had its own collection of these groups.

The Lithuanian associations ranged from music to social work. Students of history had formed *Talka* (Assistance) in March 1987 for the purpose of preserving historic monuments, first of all in Vilnius's Old City. *Žemyna* (the Lithuanian goddess of the earth), originally called *Santarve* (Alliance), had come into being in May 1987 as a result of the Communist Youth League's concerns with ecological problems, discussing topics ranging from Ignalina to the pollution of the Baltic. Economists and philosophers were freely discussing questions of history and even religion under the umbrella of the *Žinija* (Knowlege) society, a group dedicated to adult education (the Lithuanian equivalent of the Russian *Znanie*). Forming an army of potential supporters out in public were other associations, especially the fans of the rock group Antis. The exchange of ideas in these assemblies stimulated development of a new public consciousness.[1]

The government silenced the groups before February 16, wanting to prevent uncomfortable discussions and undesirable resolutions. When they resumed their activity in March and April, feelings ran high; the topic of why the government had felt it necessary to stifle discussion and to call out the druzhenniki added a new dimension to academic arguments. The Žinija society refused to allow the economists and philosophers back into its building, and they eventually found a new home for meetings in the building of the Artists' Union.

In a meeting at the Artists' Union on April 20, Arvydas Juozaitis, a philosopher, electrified his audience with his paper "Political Culture and Lithuania." Beginning with a discussion of Gorbachevian calls to develop "political culture," that is, political activity outside the sclerotic bureaucracy, Juozaitis complained about Lithuania's "falsified history" and argued that the activity of the Bolsheviks and the Lithuanian Communists in 1918–1919 had had "nothing to do with national sovereignty." The present government, he concluded, relied on force and threats, not laws: "the threatening ecological situation alone" should be enough to drive the people to seizing control of their own lives. Lithuania, he suggested, constituted "the last bastion of Stalinism in the Baltic."[2]

Juozaitis later explained that he had written his talk as a reaction to the events of February 16. Watching the druzhenniki take charge of Vilnius's streets, he had felt the need to do something, "but what?" he asked himself. He was not a terrorist, and therefore he "decided to deliver a public lecture, pure truth, to say everything." He prepared his talk in March, but the opportunity to read it came only in April.[3] His message, however, was still limited to the world of the discussion groups; it could not yet reach the public's consciousness.

The day after Juozaitis's talk, public debate began over a different issue, Stalin's deportations of Lithuanians to Siberia—since in Moscow one spoke of Stalin's use of terror, rule, couldn't the Lithuanians presume that Stalin had been equally harsh and arbitrary in their land? In an essay entitled "The Dizziness of Illusions" and published on April 14, Antanas Augus, a historian, had indicated that the "bandits" who had opposed Soviet rule had deserved their fate of deportation. Bourgeois nationalists, moreover, had provoked Stalinist repression in Lithuania. This interpretation seemed standard fare; Lithuanian historians had been writing this way for years; now, however, it could not go unchallenged.

On April 21 an instructor in political economy at the Vilnius Pedagogical Institute, Saulius Pečiulis, counterattacked, comparing Augus's article to Nina Andreeva's celebrated criticism of perestroika in her "letter to the editor" published in *Sovetskaia Rossiia* (Moscow) on March 13. In Andreeva's case, after a long silence the Central Committee of the Soviet Communist Party had just recently rejected her arguments, and Pečiulis hoped to build on that position. Augus's essay, he argued, represented a rejection of the ideals of perestroika and renewal.

Soviet Lithuanian historiography, Pečiulis complained, had "tried to blame all Lithuania's postwar tragedies on various 'residents' and on Western radio stations." Speaking ironically, Pečiulis observed, "It would seem that repressions took place in the whole of the Soviet Union as a result of Stalinist political errors and crimes, but in Lithuania only as a result of bourgeois nationalists and Western radio voices." Lithuanian peasants, he argued, had naturally resorted to violence to resist the "serfdom of collectivization." Agreeing that no one could "justify the nationalists' use of terror," he insisted that Stalinism had itself brought about the postwar violence in Lithuania."[4]

The party had to respond to Pečiulis's statement, and *Tiesa*, its major organ, published a "letter to the editor" from Juozas Jermalavičius, a member of the Institute of Party History, accusing Pečiulis of having written "one-sidedly and irresponsibly." Using standard polemical terms—"dilettantish superficiality," "repetition of the stereotypes of the enemy's propaganda," "subjectivist position," "antiscientific views"—Jermalavičius wrote of "class struggle," reactionaries, and fascist sympathizers. He pointed out that opposition to Soviet rule predated collectization, and he denounced "the imperialist reaction that, having started the 'cold war' against socialism, activated various anticommunist diversions," exploiting the "shortcomings and errors" of socialist construction in Lithuania.

Just as Pečiulis had distanced himself from "nationalist terror," Jermalavičius assured readers that he had no wish to justify Stalin's "cult of personality." Historians, to be sure, had much yet to do in clarifying the bad effects of Stalinism, but Pečiulis had allegedly failed to deal with "the complex of objective factors behind this inevitable historical development." The Lithuanian people, Jermalavičius insisted, had made their own choice in favor of socialism; violence after World War II had resulted from the bourgeoisie's resistance to socialism.

In earlier times, Jermalavičius's response could have stopped here—his opponent would have been crushed by the power of his pen, reinforced by the authority of *Glavlit*, the state censorship agency. In the fall of 1988, a Moscow journalist exclaimed, "The most surprising thing is the total absence in Riga, Vilnius, and Tallinn of the powerful academic teams of historians, ethnographers, social psychologists and economists who should have addressed the novel situation in our society as early as last summer."[5] Jermalavičius was fulfilling this function, but the reaction to his efforts was completely unexpected.

Jermalavičius went on to explain that the purpose of the deportations had been "to weaken the social base of bourgeois terror." The "people who suffered innocently constituted an insignificant part of those displaced," he continued, and Pečiulis had violated "truth" in speaking of "mass deportations to Siberia of innocent residents of Lithuania." In denying the glorious achievements of socialism, Pečiulis's article "sounds like an extremist challenge to the older generation of toilers in Lithuania." *Komjaunimo tiesa*, the organ of the Lithuanian Communist Youth League that had published Pečiulis's essay, furthermore, should understand that such articles served no constructive purpose: "With slander you do not argue, you just reject it."[6]

Upon first reading Jermalavičius's essay, many feared

that perestroika in Lithuania had come to its sudden end. "The article," wrote Petras Braženas, secretary of the Lithuanian Writers' Union, "was understood—this too the result of many years' bitter experience—as a program piece."[7] When Vasily Emelianov, editor of the Russian-language *Sovetskaia Litva,* complained about "bourgeois nationalism and clerical extremism," their fears increased. Jermalavičius's article became a call to battle; as one commentator later put it, Jermalavičius, "without wanting to do so, matured the revolutionary situation in Lithuania."[8]

Jermalavičius found himself standing alone; when the counterattack came, no one rose to his defense. In the fall of 1988 even the Institute of Party History distanced itself from his views, saying that he had "distorted historical truth about Stalinist deportations of citizens of the Lithuanian SSR" and had "contradicted the humanistic and democratic principles of the ideology of perestroika as propagated by the Communist Party."

The institute's director, Vanda Kašauskiene, publicly complained that the party official who had ordered the piece had failed to support the author. The finger pointed at Česlovas Slyžius, the head of the party's Section for Propaganda and Agitation, who had presumably acted at the orders of Mitkin, the second secretary.[9] As the director of the Institute of Party History, however, Kašauskiene had presumably endorsed Jermalavičius's "letter." If she had any doubts about it, she could have appealed to Lionginas Šepetys, the party's ideological chief, who stood between Mitkin and Slyžius in the hierarchy. Šepetys privately told colleagues that he had approved the text without having read it—a standard excuse for officials caught in such a situation—but speaking publicly on television on November 4, he categorically denied that he had ordered the article. No matter how one reconstructed the chain of command, Jermalavičius discovered that he had no supporters.

Although Pečiulis, in starting the discussion, had tried to pin Nina Andreeva's name to Augus, Jermalavičius now received the ignominious title of "Lithuania's Nina Andreeva." After the first shock, criticism quickly developed, and the momentum soon flowed in the other direction. On May 12, *Gimtasis kraštas*, a weekly newspaper in the forefront of reform, published a number of angry letters objecting to Jermalavičius's views. "The professor has far surpassed his colleague from Leningrad [Nina Andreeva] with his orthodoxy," wrote one. "The ideology of Stalinism up to now has many defenders even among declared supporters of perestroika," said another. "Why is the professor silent about the prewar deportation?" asked a third. A fourth declared, "Prof. Dr. J. Jermalavičius defends, even unjustifiably, Stalin's repressions and slanderously accuses those who first pointed to the injustice of Stalin's repressions in Lithuania. . . . J. Jermalavičius has boldly declared that he is a Stalinist." The newspaper was receiving up to seventy letters a day concerning Jermalavičius's article.

Stalinist deportations now became a daily topic of concern even in the press. Writing in *Literatura ir menas* of May 28, the poet Justinas Marcinkevičius discussed a memoir written by Dalia Grinkevičiute recounting how she was deported in 1941 at age fourteen. Marcinkevičius interpreted the Soviet action as having been aimed at the Lithuanian intelligentsia, not just at "harmful profascist elements," and he compared this with Nazi plans to destroy the Russian nation by striking first at the intelligentsia. Some emigres had long criticized Marcinkevičius as a "regime poet" but, well known for his interest in historical subjects, he now emerged as one of the leading spokespersons of the new Lithuanian national consciousness.[10]

When the full text of Grinkevičiute's horrific memoir appeared in the August issue of the monthly *Pergale*, it stunned the reading public and immediately took an important place in their collective memory as an oppressed nation. Life could obviously be worse than death: on her deathbed Grinkevičiute's mother had exclaimed, "Why didn't they just shoot us at the wagon doors?" Women shuddered at the account, and their husbands quietly told one another that for men the situation had been even worse. Only one out of eight of the deportees of 1941 was said to have survived exile in Siberia.[11]

Grinkevičiute was now dead, but the discussion and publication of her memoir opened many doors. The deportees of the 1940s had been permitted to return home in the late 1950s and early 1960s only on the condition that they not discuss their experiences in Siberia. This constituted another in the series of documents that they had been forced to sign and respect over the years, and they had indeed remained silent. Grinkevičiute's story evoked memories that they now dared to recount in ever-louder voices.

The party leadership found itself forced to display understanding and even sympathy. On May 13 Šepetys called for a positive reevaluation of the role of the Catholic Church in Lithuanian history and, in *Tiesa* of May 21, Kašauskiene acknowledged that "socialist deformations" had claimed innocent victims. In June

1941, the authorities deported 12,562 residents of the republic (7,439 families) and arrested 3,649 "for anti-Soviet activity." Although the Soviet regime had had real enemies, "the mass deportation of people was not entirely justified and cannot be justified by anyone." The action was even deemed counterproductive in that some people designated for deportation escaped and "terrorized the Soviet activists" when the Germans attacked a week later.[12]

At the beginning of May a group calling itself the Lithuanian Freedom League, *Lietuvos laisves lyga,* issued a call for a mass demonstration on May 22 to mark the fortieth anniversary of the mass Stalinist deportations of 1948. The organizers declared that "our members cannot sign this statement, because they will be arrested and will not be able to take part in the demonstration,"[13] but few people could have been in doubt as to who was behind the action—the militia brought in Terleckas and Bogušis, organizers of the demonstration of August 23, 1987, for questions and threats. The authorities in turn endorsed a counterdemonstration on May 21 commemorating the "innocent victims of Stalin" and held at the monument honoring the memory of Zigmas Aleksa-Angarietis, a Lithuanian Communist executed by Stalin in the 1930s.[14]

The gathering on the twenty-first of that month, officially sponsored by the "Creative Unions," an amalgamation of artists, writers, and musicians, undermined the dissidents' call for action on the twenty-second, and the authorities brought out their own noisemakers to disrupt those who assembled in Gediminas Square. The government's representatives, however, were unable to deflect the rising current of criticism. Jermalavičius himself evoked ridicule and laughter from an audience when he made the claim that the workers of Lithua-ania themselves had drawn the lists of persons to be deported.[15]

The popular discussion of Lithuania's history put the spotlight on the work of the history establishment. In *Komjaunimo tiesa* of May 31 Liudas Truska complained, "Much of our work consists of stereotypes, prearranged schemes, unsupported by the imperatives of scientific methodology." He called for reconsideration of a number of historical questions, including the role of the Catholic Church in Lithuanian history, a reevaluation as to whether the incorporation of Lithuania into the Russian empire had really been a positive factor in Lith-uania's historical development, and a serious examina-tion of the problems of socialism in Lithuania. "It is paradoxical," he noted, "that in a time of general inter-est in history, the authority of the historians themselves has fallen."

Historians felt pressures from all sides. The au-thorities excused themselves in the discussions of "blank spots" in history by saying that the historians had handled their own affairs and should take the blame for what was wrong. Many sectors of the public began to say openly that they never had believed the historians anyway. There were, to be sure, exceptions such as Regina Žepkaite of the academy's Institute of History, who had won respect on all sides by carefully making her way through the stereotypical demands of the profession to forge a systematic picture of Lithu-ania's international position between the two World Wars. In the summer of 1988 she received a state prize for her work, and at the same time, riding the wave of popular interest in history, she also found herself more and more in demand as a speaker.[16]

On May 31 and June 1, responding to the demands for new history, the academy's Institute of History hosted a meeting of historians from all over the republic. Although in March the organizers had issued invitations to some 300 historians to submit papers, only 24 responded; their contributions represented the entire range of the new historiographic debates. Older conservatives like Šarmaitis and Navickas lined up against younger revisionists.

In the keynote address, Šepetys, who was a corresponding member of the Academy of Sciences, reviewed Lithuanian historiography since the war, praising the historians' efforts and noting that the "blank spots" that existed were not necessarily their fault. The party had dictated the celebration of specific dates, defining "facts, arguments, conclusions, and the world historical significance." Demagogic phrases covered scientific shortcomings, and historians "for understandable, but scientifically unjustifiable, reasons" had avoided discussing controversial views, processes, institutions, and personalities. History had thereby become "not a science but an object of politicking.

Despite his support of "science," Šepetys was himself a politician. Speaking in April with a correspondent of *Moscow News* , he had been more pointed in discussing the shortcomings of Lithuanian historiography, blaming it for much of the regime's problems with national feeling. Asked about "extremists" in Lithuania, he explained that this group was made up of "people 'offended' by the Soviet system," together with "some of the nationalistic-minded Catholic clergy," and also "nihilists, many of whom we created ourselves. We did this by not telling the truth and concealing facts. . . . We did not teach Lithuania's history properly. . . . Lastly, extremists include those who idealize the past. Both the distant past and the recent, bourgeois past."[17]

Addressing the historians, Šepetys emphasized the importance of ideology in the study of history: "Historical science, as recent experience has shown, will remain an object and tool of ideological struggle. The professionalism of historical research will determine much as to who will have the first initiative in this struggle: we or our ideological opponents." Foreign historians and politicians, "hostile to socialism and its principles," he warned, stood always ready to take advantage of shortcomings and failures of Lithuanian historiography. The new "pluralism" represented by heated historical discussions was welcome, but historians had to remember that "Marxist-Leninist conceptions" constituted "our most important principle." Historians had to help "the seekers of historical truth from becoming lost in the complicated labyrinths of the past."

After reviewing the status of research in earlier periods of Lithuanian history, Šepetys considered the Soviet period, where historians had depicted "the basic orderliness and development of socialist construction" but had not paid sufficient attention to the "contradictions and difficulties of the period," including: Stalinist repressions, deportations, the sharp class struggle, and the violation of Leninist principles in the collectivization of agriculture: "Historians must examine these problems more boldly."

The attention given to the "blank spot" of February 16 had caught the Lithuanian historical establishment unprepared, Šepetys pointed out and, although they had responded ably, there remained much work to be done: "Although the bourgeois Lithuanian state was suppressing the proletarian revolution, warring against the Soviet republic, the declaration read on that day by the Lithuanian Taryba showed how strong the blast of the October Revolution was in destroying the Tsarist prison of peoples. The act of February 16, 1918, had a certain significance in the struggle of the Lithuanian people for statehood. It did not become a symbolic date without reason, one the Lithuanian bourgeois parties would later select as the date of the rebirth of the state and establish as the national holiday of the republic of Lithuania." It remained for Soviet historians to study the history of the Lithuanian republic "from clearly class positions."[18]

In general, the historians welcomed the thrust of Šepetys's speech at their conference; he had supported various of their own calls for improvement of their working conditions. Their subsequent papers and discussions in fact revealed a new diversity in historical thought. Navickas spoke of "historical truth," Jermalavičius on the "class struggle in Lithuania," and Robertas Žiugžda on the events of 1939. Truska spoke on collectivization and Eidintas on Smetona. The conservatives railed against "nationalism," but the new liberal wing of the profession fired back.

The reformers came out of the conference satisfied that they had wrought havoc with the standard interpretation of "socialist revolution" in Lithuania in 1940. When Soviet power was first established in Lithuania, it was common to speak of it as having been made possible by the arrival of the Red Army. Under Moscow's eye, the Lithuanians had elected a "People's Sejm," *Liaudies seimas*, which had in turn applied for admission to the Soviet Union. In the 1950s, historians spoke of "socialist revolution" as having occurred after the meeting of the "People's Sejm"; after 1965 the "socialist revolution" became a historic phenomenon independent of the Red Army. In May 1969 a historical conference in Tallinn blessed the model of socialist revolution, and in the 1970s this became historical truth. The Lithuanian people, like the Estonians and the Latvians, had presumably carried out a socialist revolution independent of Moscow's influence and had voluntarily requested admission into the USSR.[19]

Specialists from the Institute of History now systematically picked apart the standard "truths" of that account. In June 1940 Soviet troops had marched into Lithuania as the result of an ultimatum from Viacheslav Molotov, the Soviet Union's foreign minister; no one had previously challenged the justice of Molotov's demands. Now Gediminas Rudis pointed out that Molotov's claim that Lithuanians had "kidnapped" Soviet soldiers constituted nothing more than a deliberate fabrication, and Vytautas Žalys demolished Molotov's claim that the Lithuanians, as part of a Baltic Entente, were planning provocative measures against the Soviet state. With these two claims debunked, Molotov's ultimatum stood as an unjustified demand for Lithuania's surrender.[20]

The party and its press organs resisted the pressures to change the image of the past. Writing in *Tiesa* of June 17–19, Sigitas Jegelevičius insisted that the resistance to Soviet rule after 1945 arose not because of misguided government policies but because of the activities and efforts of foreign radio voices and "diversionary centers." The resistance, moreover, allegedly hurt the people as a whole more than it hurt the government; this period, he concluded, must be considered one of civil war, class war, complicated by both foreign propaganda and the excesses of Stalinism.

Changes in party history were nevertheless on the horizon. On June 21, celebrating the fortieth anniversary of the Institute of Party History, Kašauskiene noted shortcomings in the group's work. In the same day's issue of *Tiesa*, Henrikas Šadžius, head of the section on the history of socialism in the Institute of History, spoke of the necessity of more careful historical study of the period. Stalinism, he declared, had diverted socialism from "Leninist principles" and had stimulated opposition in Lithuania. He put the number of "repressions" at almost 200,000. The failure of Soviet historians to explain the problems of the period of 1940–1951, he argued, had allowed "historians of enemy ideology" to present their own concepts of independence as the people's will.

A week later, on June 26, Mindaugas Barysas, a veteran journalist, reviewed recent letters to *Tiesa* and concluded that the newspaper was in the forefront of the campaign to set history on its proper track. Although some thought it might have been better not to publish Jermalavičius's article, others saw the article as having helped to polarize thought on Stalinism's impact in Lithuania. Stalinism, Barysas concluded, must be pinned to the post of shame and examined.

Amid calls that historians must be more bold, new research emerged. Writing in *Komjaunimo tiesa* of June 28, Liudas Truska analyzed various statistical records, especially land records, and put the number of deportees in 1941 at 30,000. He estimated the total deportations from 1940 to 1951 at 200,000 to 240,000, perhaps 10 to 12 percent of Lithuania's postwar population. In August *Kulturos barai*, the monthly organ of the Lithuanian Ministry of Culture, began the serialization of Šapoka's *History of Lithuania*. The editor's original plan was to publish the work up to its account of the 1860s in Lithuania, the time of "Muraviev the Hangman." The journal's success—from December 1987 to September 1988 its circulation doubled from 12,500 to 25,000—led the editor, Vilhelmas Chadzevičius, to reconsider. "Who knows?" he said to me in late September in response to my question whether the reprinting of Šapoka would stop with Muraviev's time. "It depends on the atmosphere—some days it rains, some days the sun shines."

There seemed no established historical interpretation immune to reassessment and argument. "The myth about the revolutionary situation in 1939–1940 and about socialist revolution in 1940 was thought up later," declared Kestutis Strumskis, a faculty member at Vilnius University. Strumskis's statement aroused discussion in party ranks, and Mykolas Burokevičius, a professor of scientific communism, issued a rebuttal, saying that Strumskis had repeated emigre arguments: Lithuania had in fact experienced "the first socialist revolution in the second general crisis of capitalism." For his troubles Burokevičius received only grief; he subsequently complained of having received objectionable telephone calls.[21]

Most notable about these statements by both conservatives and reformers was the fact that they were writing for the daily or the weekly press. It was a standard practice that one could speak more freely in periodical works. One could experiment with a newspaper article; one had to be ready to defend one's theses in a book. A book, moreover, could take years to publish. At the same time, however, as the historians turned to the public, they found they had no monopoly on historical themes. There were challengers aplenty coming from other intellectual disciplines in this era of expanded historical consciousness.

In the debate the established truths of Soviet Lithuanian historiography were disintegrating rapidly. Conservatives hung on to their sacred icons of "socialist revolution" and "class struggle," but their critics dominated the press, at least the Lithuanian-language press. Historians like Kašauskiene and Šadzius struggled to reassemble the crumbled parts, but building the old structure had taken forty years, and it had been nurtured in a very controlled environment. Building a new one in the intellectual free-for-all that was now developing would be an enormous task.

The main problem that the party historians had yet to resolve was how to separate Stalinism from the history of socialism in Lithuania. In the Soviet Union as a whole, one could turn back to Lenin or rehabilitate a Nikolai Bukharin, but "socialism" had come to Lithuania borne by Stalin's lieutenants. One had to believe strongly in the ideals of socialism to find a way to separate the ideal from the facts of Stalinist policies, and then there still remained the task of convincing others. The conservatives had once enjoyed a monopoly of power that had given their words cogency; now reduced to struggling with only ideas, they felt disarmed and set upon.

3

Birth of Sajudis

At the beginning of June a new force entered the life of the republic: Lietuvos Persitvarkymo Sajudis—the Lithuanian Movement for Perestroika or, as Sajudis spokespersons came to prefer, the "Lithuanian Reform Movement"—came into being as a response to calls from Moscow. To reinforce his program of perestroika, Mikhail Gorbachev had summoned a special party gathering in Moscow, designated as the Nineteenth Party Conference, at the end of June, and the public debates in preparation for the meeting aroused new excitement. When the party encouraged social groups to submit nominations for the Lithuanian delegation to the conference, the intellectuals responded with enthusiasm, drawing up lists of candidates and submitting topics to be raised at the conference.

For the Lithuanian Writers' Union, as for other "creative" unions, such encouragement intensified what they had been doing for months, expressing concern about the state of Lithuania's environment and the parlous future of the Lithuanian language and national culture. In March the writers published a manifesto condemning the central government's ecological policies in Lithuania, speaking of "a colonial style of management," and complaining of pollution in the air, water, and ground. In April they called for Lithuanian to be made the official language of the republic, for the restructuring of the school curriculum so as to use Lithuanian history as the foundation for the teaching of all history, and for greater public discussion of any further large-scale industrial development within the republic. A month later the "creative artists" of Lithuania called on the Nineteenth Party Conference to "strengthen the sovereignty of the national republics," to give each republic greater control over its own economy, and to support the development of the national culture in each republic.[1]

Despite such activity the Lithuanians seemed slow to translate their words into actions, especially as compared to the startling developments to the north in Estonia, where a Popular Front had been organized and calls for economic autonomy had arisen. Observers abroad spoke of "Lithuania's generally more conservative approach" to questions of the day and of "the Lithuanians' cautiousness, their determination not to trespass the limits of Soviet official toleration."[2]

Toward the end of May two events galvanized the Lithuanians into action. Emissaries from Estonia arrived in Vilnius and talked with Lithuanian intellectuals about the goings-on in their republic—the Lithuanian press at this point was for the most part still devoting only silence to reports from Estonia. Then, on May 28, the party leadership announced the list of delegates to the Nineteenth Party Conference in Moscow. Despite all the publicized "democracy," old-guard names predominated in the list; it included only two members of the Academy of Sciences, one writer, and a couple of doctors. The Central Committee had made its decision at an unannounced, secret meeting at a time when nominations were still being discussed in the press. With only three representatives of the world of scholars and creative artists on the list, the intellectuals complained that the Lithuanian party leadership had violated Moscow's recommendations and that the makeup of the delegation constituted a victory for the bureaucracy rather than for supporters of perestroika.

The "unofficial associations" buzzed with indignation. These delegates to the Party Conference had been selected, not elected, declared Vytautas Žemaitis in the *Literatura ir menas* of June 11; the entire process had followed old patterns without the least concession to perestroika. All agreed that Vytautas Martinkus, the head of the Writers' Union, would carry a difficult burden to Moscow as the only representative of Lithuania's creative intelligentsia. The intellectuals' feelings quickly crystallized around the model that the Estonians were offering.

Several "unofficial associations" came forward with proposals for action. Gathering on May 30, representatives of the economists' club, Talka, and Žemyna learned that the Presidium of the Academy of Sciences had formed a commission to propose changes in the constitution of the Lithuanian SSR in the spirit of perestroika, glasnost, and democracy. Spokespersons for the clubs contacted Eduardas Vilkas, secretary of the Academy of Sciences Presidium and chairman of the constitutional commission, and won his approval for a general meeting on June 3 where interested parties could share their own views on perestroika.

Tiesa's announcement on June 2 of plans to develop
further the industrial complex running through the
Lithuanian cities of Kedainiai, Jonava, and Mažeikiai
raised new concerns. On the one hand, such industrial
development posed the threat of increased pollution of
the ground and water of Lithuania and, on the other, it
promised a renewed migration of Russians into the republic and the corresponding diminution of the role of
Lithuanians in their own land.

On June 2 a meeting of concerned intellectuals and
other public figures crowded the Academy of Science's
meeting hall on the outskirts of Vilnius to discuss the
subject "Will we defeat the bureaucracy?" They agreed
on the desirability of a new social organization aimed
at protecting constitutional rights. The meeting with
Vilkas's Constitutional Commission the next day would
provide the occasion for action.

After a session of the commission in the morning of
June 3, Vilkas presided over a special meeting in the
evening. Some five hundred people crowded into the
major conference hall of the Academy, located on Lenin
Prospect in the heart of Vilnius; they included academy
workers, writers, artists, journalists, students, and en-
gineers, all with no special mandate other than a passion for some sort of positive action in response to the
visible problems of Lithuanian society.[3]

As the speakers became more intense and ardent, Vilkas lost control of the meeting. No one, he complained,
seemed interested in the commission's views: "It is now
clear that we do not want to meet any more with such
a stormy public; this is a useless effort." He tried to
end the meeting—some later thought that his opposition was part of a grand plan to give the Sajudis even
more credibility as a spontaneous popular creation—

but the assembly went on to demand the formation of some sort of committee.

The speakers demanded daring and boldness. "Three years we have tried to conquer [fear]," said Arvydas Juozaitis, "and only today is it beginning to leave." Vytautas Landsbergis, a music and art historian, proclaimed, "We want something constructive, operative. Not sometime, but now." Zigmas Vaišvila, a young physicist, urged the assembly to nominate candidates to an Initiative Group: "We don't have to call it a popular front if that word frightens anyone." Over Vilkas's continued protests a total of thirty-six names won the approval of the assembly: the Initiative Group of the Movement for Perestroika in Lithuania was born.

The group later denied that its membership had been determined in advance. Privately, some leaders admitted to having drawn up a list of some ten names in advance, but they insisted that most of the names had arisen spontaneously at the meeting. The gathering rejected some nominees, like Sadunaite, and elected others, like Petkevičius, in absentia. Sajudis leaders argued that the failure of the press and of the party leadership in Lithuania to dedicate itself to a program of reform had "reared and developed a feeling of a lack of appreciation"on the part of the intellectuals and had forced them to take the initiative of forming an independent social organization. "Openly, democratically, each candidate was elected by applause," recounted one summary of the meeting; "Have you ever seen a more democratic election?" asked another, contrasting the process to the Central Committee's procedures in naming delegates to the party conference.[4]

The newly elected Initiative Group immediately retired to the smaller meeting room behind the great hall of the academy, and its members resolved to meet at least once every week in the future. In the spirit of their founding, they agreed not to elect a chairman; everyone in the committee was equal. At the end of any given meeting, the group would select its presiding officer for the next meeting.

The group nevertheless had to have some standing officers. Julius Juzeliunas, a composer, took the post of treasurer, and observers unanimously agreed that his name offered the best possible guarantee that the accounts would be correct "to the last kopeck." Arvydas Juozaitis and Arturas Skučas became the "secretariat" of the group, and Juozaitis eventually became the editor of the group's irregular publication *Sajudžio žinios* (Sajudis News). Alvydas Medalinskas, a young economist, undertook organizational questions, handling details of maintaining order at meetings and public rallies.

The committee's search for democracy at times would have confusing consequences. No single member had the right to speak in the name of the group, but the group at times considered it in order to censure a member for expressing a wayward opinion. When Arturas Skučas attacked the party leadership and called for a special party congress, the group called his article "incompetent and irresponsible." This in turn evoked a protest from Arunas Degutis, one of the editors of *Šajudzio žinios*, who complained that "if a government can stay out of a dispute, it should."[5] Despite such arguments, however, the committee members, who had previously barely known one another in their respective specialized worlds, grew in their mutual understanding and respect.

At first the Initiative Group had trouble finding a regular place to meet, but eventually the Artists' Union, of which the president, Bronius Leonavičius, and the secretary, Arvydas Šaltenis, were members of the committee, offered it a home. The artists' generosity had its costs: thugs broke windows in the house, located on Kosciuszko Street not far from a militia station, and the union insisted that Justas Paleckis, the supervisor of cultural affairs in the Central Committee, come to view the damage. In addition, Leonavičius had his misgivings about the disruptions caused by the large crowds that came into the building in connection with Sajudis's work, but the cause of Lithuania's renewal seemed to be worth the sacrifices involved.

The Initiative Group also resolved that its meetings should be open to the public. A curious confrontation developed with the party when the Central Committee's supervisor of higher education, Stasys Imbrasas, asked whether he should stay and listen to the discussions. The Initiative Group saw no reason why he should, and it voted that he leave. "Sajudis refuses to cooperate with party organs," Imbrasas huffed as he left the room. Lionginas Šepetys subsequently suggested that the committee accept the role of an advisor to the Central Committee and not seek public support, but Sajudis leaders eventually resolved to take their cause to the Lithuanian people. Meetings would be open; anyone who so wished would have a chance to speak.

In the tradition of Soviet politics, the group first of all needed to define its program. At its first formal meeting on June 8 it formed a series of special commissions and, on June 13, the commissions presented provisional programs. Their reports were not meant to be formal statements of Sajudis; rather, they indicated general lines along which the group intended to focus discussions.

The group gave every indication that it intended to work within the existing Soviet structure in accordance with the principles of Gorbachev's reform program.

The Social Commission, headed by Bronius Genzelis, a philosopher at the University of Vilnius, targeted the bureacracy as its opponent, calling it "a new class of exploiters and parasites." The commission proposed: (1) to end the privileges of the *nomenklatura*, the Soviet bureaucratic elite; (2) to raise the workers' standard of living; (3) to improve the funding of social help; (4) to review social funds and investment in industry and social matters; and (5) to hold officials, including the party apparatus, accountable for their decisions. Although functionaries of party and government might find these proposals objectionable, Gorbachev himself would hardly raise any protest.

The Cultural Commission, headed by the writer Vytautas Bubnys, proposed: (1) to mobilize the intellectuals' unions in support of saving Lithuania's cultural heritage; (2) to remove the "blank spots" in Lithuania's cultural heritage; (3) to establish social control of the maintenance of cultural monuments; and (4) to pursue closer cooperation with the emigration in cultural matters. The emphasis on cooperation with the emigration, in the sense of there being one unified Lithuanian culture throughout the world, found considerable resonance in Lithuanian affairs in the next six months.

Film Director Arunas Žebriunas headed the Commission on National Relations, focusing on: (1) returning Lithuania's national history to the people and publishing significant documents; (2) recognizing Lithuanian as the official language of the republic; (3) resolving the problems of minorities in Lithuania; and (4) establish-

ing Lithuanian schools outside the boundaries of the republic. In the months to come, the so-called national
question would require that they consider the demands
of the other national groups in Lithuania but, at this
point, Sajudis leaders seemed concerned only with the
demands of their own people.

Academician Antanas Buračas, as head of the Economic Commission, called for: (1) economic and political self-sufficiency for Soviet Lithuania; (2) price reform; (3) limitation on interrepublic migration; (4) more
rational and ecologically safe management of natural
resources; and (5) development of trade. Kazimiera
Prunskiene, an economist, added a call for republican khozraschet, meaning that the Lithuanian economy
should produce a "profit" for the republic. The relationships between republican khozraschet and republican
economic self-sufficiency would be at best confused in
the months to come, but the term "self-sufficiency,"
samostoiatel'nost' in Russian or *savarankiškumas* in
Lithuanian, was deliberately chosen to avoid the political connotations of "autonomy" or even "independence." The question of who should control Lithuania's economy would arouse great debate in the coming
months.

Since there was an acknowledged shortage of "socially active lawyers" in the group, Vytautas Tomkus, a
journalist, spoke on behalf of the Legal Commission,
and the problems he identified included: (1) duplication
of effort between the republican and all-union Justice
Ministries; (2) the inability of Lithuanian laws to differ
from all-union laws; (3) the "strong economic mafia"
operating in Lithuania; (4) the government's overreac-
tion to foreign propaganda and demonstrations such as
those marking February 16; and (5) the de facto prohibi-

tion of demonstrations by the Vilnius city Executive Committee. These demands emphasized one of Gorbachev's own desiderata, namely the establishment of a state of laws in which open legislation, not the will of administrators carrying out secret directives, provided the norms of social and political behavior.

Speaking for the Ecological Commission, Zigmas Vaišvila pointed to pollution as the major problem and identified as the "hottest points" for the Sajudis's program: (1) regular information about water, air, and land pollution; (2) observing the complex plan for preserving nature adopted by the government two years before; (3) support for the Žemyna club's efforts to pursue ecological questions. Ecological concerns quickly became one of the strongest rallying points around which Sajudis could collect support.

Vaišvila uncovered the "hottest" point of all when he inaugurated critical discussion of the Ignalina nuclear power plant near the city of Sniečkus with his article in *Komjaunimo tiesa* on June 9, pointing out problems at the plant.[6] Lithuanians reacted strongly, raising questions about the site that had never been discussed publicly before, the major one concerning the safety of this plant that had been built on the model of Chernobyl. With people using such strong words as "genocide," the Lithuanian government soon found common ground with its citizens, and it posed its own questions to Moscow.

"Ignalina" and "Sniečkus" also became code words for the nationality problem in Lithuania. The vast majority of the people associated with the nuclear plant were Russians. A Russian woman from Sniečkus told me that she and her friends relied on Moscow for their cultural life—television and newspapers—and that if one wanted to read *Sovetskaia Litva*, the Russian-language newspaper of the Lithuanian Central Committee, one would have to subscribe to it since it did not usually appear on the newsstands. The isolation of Sniečkus and Ignalina from the mainstream of Lithuanian cultural life intensified the conflict over the plant.

Imbrasas, who was at this point still an observer, expressed satisfaction with the group's readiness to work with official agencies, but he declined to comment any further on the proposed activities. The group in turn indicated that it was ready to challenge the party: Algirdas Kauspedas, an architect and leader of the Antis rock group, repeated popular objections to the makeup of Lithuania's delegation to the Nineteenth Party Conference, and he proposed that Sajudis organize a public meeting with the delegates. Others suggested that the delegates be identified as "designated" representatives rather than "elected."[7]

Notably absent from the Sajudis program as tentatively defined at this point was any political program. Although Sajudis had come into being in no small way as a result of hostile reactions to the naming of delegates to the Nineteenth Party Conference, the Initiative Group produced no program for intra-party democracy, much less a multiparty system. Sajudis spokespersons, insofar as anyone dared to speak for the entire group, insisted that the "movement" was just that, a commonly agreed sense of reform without any intention of becoming a permanent organization, much less a political party. Speakers repeatedly insisted that once the party had unreservedly dedicated itself to perestroika, the "movement" would dissolve itself. Time was to show, however, that there were elements in Sajudis dreaming of becoming a political force.

Another major area of Lithuanian life ignored in Sajudis's program was religion and, more specifically, the role of the Catholic Church in Lithuania. Despite the Stalinists' best efforts, the church had survived the bitter postwar years, and with the publication of the *Chronicle of the Catholic Church in Lithuania*, begun in 1972, believers had established the church's position as the major institutional alternative to Soviet rule. Over the years I had even heard Lithuanian professors of atheism complain of their difficulties in battling the church, although government officials wielded close control over appointments and transfers of church officials. The regime's pressures for atheistic education, combined with its policies encouraging assimilation, gave the church a special mission as a repository of Lithuanian national feeling under Soviet rule.

The church had entered a new era in 1988 with the decision of Pope John Paul II to name the bishop of Kaišedorys, Vincentas Sladkevičius, first the head of the Lithuanian Council of Bishops and then a cardinal of the Catholic Church. Under his direction were 686 Catholic priests, a number insufficient to handle the needs of the 630 functioning Catholic churches in Lithuania. The 137 seminarians in Kaunas had produced 27 new priests in their most recent graduating class. According to church figures for 1987, 32 percent of the babies born in Lithuania had been baptized, and 35 percent of the dead had been buried with religious rites, while 18 percent of the marriages in Lithuania had been celebrated in churches.[8] Sladkevičius had dared to challenge the government on more than one occasion in the past, and now he acted even more firmly. As he told me in October, "After I became a cardinal, I became bolder."

The intellectuals who made up the Initiative Group

of Sajudis were the products of an educational system
that had aggressively disqualified religious believers
from intellectual professions and pursuits. Although
some members of the group had maintained some religious convictions, on the whole Sajudis and the Catholic Church each had its own distinctive program. The
church would not be ready to tie its fate to a temporal
grouping of intellectuals, and in turn the intellectuals
wanted genuine freedom of conscience as promised in
the Soviet constitution. In the summer of 1988 they
were going the same general direction but by different
paths.[9]

Yet another force in the land with which Sajudis
would have to reckon was the Lithuanian Freedom
League (Lietuvos laisves lyga, or LFL), a group of dissenters demanding Lithuania's independence whom the
authorities insisted on calling "extremists." The league
first announced its existence in May, declaring that it
had been operating since 1978 as an underground organization with two tasks: "to raise Lithuanian national
consciousness and to develop the idea of an independent
Lithuania."[10] On July 3, after Sajudis had been functioning for a month, the members of the league publicly
identified themselves and issued their program. To no
one's surprise, the league's council included the organizers of past demonstrations: Terleckas, Cidzikas,
Bogušis, and Sadunaite.

As published, the league's program differed little
from the announced aims of Sajudis. It demanded the
principle of Lithuanian citizenship, the establishment
of Lithuanian as the official language of the republic,
and Lithuania's right to maintain its own army. Its cultural program demanded greater attention to Lithuanian history and permission for religious instruction in

schools. The group called for the establishment of "historical truth" about the events of 1918–1919 and 1939–1940 in Lithuania, condemnation of the internal and foreign policy of Stalinism, and the full rehabilitation of all persons deported from 1940 to 1953 as a result of "Stalinist genocide in Lithuania." Its economic program called for a separate republican currency and restrictions on migration from other Union republics. Its "human rights" section demanded freedom of personal convictions, freedom of speech, abolition of internal passports, full right of emigration, and the release of all political prisoners. Above all, the league wanted to make clear its dedication to the principle of Lithuanian independence, "a free Lithuania in a confederation of European nations." The realization of the various planks in its program, it declared, "will create the bases to restore Lithuania's sovereignty and independence."[11]

Among the league's leaders Terleckas and Sadunaite enjoyed a special renown at this point for having been part of a group of prominent Soviet dissidents with whom U.S. President Ronald Reagan had met during his visit to Moscow in late May. *Tiesa* had criticized that meeting, whereas emigres and dissidents welcomed it. Ironically, Terleckas and Sadunaite were rather dissatisfied with it because its highly structured format gave them no opportunity to make their own case.[12]

The official establishment took note of the Freedom League at the beginning of August, calling it a throwback to the dreams of liberation at the end of World War II. Claiming again that "radio voices" had evoked the league, *Tiesa* pointed out that the group wanted to work with Sajudis; the authorities thereby apparently hoped to compromise both groups.[13] Although *Tiesa's* attack would later be frequently cited as a comprehensive exposé of the league, it in fact offered little real information about the group or its program.

The members of the Initiative Group were themselves somewhat divided in their attitudes toward the Freedom League. The league's program essentially coincided with the aims of Sajudis, but one could not be too sure what the league's hidden agenda might include; many members of the Initiative Group considered the league too "nationalist," and some even referred to it as "extremist." Some other Sajudis members, however, actually welcomed the league as a sort of "finger of God," offering a position on the left that made it easier to occupy a centrist position. Several members of the Initiative Group undertook to establish contact with the new group, and for their efforts they discovered that they had "tails": they were being followed by Saugumas officials.[14]

Supporters of the league, especially in the emigration, viewed Sajudis as too cautious, although they eventually gave it credit for helping "the Lithuanian creative intelligentsia to recover its voice and its self-respect."[15] Sajudis and the league, they acknowledged, had put forth similar programs, but the league, they insisted, wanted an independent Lithuania and would not put up with the diplomacy and pussy-footing of the Sajudis intellectuals, who were in fact a part of the system. The league looked for confrontation: to ask the government for permission to hold a rally, declared Terleckas on one occasion, "would betray all our principles. They kick us, hit us and keep us under house arrest. That's why we don't ask for permission."[16]

Some league supporters, moreover, considered Sajudis cool or even unfriendly to the Catholic Church and other fundamental Lithuanian traditions; the league, by way of contrast, tried to identify itself with the church. Sadunaite, for one, tended to be identified as a Catholic rather than as a political dissenter.[17] Church officials, including Cardinal Sladkevičius, however, shied away from tying their institution's fortunes to any passing political movement, especially after the government showed increasing signs of willingness to deal directly with church officials.[18] Both the league and the church, of course, found their work facilitated by Sajudis's activity.

Although Sajudis gradually united people of all vocations in Lithuania, intellectuals provided the leadership of the movement, and about half the Initiative Group, seventeen, were party members. The party members justified their participation with the thought that they wanted to encourage the party leadership to accept the imperatives of perestroika, and they provided important channels for communication with the authorities in Lithuania. To be sure, when Sajudis members began to rise in the party hierarchy, a new set of problems would surface, but this situation was as yet far in the future. For the moment, the party members in the group had to defend their activity from higher-ups in the party itself.

Other subgroups within the Initiative Group gave Sajudis special entries into public life. Writers such as Bubnys and Petkevičius, the opera singer Vaclovas Daunoras, and the poet Sigitas Geda all gave the movement considerable public visibility; academicians Antanas Buračas and Raimundas Rajeckas, together with other personnel of the Academy of Sciences, gave it political clout; and younger members of the group such as the philosopher Juozaitis and the economist Medalinskas gave it youthful energy.

Notably absent in the membership of the Initiative Group were historians. One was elected, Inge Lukšaite, a specialist in Lithuanian cultural history, but she immediately resigned saying that she had simply too much work to do justice to such a responsible task. Her resignation left the Steering Committee with just two women and no historians.

Although some observers bemoaned the absence of workers in the Initiative Group, its members were unabashed by their occupations. Vytautas Petkevičius was particularly outspoken on this account, insisting that one of the problems of the Lithuanian Communist Party itself was its past discrimination against intellectuals in its membership and leadership. Intellectuals, he argued, "must organize government and lead society. We know well where Lenin's romantic statement 'Any cook can administer the state' has led us."[19]

Petkevičius was one of the Initiative Group's most visible and controversial figures. Frequently said to be a former "defender of the people," *liaudies gynejas* or *stribas,* depending on one's point of view, he was a popular novelist whom some now considered the conscience of the establishment. Others, however, refused to forgive his past. Asserting that Lithuania's future was inconceivable outside the Soviet Union, Petkevičius held a prominent position in Sajudis's public activities through the summer and fall although, as its program became more demanding, he tended to hold back.[20]

Whatever the visibility of the older members of the Initiative Group, it was the youth who carried Sajudis's message through Lithuania in June and July. For many members of the older generation, Lithuanian youth had in fact seemed apathetic; rejecting the formal history in school and also rejecting the oral history of their elders, they seemed on the whole to have little national consciousness. The younger section of the Initiative Group, however, spoke the requisite language for communication. From June 20 to July 2 a group of bicyclists toured the republic, organized by the Žemyna society with the support of the Central Committee of the Komjaunimas, the Communist Youth League. Their effort, covering nine hundred kilometers and twenty-four cities, began as an ecological crusade aimed at making the people aware of problems of the environment but, as local officials hindered their efforts, they became more political. In Sniečkus they experienced an ugly confrontation with the Russians. Nevertheless they carried Sajudis's name throughout the republic.[21]

The Initiative Group also decided that it was necessary to publish a newsletter. In the words of Algimantas Čekuolis, the editor of *Gimtasis kraštas*, the group had to establish a "forum as a means of mass information" against "a wave of reactionary opposition" to Sajudis. The result was *Sajudžio žinios* (Sajudis News), printed in a small format that did not require submission of copy to Glavlit, the state censorship. Beginning with the third issue, dated June 28, the publication adopted a formal masthead: *Sajudžio žinios: Lietuvos persitvarkymo sajudžio leidinys* (Sajudis News: Publication of the Movement for Perestroika in Lithuania). The first issues carried names of writers but designated no editor. No. 16 of August 2 identified Gintaras Songaila (no relation to the party secretary) as the editor but, beginning with no. 18 of August 8, Arvydas Juozaitis officially became editor. The publication was distributed free, and readers were urged to pass the copies on when finished with them.

At its birth Sajudis seemed an oddity; legally it

amounted to little more than the "unofficial" associations out of which it had grown. The press paid little attention to it; only *Gimtasis kraštas* and *Vakarines naujienos* (Evening News), the daily organ of the Vilnius party committee and of the Vilnius city council, published the list of members of the Initiative Group. Party officials apparently considered it a nuisance that would perhaps disappear if one isolated it. During the first two months of its existence, the group found itself engaged first of all in a struggle for survival, identity, and recognition.

4

The Period of Mass Rallies

From the start the Initiative Group continually had to redefine its relationship with the "extremists," as critics referred to the Freedom League and any other individuals who opposed Soviet rule in Lithuania. It also had to decide on the mode and forms of its own appeal for public support. On June 13, this involved the practical question of how to respond to the Freedom League's call for a public demonstration the next day, June 14, to commemorate the mass deportation of 1941. Should the Initiative Group take part? Should it stage its own observance? The group had no stable place in Lithuanian society, the authorities might yet step in to crush it, and now it had to decide just how bold it dared to be. The public gave strong signs of wanting to observe June 14 in some way: how should the group respond?

The discussion tested the group's resolve. Rumors suggested that military and militia units would deal summarily with demonstrators. "These were intellectuals," Arvydas Juozaitis later recalled, "they could not just enter into a pushing match with the military, they were not some sort of headstrong youths. . . . Čekuolis suggested that we each do as we saw fit, go to Gediminas Square if you want. . . . And so it came out, neither this nor that, personal self-determination."

After the meeting ended, some twenty to thirty people went off by themselves further to discuss what to do. Kaušpedas, the leader of Antis, suggested organizing a concert; he tried to call the city of Kaunas to order the necessary equipment but could not get through. The group finally decided that it had to sponsor its own meeting, and through the help of one of its members, Kazimiera Prunskiene, an economist, it obtained a room at the Institute of Agricultural Economics. "Less than half of the members of the Initiative Group showed up," Juozaitis noted, "almost all of the youth wanted to go to the Square to hear Terleckas speak."

According to *Vakarines naujienos*, rival groups formed in Gediminas Square. About 100 to 150 Sajudis supporters listened to speeches marking the anniversary of the mass deportation in 1941: "Such a painful period of our history should never be repeated," served as the theme of the meeting. At the same time, the newspaper continued, other demonstrators assembled with their own "subjective interpretation of historical facts" and even raised the national tricolor. According to emigre accounts, which cited sources in the Freedom League, 6,000 demonstrators condemned the deportations of 1941, expressed solidarity with Armenian claims to Nagorno-Karabakh, and demanded the return of the cathedral to the Catholic Church. Militiamen reportedly turned latecomers aside "to an officially sanctioned event held elsewhere by a newly founded club of Lithuanian intellectuals promoting Gorbachev's policy of perestroika."[1] The Freedom League and its emigre supporters considered Sajudis a government stooge.

When a demonstrator first raised the yellow-green-red banner on Gediminas Square, spectators felt both exultation and fear. A young man told me that he trembled just taking pictures of the event. When no arrests took place and the state somehow withstood the challenge, one could be sure that the flag would soon make other appearances. That in itself represented a major psychological victory for the Freedom League. It had dared to act, and it had gotten away with it.

Sajudis still had to define its own public persona; it faced severe handicaps. It had no channel to appeal to the emigration. The league had the support of the emigres, and it scornfully pictured Sajudis as pro-Gorbachev, perhaps even a government front. The Initiative Group had trouble even putting its finances in order. In the absence of authorization to establish an official bank account, Juzeliunas had to keep the group's funds in his own account. The issue became still more urgent when the group's public meetings began to draw large crowds and the contributions reached sizeable proportions.

The authorities continued to withhold recognition, and the party leadership remained hostile, this despite extensive personal ties between individuals on both sides of the barrier. As a result Sajudis functioned in a semilegal twilight zone; its publication *Sajudžio žinios* similarly existed uneasily. Paradoxically, the Initiative Group's problems increased its popular appeal; it represented forbidden yet accessible fruit. In the light of Gorbachev's calls for local initiative against bureaucracy, moreover, the position of the party became increasingly unstable, however much party leaders might want to denounce the new group as a pack of nationalists.

In a meeting held at the Writers' Union on June 17, Šepetys granted that Sajudis represented "some of the most serious forces of our scientific and creative intelligentsia," and he urged the group to submit ideas and proposals to the Central Committee, the Lithuanian Supreme Soviet, and the Lithuanian Council of Ministers. When he reported, however, that party and government had formed commissions to which Sajudis members had been named, members of the Initiative Group objected, insisting that they, and not the authorities, would name representatives to any proposed commissions. Šepetys quickly backed away, saying, "Let's go ahead as if I had not read you that list." At the same time, he declared that the list of delegates to the Nineteenth Party Conference would stand as announced, and he questioned whether various of Sajudis's demands were not signs of undesirable nationalism.[2]

The party also tried, unsuccessfully, to weaken the Initiative Group from inside. Mitkin threatened a member of the Academy of Sciences for his participation in the Initiative Group; the man in question refused to resign. Mitkin found the academy a formidable opponent. In *Komjaunimo tiesa* of June 15, Algimantas Liekis, party secretary of the academy's Institute of History, challenged the manner of naming delegates to the party conference and also criticized the process whereby the party second secretary came from Moscow. On June 21 the academy called for Mitkin's removal as party secretary.

Sajudis quickly became more bold. After the demonstrations on June 14, Juozaitis and Prunskiene had gone to Estonia to observe the work of the Popular Front there, and they returned with enthusiastic stories of the power of mass meetings. On June 21, Sajudis sponsored a demonstration outside the Supreme Soviet building, attended, according to its own estimate, by over five hundred persons, protesting the destruction of historical monuments in Trakai and the "suffocation of glasnost" in Lithuania. Speakers "invited the public of Vilnius to organize new protest actions, to oppose policies of cultural destruction and the restriction of human rights."[3] According to Juozaitis, this demonstration was the work of the youth in the Initiative Group: "The academic members came to see what the youth was doing! This was suprising to them, but we just closed our eyes and went on with the demonstration. The public now saw that it could believe this organization."

Meeting on the twenty-third with party leaders, Sajudis party members demanded formal recognition. Romualdas Ozolas, by training a philosopher and by profession editor for the Mintis publishing house, carefully explained what Sajudis stood for, "because," as he put it, "information about it, its goals, as of yet has not reached the press, radio or television." Arunas Žebriunas called for filling in the blank spots of history: "It is time to publish the documents concerning the most painful moments of Lithuanian history." Vytautas Martinkus, the president of the Writers' Union but not a member of the Initiative Group, declared that the party's critical reactions to Sajudis did neither side any good, and he urged that the party recognize the group.[4] The Sajudis representatives eschewed long-range ambitions, insisting that their movement was "not a party and probably not an organization, but rather a movement, a wave, which will disappear when its mission is accomplished."[5]

The next day, June 24, Sajudis established its place in the public's heart by sponsoring a meeting in Gediminas Square with the delegates to the Nineteenth Party Conference. When Sajudis leaders demanded the meeting, Songaila, the party leader, did not know how to respond, but Algirdas Brazauskas, a Central Committee secretary, indicated he was ready to represent the party in such a gathering. On June 23 Brazauskas, perhaps to strengthen his public image, announced that the Cabinet of Ministers had decided to request that Moscow stop plans to construct the fourth unit of the Ignalina complex, which Vaišvila called "the greatest and most absurd monument of Stalinism and Stagnation in Lithuania."[6] The gathering in Gediminas Square would in fact launch Brazauskas into a new political career.

A crowd estimated at 20,000 persons filled the square and stood for three hours in the rain, waving pictures of Gorbachev, signs such as "Freedom to Lithuania in the Family of European Nations" (a slogan of the Freedom League), and a number of tricolor flags. When some party officials hesitated to take the podium in front of such a crowd, Brazauskas reportedly clapped his colleague, Vilnius party leader Kestutis Zaleckas, on the back and pushed him forward, saying, "Come on, let's go." Brazauskas himself demanded that the tricolor immediately in front of him be lowered before he spoke. As he later recalled, "That was a time when, going onto the stage, I said, as long as those flags wave, I will not speak. I began to speak, and again they raised the flags."[7] Brazauskas took no note of the flags, and they continued to wave.

Vytautas Landsbergis gave the major speech for Sajudis, recounting the grievances of the public and telling the delegates that, although they could not call themselves "popular" delegates, "they can become our delegates" if they truly represented Lithuanian interests at the conference. He welcomed the delegates' announced intention "to recover the economic, cultural and political sovereignty of the republics [of the USSR]," but he warned that first one must "organize a just state and guarantee that legal principles will not be violated." The delegates' program, he insisted, contained contradictions and cautiously vague statements. In conclusion he called for restraint and sobriety on the part of the spectators in order not to compromise the impact of this mass gathering.[8]

Landsbergis's call for sobriety was a note often to be struck in the succeeding months. Alcoholism unquestionably was a major social problem in Lithuania, as in the rest of the Soviet Union, and Gorbachev's campaign against drinking had had only little if any success. Sajudis leaders repeatedly wanted to inspire their supporters to avoid demon rum. The authorities could only applaud such thoughts, and in fact more radical groups had reportedly infiltrated the Temperance Movement as a means to stage legal meetings. In turn, one heard stories of individuals who had given up drinking as their recognition that social reform was the road to individual reform and as a sign of their determination to be worthy of taking part in the process of national revival.

During the meeting on the twenty-fourth, spectators, as is the Soviet practice at public speeches, sent up notes with messages and questions, sometimes hostile, even insulting, and occasionally even challenging the speakers' personal behavior. Among the notes on this occasion were: Will Brazauskas give up his privileges? Send Sajudis's program instead of the party's to the conference! Can the meeting send its own delegate to Moscow? When will the tricolor be returned? Will the military obligation for university students be dropped in 1990 as promised? Remember the Lithuanians in Belorussia! When will the government return the Church of St. Casimir to the believers? The public's growing inclination to challenge the government and to support Sajudis was obvious.[9]

Sajudis also used the occasion to intensify its campaign against Mitkin. Speaking in Gediminas Square, Petkevičius criticized Mitkin's role in Lithuanian affairs, declaring he could not tolerate "that in my native land an uncultured man demands that I speak Russian." He received an ovation when he announced the academy's call for Mitkin's removal. A few days later the Writers' Union added its voice to calls for Mitkin's removal.[10] Mitkin remained at his post, but his position was becoming increasingly vulnerable.

Sajudis's own program for the delegates to the party conference focused on several points already raised by Gorbachev and on several that were distinctively Lithuanian, demanding self-rule, sovereignty, and a variety of cultural rights. The call for a "government of laws," in which legislation and not party edicts would rule, seemed clear enough. Gorbachev's calls for khozraschet had metamorphized into a call for "regional khozraschet." Lithuanian activists, copying the Estonians' initiative, translated this into "economic self-dependency" for their republic. Greater local control over the economy would facilitate a sane ecological policy aimed at improving the natural environment.

The distinctively Lithuanian parts of the program focused on culture in general, language, and history. The system of "bilingual education" should be modified to improve the teaching of the Lithuanian language; the Lithuanian language should be the official language of the republic; the teaching of Lithuanian history should be improved; and there should be no limits imposed on the development of the national culture.[11]

Even after this demonstration had shown Sajudis's popularity and growing strength, the authorities still refused to recognize the group. The media had not announced the meeting on Gediminas Square; Sajudis supporters had advertised it by poster and word of mouth. In reporting on the proceedings, ELTA, the Lithuanian telegraph agency, did not name Sajudis as the gathering's sponsor, suggesting instead that the Central Committee had taken the initiative in communicating with the people. The meeting of the twenty-third was said to have been with "representatives of the republic's intelligentsia," and the one of the twenty-fourth was with "society." The intelligentsia, moreover, were said to support the party line. ELTA summarized Landsbergis's speech in one sentence as having called attention to "forces that were hindering" perestroika, and it reported that "a small group of nationalists, who had already more than once called attention to themselves masquerading under the slogan of perestroika, tried to divert the course of the meeting to discredit the ideas of reform and thereby to hinder democratization." The crowd's majority, however, "demonstrated its dedication to the party's program of perestroika and concrete deeds."[12]

Sajudžio žinios of June 28 called for a demonstration to protest "against the mass media's disseminating false information" about Sajudis's work. On the twenty-ninth demonstrators gathered in front of ELTA's office on Lenin Prospect to complain that the agency had failed to show "good will" toward Sajudis and that the agency's coverage of the meeting in Gediminas Square constituted the "apogee" of its dilatoriness. ELTA's director came out to speak with the demonstrators and pointed out that his was a government agency and it did as it was told.[13]

The demonstration in front of ELTA concerned mainly the morning dailies that had simply repeated the agency's cold and misleading reports. Čekuolis's *Gimtasis kraštas* had long been in the forefront of reform; in reporting the assembly of the twenty-fourth in Gediminas Square, it called the delegation to the Nineteenth Party Conference the most important group to leave Vilnius for Moscow since the committee of the People's Sejm had gone to Moscow in 1940 to arrange for Lithuania's incorporation into the USSR. *Vakarines naujienos* had already published Ozolas's statement to party leaders on the twenty-third.[14]

After the demonstration, *Tiesa* of June 30 dutifully reported the demonstration, but without pictures, and declared that ELTA officials had met with Sajudis representatives to discuss how to cooperate better in the future. *Komjaunimo tiesa* went much further, offering a brief account of Sajudis's existence and work, together with a picture of the demonstration including placards critical of ELTA. Television, however, remained silent.

At the end of June and the beginning of July, attention turned to Moscow and the Nineteenth Party Conference. The delegates themselves had not known what to expect; when they discovered, for example, that there were no representatives of the Lithuanians, Estonians, or Latvians in the Nationalities Commission of the conference, and when they received prepared draft resolutions on various crucial questions, they feared for the worst—things seemed as of old. But then the Nationalities Commission added representatives of the three Baltic peoples, and the resolutions were opened for discussion.

Gorbachev's opening speech to the conference stressed the need to avoid national exclusiveness, and he argued that "a person of any nationality should have equal rights in any region of the country."[15] In the Nationalities Commission the Russian chairman blocked the Estonian proposal to discuss economic self-dependency of the republics, while he strongly endorsed the principle of bilingualism. The Estonians, however, persevered, and the conference's final resolutions emphasized "federation" and "the development of the independence of the union republics," "self-dependency of regions," and "radical economic reform." The final resolutions also called for continuing bilingual education and mastering the Russian language but emphasized the need to develop the languages of the minority nationalities.[16]

When Songaila addressed the conference, he confessed to certain errors in organizing the Lithuanian delegation: "Preparing for the conference was a great school for democracy within the party. This was difficult, since there was a certain amount of confusion, especially in the procedure for electing delegates to the conference." He went on to support the use of national languages in the republics of the Soviet Union.[17] In all, he did nothing to call the attention of the conference's organizers to the Lithuanians.[18]

Leaving Moscow, the Lithuanian delegates nevertheless argued that they had done their share in convincing their colleagues to remember the problems of the minority nationalities, and on returning home they found a Lithuania that had itself changed. A Baltic student festival in Vilnius, known as "Gaudeamus," had excited the population by raising the national flags of all three Baltic nationalities—the Estonian students had come prepared with appropriate flags for their Latvian and Lithuanian comrades—and although Lithuanian television authorities tried to destroy all the tapes of controversial scenes, a groundswell of national feeling was creating an expectant atmosphere for the planned public meeting with the conference delegates.

On July 8 the delegates met first with Vilnius "society" in a standard, controlled environment. Songaila told his constituents that he had been impressed by the conference and by the vigorous way in which his fellow delegates had prepared. The republic now had the task of pursuing the concept of economic self-dependency and of maintaining the principle of bilingualism even while working for the development of the Lithuanian language. He also warned against precipitous actions by would-be reformers. Songaila's presentation received the approval that he could expect from this audience.[19]

The atmosphere the next day in Vingis Park, where Sajudis had arranged for the delegates to confront a mass gathering, was quite different. *Komjaunimo tiesa* set the stage on the morning of the ninth by giving Songaila's speech space on the first page, splitting the second page between five columns on problems of alcohol and drug abuse in Lithuania and three columns on the history of the colors of the Lithuanian national flag, and half of the third page again to Songaila and half to an article on Ignalina by Vaišvila. The editors of *Komjaunimo tiesa* liked to make their Saturday issue provocative, and this particular issue more than fulfilled their goals.

The article on the flag, written by Edmundas Rimša and Gediminas Rudis of the Institute of History, explained that in pre-Soviet times the Lithuanians traditionally had flown two flags, one with a white knight against a red background, and the other the tricolor, developed in its yellow-green-red form by a commission in 1917 and 1918. The presidential flag in independent Lithuania carried a schematic outline of Gediminas's castle, known as "the pillars of Gediminas" (Gedimino stulpai). The tricolor, the authors concluded, had come from the people: "The democratic character of this principle raised no doubts that there is no basis to suppress it or to call the flag 'only Smetona's' or 'only bourgeois.'" The "knight" and the "pillars," they added, had gone into battle at Žalgiris (Grunwald) against the German Teutonic Knights in 1410. For the newspaper's readers, the article constituted a call to carry flags to Vingis Park that afternoon.[20]

Sajudis added its own word on the topic: in its seventh issue, dated July 7, *Sajudžio žinios* offered "a jurist's opinion: 1. walking in the street with flags is not a violation of the public order; 2. the national colors are not legally prohibited." These assertions would not necessarily stand up in a Soviet court of law, but they were obviously meant to encourage people to action.

The flags flowed into the park that afternoon, borne by an estimated 100,000 people—new homemade flags quickly sewn for the occasion, as well as obvious relics of the prewar period with mothholes in their woolen fabric. Gediminas's pillars were there, the white knight was there, and the tricolor was every where. *Komjaunimo tiesa*'s representatives congratulated themselves

on their newspaper's role in preparing the display,[21] but
the Estonian students had played perhaps a greater role
in preparing the atmosphere. Although organizers had
made plans to display the Soviet flag, "somehow or
other" the supporting ropes had been cut, and there
were no Soviet flags to be seen.[22] Accompanying the
flags in the crowd were banners: "Return the National
Flag of Lithuania," "Sovereignty for Lithuania," "Enemies of Sajudis Are Enemies of the People," "Songaila,
Our Shame" (in honor of Songaila's speech the day before as printed in the morning papers), and "Clean Up
Our Consciences and Our Rivers."

Such a large group represented a unique opportunity
for pollsters and sociologists, and they were there in
force, distributing over 3,000 questionnaires among the
spectators. Two thousand respondents added comments
to their answers. Sociologists reported that over two-
thirds of the respondents were from Vilnius, about
12 percent from Kaunas. People between the ages of
twenty-one and thirty constituted over 25 percent of the
respondents, with people in the range of forty-one to
fifty about 23 percent and people thirty-one to forty
about 22 percent. Over 70 percent of the respondents
were "specialists and administrators," 10 percent were
workers, 13 percent students. On a scale of 5 points, the
spectators evaluated the results of the Party Conference
as 2.7 and they evaluated the report of the Lithuanian
delegation on its work as 1.9. The work of Sajudis,
by contrast, they gave a 4.4. Written comments complained about the lack of glasnost in the republic's press
and the general slow pace of perestroika.[23]

A subsequent telephone poll revealed similar dissatisfaction with the work of the Nineteenth Party Conference. Without specifying how many respondents they

had polled, the group reported that their target group roughly corresponded in nationality to the makeup of the city's population: 51 percent Lithuanians, 25 percent Russians, and 13 percent Poles. Asked whether they had received "enough" information on the conference, only 36 percent of the Lithuanians said yes, while 63 percent of the Russians and 67 percent of the Poles were satisfied. The Lithuanians gave it a grade of 3.6 (on a 5-point scale), whereas Russians and Poles both gave it 4.0. All groups agreed by a large margin that Gorbachev had succeeded at least in part in having the conference approve his program. Eighty-five percent of the people knew of Sajudis's work, 94 percent of the Lithuanians as opposed to 80 percent of the Russians and 72 percent of the Poles. Sixty-eight percent of the Lithuanians were hopeful about Sajudis's work, but this optimism was shared by only 37 percent of the Russians and 28 percent of the Poles.[24]

The crowd in Vingis Park on July 9 was overwhelmingly Lithuanian, and the delegates who now appeared before it knew even without polls that it would be critical of what they had to say. Songaila obviously preferred not to appear before such a gathering; the task of explaining that "the party had initiated perestroika and the party will lead it" fell again on Brazauskas.

Since Sajudis could not use the media to advertise the gathering, the very size of the crowd represented a great triumph—"VICTORY!" proclaimed *Sajudžio žinios* of July 16, "A MIRACLE happened." Juozaitis opened the festivities with the observation that Sajudis had brought the people "together with words. . . . In the beginning was the word. . . ." Militiamen were not to be seen; young men with green armbands displaying Gediminas's pillars kept order. Should there be any problem with the regular forces of law and order, the Sajudis guardians informed the spectators, the people were simply to fall to the ground and offer no resistance. There was no trouble, and even the official press respectfully noted the orderliness of the gathering.

After Petkevičius had reminded the crowd that there was no place in Lithuania for nationalism or chauvinism—"We distance ourselves from any extremist chauvinist or nationalist hotheads and we have nothing in common with them"—Brazauskas insisted that in order to achieve economic self-dependency, "we will have to work harder." The Lithuanians, he declared, still consumed more than they produced. When the crowd greeted this statement with whistles of disagreement, he emphasized, "That's the way it is." As a counterthrust, he then announced that the Lithuanian government had stopped funding of the construction of the third unit of the Ignalina nuclear complex, and he declared that since the people had shown such dedication to the tricolor flag, the party and government would soon be legalizing its display.

This news evoked enthusiastic applause, and the crowd began chanting *"Lie-tu-va, Lie-tu-va"* (Lithuania, Lithuania) and then sang the forbidden *National Hymn*. Sajudis had distributed 30,000 copies of the words to the anthem and had prepared a chorus for the occasion. Although the crowd's singing was rather muddy, the participants' enthusiasm and sincerity nevertheless made it a memorable moment. Only later did the public learn that Brazauskas had had no authority to make his statement on legalizing the flag; he had done it on his own initiative on the spur of the moment.[25]

Sajudis speakers and delegates went on to speak of the accomplishments of the conference and of the tasks still lying ahead. Ozolas summarized Sajudis's program; Sigitas Geda stirred the crowd with his statement, "We have all grown up in the shade of Satan"; and Jokubas Minkevičius, a philosopher, brought cheers by suggesting that instead of *persitvarkymas* (i.e. perestroika), the Lithuanians should perhaps be better speaking of *atgimimas*, "rebirth."[26]

Brazauskas eventually returned to the microphone to announce that when he spoke earlier, he had been using "official" statistics. Now, he declared, he knew better, and Lithuania in fact did produce more than it consumed. Having won the crowd with this statement, he went on to declare that the party and the government had now decided to ask the academy's Institute of Language and Literature to prepare documentation for legislation making Lithuanian the official state language of the Lithuanian Soviet Socialist Republic. Again the crowd roared its approval.

Some commentators later complained that although this gathering was supposed to be a meeting with the delegates to the Nineteenth Party Conference, the majority of speakers represented Sajudis.[27] The meeting was in fact a major Sajudis rally, as witnessed by the resolutions that emerged. Vaišvila won support for opposing the construction at Ignalina, and the group approved a telegram to Gorbachev supporting a plebiscite or referendum in Karabakh.

Perhaps the most startling result of the meeting was the resolution calling on people to boycott the party newspaper *Tiesa* (Truth), which *Sajudžio žinios* called "the most significant monument of Stagnation."[28] Read by Arvydas Šaltenis, the resolution condemned the newspaper for its policies in general, for its having published Jermalavičius's article, and for its "tendentious or mendacious" reporting. Therefore, it concluded, the people should agree not to subscribe, buy, or read the newspaper and to urge friends to do likewise.[29] The crowd accepted the resolution by voice vote.

The boycott injected a new dimension into Lithuanian politics. Party spokespersons complained that Sajudis did not understand the meaning of democracy and the principles of freedom of the press. In August, Juozaitis claimed that in one month's time *Tiesa*'s circulation had dropped by at least 40,000 copies.[30] *Tiesa* representatives insisted to the contrary that the boycott had had no effect, but for months thereafter one could still find copies of *Tiesa* lying unsold in kiosks when all other newspapers had long since disappeared.

Arguments also ensued as to whether the boycott had any effect on *Tiesa*'s editorial policy. Again, *Tiesa* spokespersons played this down. The editor of *Tiesa*, Albertas Laurinčiukas, already under attack by the Writers' Union, reportedly had a heart attack the day before the meeting in Vingis Park, and therefore, one *Tiesa* correspondent insisted to me, the boycott obviously had no influence on his disappearance from the newspaper and subsequent retirement.

Whether from the boycott, Laurinčiukas's illness, or the confusion of perestroika, however, the newspaper went through significant changes in the next few months, although it still carried Laurinčiukas's name as editor. The party Central Committee was unable to decide on a permanent replacement for him, and the assistant editor, Mindaugas Barysas, had to take the responsibility on a provisional basis until he officially became editor at the end of the year. Such was the confusion of the day in party ranks that Barysas was not even a member of the party Central Committee.

In all, the gathering in Vingis Park constituted a major achievement for Sajudis; it enjoyed considerable moral support and in addition collected 28,650 rubles in donations. Critics complained that it still lacked a "program"; it seemed to reformulate its program at every rally. They also warned that it must keep its distance from "extremists" who obviously wanted to attach their own causes to the Sajudis banner. This, the conservatives kept repeating, is a time for real work, not just words.[31] But Sajudis was growing.

The references to "extremists" referred to the Freedom League. Both the league and government wanted to give Terleckas and other league representatives a prominent role in Vingis Park. A television film about the meeting in Vingis Park, *Rebirth of a Nation*, distributed in the United States with an English-language commentary, paid considerable attention to Terleckas's presence, even though he played no role in the proceedings, and many émigré commentators went out of their way to give the Freedom League a place at all the mass meetings organized by Sajudis.[32] Conservative émigrés, still suspicious of Sajudis as being some sort of Communist ruse, preferred to give their support to the Freedom League.

The relations between the two groups faced another major test almost immediately after Vingis Park. The Lithuanian Temperance Movement announced a meeting in Gediminas Square for July 12, the anniversary of the treaty between Soviet Russia and Lithuania in 1920 that recognized Lithuanian independence. In Sajudis's name, Ozolas and Petkevičius announced that their group would take no part in the observation. As many Sajudis members understood it, the Freedom League had established itself on the left wing of the temperance organization, and they preferred to stay clear of any association with either group. "The Initiative Group refused to extend its support to today's unofficial demonstration, considering it too radical," snorted the Lithuanian Information Center in Brooklyn.[33]

The demonstration went ahead despite efforts of militia and druzhenniki to block it as having no official permission. Late in the afternoon the demonstrators, many waving flags, gathered in front of the cathedral/art gallery. Since militia had detained Terleckas, Vytautas Bogušis opened the meeting by insisting, "Freedom is never granted as a gift by one nation to another. Freedom is always won at the price of great sacrifices." The meeting lasted for about an hour before breaking up.[34]

Spectators reacted in many different ways. A newspaper correspondent criticized the "extremists" as having been "provocative" and insisted that "there was no meeting." Demonstrators accused the militia of having used rubber truncheons. According to émigré sources, "tens of thousands" of people were prevented from joining the meeting. Sajudis declared the government's action against the meeting to be unconstitutional. A few isolated voices suggested that Gediminas Square should be reserved for more important subjects.[35]

Sajudis suffered no loss of prestige for having remained apart from the July 12 demonstration, and it expanded its own activity into new areas. On the fifteenth the group organized a demonstration near the Supreme Soviet against the Ignalina power plant. On July 19 supporters set up on Gediminas Square an exhibition of photographs of Sajudis activities, and they kept it up to date over the succeeding months. On July 20, wearing tricolor caps, another large group of cyclists set off from

Vilnius to carry an ecological and national message, "Lithuania My Home," throughout the republic.[36]

A "Rock March," a series of rock concerts moving through Lithuania, culminated on August 7 with Juozaitis's standing before 7,000 fans in Vilnius, backed up by Antis, tricolor in hand, urging the young people to be grateful to the older generation who had saved the colors through the dark years of repression. The crowd responded with the chant, *A-čiu, a-čiu, a-čiu* ("Thank you, thank you, thank you"). Juozaitis went on to thank émigrés who had nurtured Lithuanian culture through the hard years; again the crowd responded with chants. "Yesterday you shouted 'metal,'" Kaušpedas called out to the rock fans. "Today you chant 'Lithuania'—that is a real rebirth!"

The combination of ecological concerns, rock music, and national feeling mobilized the youth of Lithuania behind Sajudis. As Juozaitis later explained, "Rock rules the masses but it achieves such a relationship of individual and mass that the individual does not lose his autonomy."[37] In 1989 he admitted to at one time having looked "very pessimistically at the function of music, but in practice I exploited that function. . . . There is a lot of freedom and peaceful spirit in the music of the youth."[38]

The government responded by seeking new restrictions on public demonstrations. When the Lithuanian Supreme Soviet announced its intention to accept a law proposed by Moscow demanding ten days' notice of a meeting and giving the city Executive Council the right to prevent any gathering, a headline in *Sajudžio žinios* cried out, "WE WILL NOT REMAIN SILENT!" and summoned supporters to a demonstration outside the Supreme Soviet building on July 26.

Although Juozaitis and Gintaras Songaila reportedly spent an hour and a half beforehand sitting in the office of Vilnius mayor Algirdas Vileikis listening to complaints about Sajudis's "anarchist" and "anti-Soviet" activity, some 5,000 persons gathered near the Supreme Soviet. Militiamen announced that this was an illegal gathering and prevented the demonstrators from approaching the building. The demonstrators moved in front of the Mažvydas Republican Library and heard Sajudis speakers denounce the proposed legislation. Bronius Genzelis suggested that citizens might recall their representatives in the Supreme Soviet, and Julius Juzeliunas added a call to complete the process of "rehabilitating" deportees by simply declaring the deportation to have been unjustified and illegal. The meeting broke up without violence.[39]

The confrontation laid the groundwork for future developments: Sajudis had become a major public force in Lithuania and the authorities were looking for ways to restrict its growth. The demonstrators had risked going ahead with an unauthorized meeting. The Supreme Soviet postponed the proposed legislation, but a few days later it accepted the new regulations.[40] Although the minister of internal affairs, Stasys Lisauskas, had previously claimed that his men did not carry rubber truncheons, they had them on this occasion, and the Lithuanians were again to see them later.[41] For the moment, the two sides were still cautiously watching each other, but physical confrontation loomed as a real possibility.

5

The Visitation

In the summer of 1988 reformers and conservatives alike paid at least lip service to Mikhail Gorbachev's program of perestroika and glasnost, however they might be interpreting them. They all expressed interest in "economic self-sufficiency." From there on disagreement reigned, ranging from arguments about principles such as whether Lithuanian should become the official language of the republic to disputes over the competence of individuals in party and government. The question of how Moscow would react loomed large in everyone's thoughts.

The forces of movement attacked on many fronts. On July 20 the linguists publicized their justification for making Lithuanian the language of the republic.[1] At the end of July the Lithuanian Academy of Sciences' Constitutional Commission made its first recommendations for constitutional reform, aiming at expanding the competence of the republican government: "One of the most important statements is that on Lithuanian territory exclusively Lithuanian laws are enforced," reported Radio Vilnius's English-language service, "while the Soviet Union will have on Lithuanian territory the competence granted by Lithuanian [laws] and not the other way around."[2] Such a provision would give Lithuania considerable political autonomy, and Moscow, as had to be expected, would surely object.

Conservatives in Lithuania countered by emphasizing traditional Soviet values, but they increasingly had to resort to non-Lithuanian media. On July 5 *Sovetskaia Litva* carried an article by Navickas arguing that history was "an exact science" and that therefore unqualified individuals should not be permitted to practice it lest their "superficiality and subjectivism" mislead the unsuspecting. On July 12, in the same newspaper, Robertas Žiugžda memorialized the 1920 peace treaty between Lithuania and Soviet Russia , and on August 3 Navickas reappeared with an article commemorating Lithuania's incorporation into the Soviet Union in 1940. Konstantinas Surblys also contributed an article on the "revolutionary situation" of 1940 to the August 3 issue of *Sovetskaia Litva*. On August 1 the Soviet News Agency TASS quoted Vytautas Astrauskas, the president of the Lithuanian Supreme Soviet, as having stated that the Lithuanian people had voluntarily joined the Soviet Union as the culmination of "a revolutionary situation."[3]

Sovetskaia Litva also kept warning of "Lithuanian nationalism," a charge that the Lithuanians resented. The charge, they argued, never seemed applicable to Russians: "What is patriotism to a Russian, for example, can easily be considered to be nationalism for a Lithuanian or an Estonian," wrote Rimvydas Valatka in *Gimtasis kraštas*.[4] Trained over the years to consider "bourgeois nationalism" something bad, the Lithuanians insisted that the feelings they were expressing should not be thrown into the negative semantic circle of "nationalism," and they also objected to the use of the word *nationalist* by foreign observers.

The Initiative Group was made up almost exclusively of Lithuanians. The Lithuanians constituted 80 percent of the 3.5 million people living in the republic; of the constituent republics of the USSR, only the Armenian had a larger proportion of native population (in 1979 about 90 percent). Russians constituted 8.9 percent of the republic's inhabitants, and the Poles 7.3 percent. The bulk of these other nationalities, however, lived in Vilnius, the capital of the republic, where the Lithuanians constituted about 50 percent of the population, the Russians about 22 percent and the Poles 18 percent.[5] As a result, all national conflicts in Lithuania were felt especially acutely in the republic's capital.

When the Lithuanians erupted with demands concerning their own culture and language, they naturally felt no need to worry about the rights of Russians, whom they considered to have enough protection from elsewhere. When the local Russians professed themselves to be "frightened" by this upsurge of "Lithuanian nationalism," however, Sajudis had to respond carefully, apprehensive of a Polish-Russian alliance that could call on allies in Moscow.

The Poles, to be sure, already occupied a special place in the nationalities policy of the Soviet Union. According to official figures some 1.2 million Poles lived in the Soviet Union, and of these 250,000 were in Lithuania. In June 1988 they received special attention as a result of the visit of Jozef Cardinal Glemp, the primate of Poland. Although they had no territory designated as their own, the Poles in the USSR enjoyed significant cultural rights, established by treaty between the Soviet Union and Poland in the early postwar years. Besides having a Catholic church in Moscow, known to locals as "the Polish church," in Lithuania they had their own schools, their own religious services in the Catholic churches, and their own newspaper, *Czerwony sztandar*, published by the Central Committee of the Lithuanian Communist Party.[6]

Lithuanians rather resented the privileges that the Poles enjoyed. During the historic union of Poland and Lithuania, lasting from the fourteenth century to the end of the eighteenth, the Lithuanian upper classes had for the most part adopted Polish culture, and in the nineteenth century the Lithuanian language had stood on the edge of extinction. Lithuanians believed that many if not most of the Poles living in Lithuania were actually the descendants of Lithuanians who had adopted Polish culture. If they insisted on remaining Polish, said many Lithuanians, why did they not move to Poland?

Between the World Wars, from 1920 to 1939, Vilnius, called Wilno in Polish, had been part of Poland, but as an isolated frontier outpost it had decayed. The Lithuanians had demanded Vilnius as their historic capital and, because of the Polish occupation of the city, the Lithuanian government, located in the "provisional capital" of Kaunas, had refused to open diplomatic relations with Poland until faced with an ultimatum in 1938. The Soviet action in taking Vilnius from Poland in 1939 and turning it over to the Lithuanians held a major place in the arguments of those who wanted to inspire Lithuanian gratitude toward Moscow.

Even in the Soviet years, however, Polish culture had

maintained its foothold in Vilnius, and in recent years the Lithuanians of Vilnius resented the practice of the city fathers in awarding contracts for restoring buildings in the Old City to Polish specialists in the reconstruction of old buildings. The Lithuanians complained that Polish visitors were buying up scarce consumer goods, making their free market into a Polish bazaar, and generally undermining Lithuanian efforts to establish full control of their own land.

The Poles of Vilnius had presumably chosen to remain in the land rather than emigrate, but they continued to look to Poland for cultural nourishment. Western Lithuania could watch Polish television; all of Lithuania could hear Polish radio, including broadcasts of Catholic masses; news that Lithuanian television would add a channel to its broadcasting brought demands to pick Polish TV. Asserting their own national identity, the Poles objected strongly to the Lithuanian practice of referring to Polish-speaking peasants outside of Vilnius as *tuteiszy* or *tuteišiai*, "locals" without a national consciousness. These people, argued *Czerwony sztandar*, were Poles, nothing else, and "that word" was in fact insulting.

When the Lithuanians started waving their flags and insisting that Lithuanian must be the official language of the republic, Russians and Poles alike reacted with concern. Conservatives argued in principle that this new national consciousness was a bad thing and even dangerous to public morals, but many simply feared for their own future—would they have to learn Lithuanian in order to remain in the republic? Whether for reasons of principle or of personal comfort, opposition developed, looking for points on which to attack Sajudis and the Lithuanians.

The Lithuanian public had no doubt that Mitkin, Moscow's eye in Vilnius, was encouraging agitation against Sajudis. "Comrade N. Mitkin," wrote Juozaitis, "not understanding Lithuanian, had particular reason to suspect our movement of nationalist plans." Whoever was behind the agitation, *Sovetskaia Litva* carried the message: the newspaper's editor, Emilianov, blandly insisted that he was not waging any anti-Lithuanian campaign, but his newspaper complained, among other things, that the concessions that Brazauskas had announced in Vingis Park had been poorly prepared.[7]

Typifying the explosiveness of the situation was the furor that arose after Vytautas Martinkus spoke to factory workers in Vilnius about his work at the Nineteenth Party Conference. *Sovetskaia Litva* recorded his argument for making Lithuanian the official language of the republic but also declared that he had expressed reservations about nationalism, demagogy, and excessive emotionalism in Sajudis's public gatherings. He reportedly criticized Brazauskas for acting too quickly in announcing the government's readiness to recognize "the flag of the bourgeois republic."[8]

Martinkus objected that he had been misquoted, but he had to resort to the pages of *Sajudžio žinios* to respond, insisting that he supported giving the Lithuanian nation back "the true symbols of its historical development." The editors of *Sajudžio žinios* added their own commments about *Sovetskaia Litva*'s "partisan and provocative" reporting.[9] *Sovetskaia Litva* nevertheless continued its campaign against the Lithuanians, on the sixth of August criticizing the thought of making Lithuanian the official language and on the tenth declaring that Sajudis had contributed to exacerbating tensions between the nationalities of Lithuania.

Although many Lithuanians considered *Czerwony sztandar* to be as hostile to Sajudis as *Sovetskaia Litva*, the Poles of Lithuania took a more moderate position than the Lithuanians gave them credit for. Poles rather naturally questioned Sajudis's image of Lithuania as symbolized by the drive to make Lithuanian the republic's official language. "I see no place there for us," declared Jan Ciechanowicz, a prominent Polish intellectual in Vilnius; "There cannot be just one official language," argued a theater administrator, "it would be nonsense for a Pole to speak with a Pole in Lithuanian." Nevertheless, with reservations, the Polish Social-Cultural Society in Lithuania accepted the thought of cooperating with Sajudis.[10]

At the beginning of August both sides tuned up their arguments in anticipation of the arrival of an envoy from Moscow, Alexander Iakovlev, a member of the Communist Party Politburo and one of Gorbachev's closest advisors. The Lithuanians understood well the importance of this visit. On August 9 seven members of Sajudis's Initiative Group met with Iakovlev's advance agent, A. Tsvetkov, the deputy director of the Cultural Section of the Central Committee in Moscow.

Moscow, Tsvetkov told the Lithuanians, was hearing "panicky characterizations of Sajudis," and therefore it was necessary to come see for oneself. Bronius Genzelis complained about administrators in Lithuania; Landsbergis criticized Mitkin; Prunskiene explained Sajudis's economic program; and Ozolas called Sajudis an essential step toward escaping from Stalinism and stagnation. Tsvetkov listened sympathetically, but in the end he suggested that the group should cooperate more with the government and eschew political activity. Be careful, he added, that extremists do not enter the organization and push the intellectuals aside as had been done in Karabakh; the Lithuanians, he warned, must avoid the "moral 'totalitarianism'" of the Armenians.[11]

On the tenth, making its own contribution toward influencing the visitors, *Sovetskaia Litva* published an interview with Jakubas Minkevičius, a member of the Initiative Group, in which the philosopher insisted that Sajudis meant to represent all the people of Lithuania regardless of nationality. The newspaper added a commentary suggesting that Sajudis was not living up to Minkevičius's noble ideals and that the Lithuanians were simply anti-Soviet nationalists.

On Thursday, August 11, Iakovlev arrived in Vilnius. His first meeting was with representatives of the Academy of Sciences, and his second was with "the creative intelligentsia." (Lithuanians laughingly declared that Iakovlev understood that the Writers' Union was a center for "nationalists" whereas the academy was a center of "nationalism.") He came to the meetings flanked by Lithuanian party officials, and the name "Sajudis" did not appear in the press, but Iakovlev's purpose was clear: he was in Lithuania to resolve the tensions between Sajudis and the party.

Juras Požela, president of the Academy of Sciences, opened the first meeting by recounting how the academy had reorganized itself so as to improve the practical application of its work in the development of the republic's economy. Economic self-dependency, he concluded, was essential: "This is not nationalism, but the wish that the republic should be the most Soviet, the most 'socialist,' in our Great Fatherland." Eduardas Vilkas went on to argue that khozraschet demanded "the sovereignty of the people, that it should have all authority in its territory, but at the same time that it should remember that its territory and the republic are a part of a unified Soviet Union."

After others had spoken of problems concerning textbooks and computers, Alfonsas Eidintas summarized the situation in historical science. "There are still many 'blank spots' in our history," he began; recent events "have shown that historical science cannot so competently answer all the questions being raised. There are problems in explaining the situation in 1939–1940 in the Baltic. Part of the public does not believe the concept of simultaneous revolutionary events in Lithuania, Latvia and Estonia." The historians must "identify the influence of Stalinism on events in Lithuania, 1939–1941, and clearly separate these phenomena from the fundamental principles of socialism. . . . Silence or the repetition of superficial truths creates a fertile field for foreign opponents and their instruments of mass communication."

After Vytautas Statulevičius, the vice-president of the academy, had spoken about ecological concerns, Iakovlev responded, noting first of all that while one could justly deplore ecological damage, scientists had to shoulder their own share of the blame in that they had approved the projects now being challenged as harmful. He then turned on Eidintas, expressing shock at the size of the Institute of History: "Your historical institute has one hundred historians! That is a huge institute of history!" With "seven historians, and at least half of them like [Evgenii] Tarle [a noted Soviet historian of the 1930s]," he declared, "do you know how renowned you would be in the whole world? But here there are a hundred historians! A hundred historians!"

Eidintas could not interrupt to correct his own error in explaining the work of the institute. There were in fact 100 employees of the institute but only 36 historians, 16 of them in the section on the history of socialism, 10 in the section on the history of capitalism, and 10 in the section on the history of feudalism. The institute was by no means so "huge" as Iakovlev had understood, but one could not correct such a distinguished visitor in public.

The social sciences, Iakovlev granted, posed special problems: "Very often the demands on them are too great: Historical findings should be based on facts, like findings in physics," independently of the existing social and political order. Admitting that in the past there had been pressures on social scientists to conform to certain standards, he suggested that older historians might not be able to make the necessary change: "Yesterday [the historian] wrote that Stalin was the most brilliant of all military geniuses; today, must he write just the opposite? How can we believe such a scholar? Let him stand back a bit." A new generation of scholars would presumably have to step in to lead the way.

Turning to the topic of republican self-sufficiency, he asserted that Lenin had identified only two questions as constituting all-union concerns—defense and foreign policy. For his own part, Iakovlev declared, he was not so sure about foreign policy. Certainly newspapers should be able to send their own correspondents abroad just so long as they could pay for this themselves— "That is what khozraschet is for!" Iakovlev's liberal interpretation of republican rights spoke directly to the hearts of the Lithuanians, but Moscow would come to regret these words even before the end of the year.

Later on in the same day, again in the company of party and government officials, Iakovlev met with representatives of the "creative intelligentsia"—artists and writers. Martinkus, speaking as the head of the Writers' Union, asserted that the intelligentsia had already taken the first steps toward perestroika and a new outlook on life: "In essence our press has never spoken so openly about Lithuania's history, its most painful and sorrowful pages, about the deportations and repressions of 1941 and of the postwar period, about the bitter fruits of hasty collectivization." Sajudis, he continued, represented a positive, albeit unprecedented, contribution toward realizing the goals of perestroika, since art itself raises the issues of "man's responsibility in the questions of daily life."

In response Iakovlev reiterated the urgency of perestroika, and he recounted the government's concerns in matters of food, nationalities, and youth. In the past the government had dealt severely, and not always wisely, with films and novels, but the writers themselves had been responsible for the censorship, he insisted; this had not been just the work of faceless figures "in the apparatus." He urged the artists to deal with the real "drama of man," and he warned that as conservatism "comes closer to a certain point, it will resist more sharply."

No one challenged Iakovlev's dialectic in this last statement, either then or later. In the 1930s Stalin had used the same polemical tactic in justifying the use of terror, saying that as the final victory of socialism came closer, its enemies would become more desperate and that therefore the government had to resort to extreme measures in order to root out that enemy. Since the late 1950s, Soviet historians had been criticizing Stalin's reasoning, but Iakovlev seemed to be endorsing it. Underlying such an image was the thought that one might need "sharper" measures to deal with "sharper" resistance to official policy, whatever it might be.

Algimantas Čekuolis then took the floor to complain about Sajudis's lack of access to the media in Lithuania. He appealed to the principles of glasnost and "democratization," and he argued that the success of Sajudis's meetings with the delegates to the Nineteenth Party Conference had shown the "political face of this movement." But why had the press maintained its stony silence? Was it a matter of disagreement? fear? orders? There was no reason to fear "maximalism or separatism"; the people were united behind Soviet power as never before. They wanted it to be open, accountable, and democratic.

Julius Juzeliunas took up the cause of the victims of Stalinism who were still suffering the legal consequences of their exile in the 1940s and 1950s. These people should not have to endure the humiliation of petitioning for rehabilitation; couldn't the USSR Central Committee automatically rehabilitate everyone? "We believe that the collective resolution of this delicate and important question will certainly help improve the public's belief in the process of perestroika." In response, Iakovlev asked for time: "You would help us if you would not hurry." He praised Juzeliunas for speaking of "Stalinism" rather than "Stalin." Stalinism, he declared, "is still not completely understandable to us."

Petkevičius brought up Jermalavičius's celebrated essay, calling it "a Lithuanian variant of Nina Andreeva's article," and he asserted that Sajudis had arisen as a reaction to the slow pace of perestroika in Lithuania. "It was necessary to arouse some sort of popular support for perestroika," he explained. As for

Sovetskaia Litva's complaints of "nationalist slogans" at Sajudis meetings, he insisted there had not been "one anti-Russian act, not one," that could be attributed to Sajudis. He concluded by complaining about Mitkin's role in the Lithuanian Central Committee.

Iakovlev chose to defend party institutions. The Politburo, he noted, had criticized Andreeva's article, but it had not called for a boycott of *Sovetskaia Rossiia* for having printed it. Boycotting a newspaper, he declared, "constituted a part of the past. Democracy consists of a clash of opinions." In reference to Mitkin, he objected to looking at the nationality of party officials, but he went on to declare that many republics wanted Russian officials. In any case, he suggested, this should not be the most important question of the day.

Closing the discussion, Iakovlev declared himself satisfied. "We have to trust and understand each other," he said, and he predicted great progress in the coming year. He told of changes in governmental organizations, in the process of economic planning, and in the electoral process. "Let us meet in the fall of next year and recall what we spoke of today," he concluded.[12]

Despite the generally soothing effect of Iakovlev's comments, there were signs of continued tension and promises of future trouble, especially over the nationalities question. A. Gelbakh, the deputy editor of *Sovetskaia Litva*, had disputed Petkevičius's assertion that there had been no anti-Russian acts. The published minutes of Iakovlev's talks with the intellectuals, moreover, gave somewhat obscure witness to the explosiveness of the nationalities question: "A. Čekuolis spoke of a crime in which the student M. Juknevičius was injured. An ELTA report about this was published in republican newspapers of August 13."

Čekuolis had wanted to offer an example of problems that he saw arising as a result of the negative image that Sajudis was receiving in the Lithuanian press; instead he aroused a prolonged storm that unloaded itself directly on his head. According to ELTA, Čekuolis told Iakovlev that two days earlier two Russian-speaking "hooligans" had attacked and stabbed a young man wearing a Sajudis badge, calling him a fascist. "No one wants to blame the Russian people," he cautioned, but the press's refusal to discuss Sajudis's program was nourishing "malicious rumors about supposed nationalism and separatism." The atmosphere in Lithuania would be considerably healthier if Sajudis received public recognition, he concluded.

Čekuolis's statement to Iakovlev unleashed a furious storm. Lithuanian Prime Minister Vytautas Sakalauskas rose to announce that the young man in question had lied about the source of his wound; it was the result of a fight with a comrade. ELTA immediately put out a news release, passing rather lightly over why the young man lied and focusing instead on Čekuolis as having publicized a socially harmful rumor and thereby having fanned hostility between the nationalities of Lithuania.

Čekuolis insisted that he had been deceived. Although some of his supporters pointed out that he had used information given him by the Ministry of Internal Affairs and suggested that he had been set up, he himself focused his wrath on the young man in question; in *Gimtasis kraštas* of August 18, under the title "Wolf, Wolf," he declared that the miscreant would have to confess in public and pull his pants down for a whipping. This imagery evoked further attacks. *Tiesa* of August 24 carried a letter from an indignant reader calling Čekuolis's explanation unsatisfactory, saying that Čekuolis was trying to make the unfortunate youth the scapegoat for his own misdeeds.

As orchestrated by *Sovetskaia Litva*, discussion of the incident aimed at discrediting Čekuolis. A set of letters published on August 28 charged the Lithuanian with having instigated "dangerous rumors," and writers insisted he had "intentionally" issued his "provocative proclamation" in an effort to arouse strong feelings against "people of the Russian nationality" and to sow "enmity between peoples." *Sovetskaia Litva*, however, stopped short of endorsing the calls for Čekuolis's removal as editor of *Gimtasis kraštas* and declared, "Let us together seek a mutually acceptable resolution of each arising question, in the spirit of the tasks of perestroika." After Čekuolis left for a visit to America and new crises arose in September, the issue finally seemed forgotten.[13]

On Friday, August 12, Iakovlev completed his round of talks in Vilnius by meeting with the leaders of the Lithuanian Communist Party. Songaila opened the discussion in traditional fashion by recognizing that the party had not done enough to further mass education and atheistic education, and he went on to complain of foreign influences that were causing trouble in the republic. The party was working to improve, but he recognized that it still had much to do.

Iakovlev, in response, ignored the details of Songaila's confession and emphasized the need for action: "I am sure that future historians, characterizing the present condition of society, will write about the exceptional dynamism and the variety of current processes, the boldness of social thought and the unusual ideas." Some of the developments, he granted, might cause "discomfort, maybe panic," but the reforms were just beginning and there would be no easy victories. The roots of present-day problems, he declared, lay "in the historical past, in the nature and structure of that old world which we irretrievably left. But in our own past too." Historians must examine those roots carefully, fully explaining the truth about Stalinist repressions: "An open and honest approach to history—this is our accomplishment insofar as it gives witness to spiritual strength and maturity of society. The weak live by myths, the ignorant are nourished by legends." The truth about the past constituted "the compass for the future."

Lecturing the party officials, Iakovlev noted that much had been done but much remained to be done. "Perestroika," he declared, "applauds initiative," and this meant that the party had to enter into a rebirth of the political process, "to study politics." Nationalities, he continued, constituted a part of human society, and a person's social and economic nature could not be separated. The distortions of national policy realized in the "period of the cult of personality and of stagnation" must be thrust into the past.

He went on to give his implicit support to Lithuanian complaints against *Sovetskaia Litva* and even against Mitkin, quoting Petkevičius: "Isn't it a paradox. I know three languages, and am a nationalist. And he who calls me that knows one—Russian—even though he has lived in the republic for more than a decade. But he is an internationalist!" The rise of national consciousness among the people had to be accepted as "one of the facts of our life." The party must build a state of laws based on healthy individuals.

Responding to conservative complaints that the creative intelligentsia knew nothing of the real problems of life, he emphasized that "perestroika began as an intellectual explosion" and that it would have been impossible without the support of "the forceful activity of the civic-minded intelligentsia. This must be stated openly." The party must reject distrust of the intelligentsia as a relic of the past. "It is commonly known that the intelligentsia is the expression of the self-consciousness of the people," and also "the architect of this self-consciousness." Iakovlev made clear to the party that it would have to accept Sajudis and to work with it in the name of "pluralism of opinions." Socialism, he declared, "cannot be nonintellectual: this is not socialism."

Lithuanian speakers both defended and attacked Sajudis. Some, like Petras Braženas of the Writers' Union, insisted Sajudis should be recognized. Šepetys and Zaleckas argued that Communist Party members in Sajudis should exert a more restraining influence on Sajudis; they expressed concern about Sajudis's intolerance of party officials. Zaleckas admitted that the party had not been ready to defend the official picture of the events of 1939–1940, and Šepetys admitted that Sajudis had arisen as a result of the party's own shortcomings. Iakovlev told them all to listen to criticism and to respond constructively to it.[14]

When he left again for Moscow, Iakovlev left behind him a changed Lithuania. He had encouraged Sajudis leaders, and he had told party officials that they must learn to work with this new force. He had completely bypassed Moscow's Russian informants in Lithuania's government and party, essentially ignoring their campaign to discredit Sajudis. For the next several months, people would be continually quoting him to make their points. His visit constituted a major turning point in the fortunes of Sajudis.

Iakovlev's position was not just a personal one, but rather an expression of Moscow's current position on the nationalities question. An article approved on August 16 for publication in *Political Survey* (Moscow) spoke of "forced resettlement" and "large-scale unlawful repressions" of minority nationalities and argued that the trouble generally in the Baltic represented "the result of serious departures from internationalist principles of socialist democracy or even of their distortion." In conclusion, the author called for "transition of the republics and regions to the principles of cost accounting."[15] On August 20 *Pravda* carried an article by Petras Braženas sharply critical of the Lithuanian Communist Party leadership.

Other forces besides Sajudis could also draw encouragement from what Iakovlev had done or not done. Church officials duly noted that he had ignored Songaila's standard reference to the need to intensify atheistic propaganda. This could not be accidental, they believed; Moscow seemed to be promising the church in Lithuania new latitude for its work.[16]

Over the next week, the party and government in Vilnius displayed a new spirit of movement, even as they continued to complain about "nationalism" and "chauvinism." The party called for improvement in the teaching of Lithuanian language and history; the pay of Lithuanian teachers in Russian and Polish schools was raised; the system of bilingual education was to be altered to begin Russian only in the third grade.

On August 17 the evening television news show "Panorama" made the welcome announcement that the government had legalized the tricolor flag and the national hymn. Brazauskas had promised their legalization in his speech on July 9 but, since no decree had been forthcoming, local officials in many parts of Lithuania still insisted these symbols were illegal. "Panorama"'s report settled the question. I was visiting friends that evening; a woman sat quietly thinking about this announcement and then murmured gently, "Our children will have what we did not . . ." By the weekend fans were carrying the tricolor to a soccer match.

Party leaders now spoke with significantly softer words about Sajudis. Kestutis Zaleckas declared that Saljudis was following policies basically in line with the demands of the Nineteenth Party Conference, but he called on party members in Sajudis to become more active so as to protect it from the influence of "extremists" and "nationalists" who were trying to exploit it for their own aims.[17]

Even Mitkin took a softer line, accepting Sajudis into the Lithuanian body politic. He told party workers that local party units should not demand that their members not participate in Sajudis support groups. Sajudis constituted an established fact in Lithuanian life, born of perestroika, it was not "an opposition party," and therefore "membership in Sajudis should not be a block to the selection of Communists to party posts."[18] Given the fact that this statement was published on the day Lithuanians planned to commemorate the Nazi-Soviet pact of 1939, some wags asked whether Mitkin had begun wearing a Sajudis button.

Sajudis itself now received more time in the press. In *Komjaunimo tiesa* of August 19 Kazimiera Prunskiene explained that Sajudis was a social movement that had no intention of becoming a political party, that thoughts that Sajudis wanted to seize power were silly, and that to demand that Lithuanian be the official language did not constitute "nationalism." *Vakarines naujienos* of August 22 even carried a formal announcement of Sajudis's meeting scheduled for Vingis Park the next day.

Nevertheless Sajudis supporters recognized that they still faced serious opposition. Although the Russians were still irritated about Čekuolis's misadventure, *Sajudžio žinios* carried a major complaint by a writer, Marcelijus Martinaitis, about the Russian campaign to discredit Sajudis as "nationalist" before Iakovlev's visit. "Chauvinism or Demagogy?" asked the newspaper's headline. *Sovetskaia Litva*, it was charged, reported small demonstrations in Africa far more carefully and sympathetically than it did demonstrations in Vilnius. A week and a half later, *Sajudžio žinios* published a complaint about the hostile editorial policies of *Czerwony sztandar*.[19] Iakovlev's visit had given Sajudis a significant boost, but the fundamental confrontation of conservatives and reformers continued.

Meeting of June 2, "Can We Overcome the Bureaucracy?" at which it was decided to form the organization that became Sajudis.

Kazimiera Prunskiene and Jokubas Minkevičius sitting on the left; Romualdas Ozolas in the light suit.

Bronius Kuzmickas.

Jokubas Minkevičius and Romualdas Ozolas.

June 3 meeting at which Sajudis was formed.

Presidium: Raimundas Rajeckas, Antanas Buračas, Eduardas Vilkas, Juozas Bulavas, Bronius Kuzmickas.

View of the Academy of Sciences hall in the course of the meeting.

Another view of the meeting.

Members of the Initiative Group hold their first meeting after having been chosen.

June 14, 1988. A demonstrator raises the tricolor flag at a rally commemorating the deportations of 1941.

June 24, 1988. Rally in Gediminas Square seeing off the delegates to the XIX Party Conference in Moscow.

The banners read: "The Central Committee Chose You, You Will Answer to Lithuania," "A Free Lithuania in the Family of European Peoples," and "The 2d Secretary of the LCP = Governor General."

Vytautas Landsbergis addresses the meeting.

Algirdas Brazauskas speaks.

Vytautas Landsbergis addresses the demonstration outside of Elta office, June 28, 1988.

July 9, Vingis Park: welcoming back the delegates to the XIX Party Conference in Moscow.

Zigmas Vaišvila and Vytautas Petkevicius.

July 12: militia break up attempts to hold a meeting commemorating
the peace treaty between Lithuania and Soviet Russia in 1920.

July 26: demonstration in front of the Mazvydas Republican Library;
in the background to the left is the Supreme Soviet Building.

August 23 meeting.

Vytautas Landsbergis.

Sigitas Geda.

Array of forces defending Gediminas Square in the evening after the meeting in Vingis Park.

Hunger Strike.

An announcement of the "Hunger Strike for Political Prisoners and Deportees."

Petras Cidzikas, with beard and white cap, explains his cause.

After August 23: the pictures of Stalin, Molotov, and von Ribbentrop went up after the meeting in Vingis Park.

End of August: an elaborate tent protected the demonstrators.

September 5: Vytautas Landsbergis and Justinas Marcinkevičius.

September 28, 1988. Troops in position.

Flags on the Square later in the evening.

September 29, 1988. Crowd milling in Gediminas Square before the opening of the protest demonstration.

Vytautas Landsbergis speaks to the demonstration. On his right stands Antanas Terleckas, on his left Zigmas Vaišvila and Gintaras Songaila.

Leaders of Lithuanian Freedom League: from the left, Vytautas Bogušis, Antanas Terleckas, Victoras Petkus.

Sajudis Convention, October 21–23, 1988.

Algimantas Čekuolis, in charge of press relations, speaks with the author.

Vytautas Landsbergis with his father.

Arvydas Juozaitis addresses the opening session. Justinas Marcinkevičius and Meile Lukšiene, co-chairs.

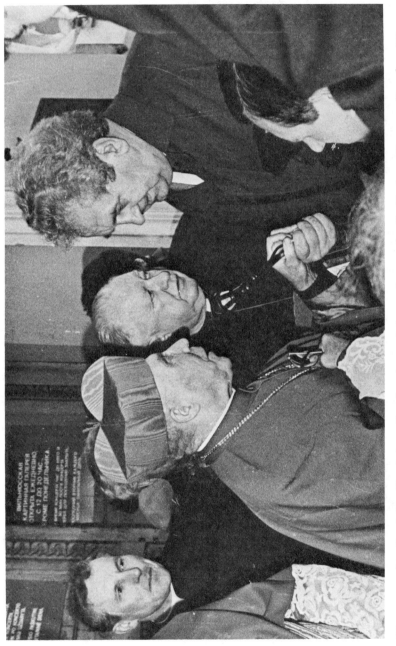

Vincentas Cardinal Sladkevicius after having celebrated mass in Gediminas Square, October 23.

The author asks a question at the press conference of October 23.

Alfonsas Eidintas answers the question. To his right: Gediminas Rudis, Algimantas Čekuolis, and Liudas Truska.

Algirdas Brazauskas addresses the convention, October 23.

——— photographs by Jonas Česnavicius and others.

6

Exposing the Secret

In the aftermath of Iakovlev's visit, Lithuanians focused their attention on the upcoming anniversary of the Molotov-Ribbentrop Non-Aggression Pact of 1939 and the question of the "secret protocols" by which the Germans and the Soviets in 1939 had divided East Central Europe between themselves. In the first agreement of August 23, Lithuania had been consigned to Germany, but in the second agreement of September 28, 1939, the Germans had traded most of Lithuania to the Soviet Union. After the incorporation of Lithuania into the USSR in 1940, a third agreement, dated January 10, 1941, had assigned one last portion of Lithuania to the Soviet Union.

The Western powers had introduced the documents at the Nuremberg War Crimes Trial after World War II but, following their publication in the United States, Soviet historians had denounced them as forgeries. "Falsifiers of history," they called historians who accepted the documents as genuine.[1] In 1987, working up to the observance of the anniversary of the Molotov-Ribbentrop pact, Radio Free Europe's Lithuanian service had broadcast a number of items pertaining to the protocols but, since the Soviets jammed this frequency, few in Lithuania seemed to have heard the programs.

Among Lithuanian writers and historians, discussion of the protocols had begun even before the 1987 anniversary. Eidintas had written about them in *Literatura ir menas*, and most intellectuals seemed to have some idea of their existence, but many apparently had no idea of what the protocols might actually say. Soviet historians in Moscow insisted that they could not find the protocols in Soviet archives and that they therefore must not exist. Accordingly, Moscow declared, they should not be discussed. The press in Lithuania dutifully remained silent.

The Estonians finally broke the silence and published the texts in the summer of 1988. *Sajudžio žinios* soon followed suit, using a *samizdat* translation of the original American publication, *Nazi-Soviet Relations*. Bronius Kuzmickas, a philosopher, put his name to the publication of the protocols and several key telegrams between Molotov and Ribbentrop. "Absolute openness about these agreements is essential," wrote Kuzmickas: silence served only to weaken popular belief in glasnost and democracy in the Soviet Union.[2]

Reacting to *Sajudžio žinios*'s publishing the protocols, Robertas Žiugžda, writing in *Sovetskaia Litva* of August 18, expressed regret that many Soviet documents of that period had not seen the light of day, and he accepted the view that Stalinist foreign policy had suffered "deformation" because of the leader's "cult of personality." Although he called the Soviet Union wise to have accepted Hitler's offer of a Non-Aggression Pact in 1939, he ad-

mitted that the division of East Central Europe constituted "a clear deviation from generally accepted norms
of international law, from Leninist principles of foreign
policy." In form the Soviet move into Eastern Poland
on September 17 might be considered "an occupation,"
but "in the perspective of securing the national self-
dependence and statehood" of the peoples concerned,
"these steps, under the conditions of the time, were
inevitable."

Despite tactical errors, Žiugžda continued, the Soviet
Union had protected Lithuania from Nazi attack. "Reactionary circles of the Lithuanian bourgeoisie" nevertheless began "to sabotage this agreement." Stalin, to
be sure, had exceeded the "normal relations between
states" by couching his demands of Lithuania in the
form of an ultimatum, but Stalinist repressions should
not eclipse the fact that the orderly establishment of
Soviet rule in Lithuania and the land's incorporation
into the Soviet Union "marked the beginning of a new
stage in the history of the country."

Žiugžda's tortured explanation satisfied few, and
there could be no doubt that something would happen
in Vilnius on August 23, 1988; the question was "What?"
On July 27 the Freedom League announced its plans for
holding a meeting. The Initiative Group had spent considerable time debating what it should do to observe the
anniversary: Would a meeting be permitted? Perhaps
there should just be some articles in the press; people
could wear black ribbons that day. Were the people
tired of having meetings and rallies?

The Initiative Group finally decided in favor of a demonstration. A letter to the Party Central Committee,
signed by twenty-three members of the group, declared

that the Soviet government should publish the 1939 treaty with all its attachments and take a clear position on it based on "today's juridical, political, and ideological evaluation." Sajudis, it assured the party, viewed "Lithuania's place in the USSR as a historical reality," but it wanted to improve that place by establishing a state governed by laws and by amending the constitution. Another letter, this one to Vileikis, dated August 12 and signed by Gintaras Songaila, Alvydas Medalinskas, and Arvydas Juozaitis, requested permission to meet in Gediminas Square, declaring, "We expect up to 20,000 participants."[3]

Over the next week considerable confusion reigned as to where the gathering might take place. The Freedom League had chosen Gediminas Square as the site for its rally. When Sajudis announced its plans to hold a meeting, the Freedom League declared that it would go where Sajudis did: "We must remain united," Terleckas told the Lithuanian Information Center in Brooklyn. "Our goals are the same—an independent Lithuania."[4] Some emigre publications, obviously relying on sources in the league, predicted that the authorities would prevent any public meeting on August 23.

Mayor Vileikis suggested to Sajudis that it should meet in Vingis Park. A member of the mayor's staff assured me that Vileikis had calculated that Gediminas Square might be too small for the crowd that would come; an emigre publication argued that Vileikis had diverted the demonstration out to Vingis Park in order to disrupt the Freedom League's plans.[5] A member of the Initiative Group later suggested to me that once the Voice of America (VOA) had announced the Freedom League's plans for Gediminas Square, the authorities decided to offer Vingis Park as a means of proving VOA wrong. When plans had been set, however, VOA matter-of-factly announced the change.

Whatever the considerations, the decision hung in the air; the "grapevine," obviously growing out of Sajudis, reported that if the meeting was to be held in Vingis Park, there would be an announcement on television; if there was no announcement, the meeting would be held in Gediminas Square. Finally on Saturday evening, August 20, Vytautas Landsbergis appeared on Lithuanian television to announce that a calm, hour-long memorial service would be held in Vingis Park on the twenty-third to commemorate the anniversary of the pact. Those who could not attend the meeting should take a moment for contemplation on their own.[6]

In the evening of August 17 a new element entered the scene when two hunger strikers, Petras Cidzikas and Algimantas Andreika, set up camp in Gediminas Square, at the corner of the cathedral/art museum outside the chapel of St. Casimir, the patron saint of Lithuania. The action had nothing to do with Sajudis. On the sixteenth Cidzikas had informed the Initiative Group of his intentions, and the group had decided to take no stand on his action—many indeed thought that the strikers would be quickly arrested. The strikers demanded that the government review the cases of eight men imprisoned or exiled on the charge of "anti-Soviet agitation" under Article 68 of the Penal Code.

The strikers quickly drew popular support, and other groups came to add their own causes to that of the original strikers. On Sunday the twenty-first, a group of six Armenians sat for a few hours under a banner declaring, "Armenia Is with You"; when they departed, they left their sign behind. Women set up candles and created a shrine of sorts in the wall of the cathedral by the place where the strikers sat. Besides expressing sympathy for the strikers, they advocated the return of the cathedral to the church.

Statements from people stopping to view the strikers both approved and condemned. "They don't know what they want themselves," declared one scornful passerby. "You can't talk about what you can't talk about," warned a cautious observer. "It will end soon, they will be taken away," predicted another. "The Russians liberated you," declared a Russian, while a Lithuanian snapped back, "But they forgot to leave!" On Sunday afternoon a priest came to say mass in the open air; in the evenings large groups gathered under specially installed floodlights to sing hymns and folk songs.

The official press took note of the strike on Friday, August 19, when *Komjaunimo tiesa* carried a report, based on information from the "organs of public order," that one of the demonstrators was under psychiatric observation. The report also recounted the charges against the prisoners on whose behalf the demonstration was taking place, speaking of one as a murderer, another as a draft dodger, a third as a homosexual. Algimantas Čekuolis, the newspaper recounted, had declared that "the Movement for Perestroika in Lithuania did not organize this action and does not support it."

Members of Sajudis's Initiative Group who sympathized especially with Cidzikas—"Starving is an extreme form of protest, a conscious sacrifice," wrote *Sajudžio žinios*[7]—criticized Čekuolis for having taken it upon himself to speak in the name of the group. In the meantime, the demonstrators posted a sign reading, "Thank you, *Komjaunimo tiesa*, for the attention." The area around the strikers now became the site of intense political debates on topics ranging from such recently tabu subjects as political and religious persecution to the secret protocols and the incorporation of Lithuania into the USSR.

Conservatives still denied the protocols' existence, and they received support from Moscow. Appearing on Moscow television on August 16 Šarmaitis insisted that Lithuania had experienced a real but peaceful "social revolution" in 1940.[8] On August 22 *Pravda* devoted a page to "letters from the republics of the Soviet Baltic"; Navickas and Domas Šniukas, *Pravda*'s correspondent in Vilnius, spoke on behalf of the Lithuanians in this forum, denouncing the Smetona regime that had ruled Lithuania until the establishment of Soviet rule in 1940.

The Lithuanian press discussed the issue of the protocols more critically, but still cautiously. Kestutis Zaleckas, head of the city's party organization, warned that the lack of documents only served to help "demagogic" and "nationalist" interests.[9] In *Tiesa* of August 20, Regina Žepkaite argued that even without the original text in hand historians had to recognize that evidence pointed to their existence and concluded that Germany gained more from the pact than did the Soviets. Although it did not satisfy those who wanted a blanket condemnation of Stalin and the Soviet government,[10] Žepkaite's article could not have been published three months earlier.

TASS, the official Soviet news agency, contributed to the discussion with an anonymous article, written in the offices of TASS-ELTA in Vilnius and published in *Literatura ir menas* on August 20. After reviewing the history of 1938 and 1939 and insisting that the Soviet Union took territory only to defend itself, the TASS dispatch printed the text of the protocol of August 23 as it had been introduced in the Nuremburg trial. The text, it suggested, seemed to have been carelessly written, a sign that it had not been prepared in advance.

On the morning of the twenty-third, Henrikas Šadžius, head of the section on the History of Socialism in the academy's Institute of History, criticized Stalin's theory of the "unavoidable sharpening of class conflict in constructing socialism"—the argument that Iakovlev had echoed—but saw the Soviet Union as having been threatened with a two-front war in 1939 and therefore forced to accept peace with Germany. Although generations of Soviet historians had insisted that the protocols did not exist, Šadžius concluded by publishing the text as printed in the West, simply warning his readers that they must read it critically.[11]

That evening the public that gathered in Vingis Park entertained no doubts about the authenticity of the protocols as published. They came in carrying tricolor flags of all sizes, most with black ribbons attached. No one could be sure how many people were there. Moscow radio spoke of 100,000, Sajudis claimed "at least 150,000," and Voice of America reported 200,000. Months later, people tended to say 150,000 to 200,000. Formally they came "to commemorate" the pact and its consequences; in fact they were there to condemn the pact.

After the meeting had opened with Juzeliunas's conducting the assemblage in singing Maironis's *Lithuania Beloved*, Vytautas Landsbergis offered his own portrait of August 23, 1939: "That day two men signed one document. Their names were Ribbentrop and Molotov. But behind them, who were evil-enough criminals, stood two others, Hitler and Stalin, whom mankind has not yet found words to describe." He pictured Stalin as hav-

ing enslaved his own country first and then having carried his system to other lands: "The earlier assertions of
some historians that this murderer of his own family
went into the street as the caring protector of the weak
cannot even convince the paper on which they were
written." Historians now have "more nerve, more freedom. We will hear their word." He declared that "Soviet
Lithuania, as we know it today, is the result of many
circumstances and actions" and that the population of
the Soviet Union still suffered from "the virus of Stalinism . . . the AIDS of Stalinism. We have to get well or
else we will die."

The next speaker was Justinas Marcinkevičius, a poet
well known for his interest in Lithuanian history. The
Non-Aggression Pact of 1939, he argued, "untied Hitler's
hands" and facilitated his victories in Western Europe.
However "politicians, historians, and ideologists" might
explain the pact, it stands as "a heinous document of international banditry," especially in the light of its secret
protocols. As for the inability of Moscow's historians to
find the text of the protocols, he scornfully commented,
"There is nothing funnier. It is absolutely clear that
Moscow will not find what it does not want to find, what
should not be found. One can search, but one should not
find." Perhaps, he added, a few Baltic historians should
enter the search as an example of "altruistic, fraternal,
international help for the benefit of historical truth."

Insisting that a people must know its own history,
Marcinkevičius offered five demands as a resolution of
the gathering: (1) to publish the Molotov-Ribbentrop
Pact with its protocols, (2) to establish a time-limit after which archival documents must be made public,
(3) to open all archives to historians and journalists,
(4) to publish a special volume of documents on recent

Lithuanian history, and (5) to prepare as quickly as possible a new program and new textbooks for the teaching of Lithuanian history in secondary schools. Marcinkevičius's proposals were out of order since the gathering was a memorial, and not a rally, but his words found their audience. In conclusion, he declared, "Long live a people freely associating with its history!"

Antanas Buračas, a member of the Academy of Sciences, also proposed a series of actions, including the possibility of joining "with our Latvian brothers" to blockade Ignalina in protest against construction of the third unit of the huge structure. He called for a special session of the Lithuanian Supreme Soviet to consider constitutional reform, for guarantees of Lithuanian cultural and economic sovereignty, for restitution of rights and property to deportees, for better relations with emigres, and for the reconsideration of the cases against people charged with anti-Soviet activity.

Buračas's call for better relations with the emigration spoke to a general effort being made in 1988 to close the gap between the homeland and the émigrés, to unite the divided islands of Lithuanian culture around the world. When I first arrived in Vilnius, I was immediately struck by a poster advertising a show of art by emigre Lithuanian artists; the art on the poster was the work of Vytautas Ignas, who lives in Connecticut. A number of émigré artists, moreover, were visiting Vilnius in connection with the show. "One nation, one culture," was a common theme in the press.

Marcinkevičius and Buračas had whipped up such enthusiasm in the crowd that Landsbergis had to remind the spectators that this was a memorial service. People carrying flags "should not wave them as if they were in a stadium; this is a different sort of gathering." The

tone of the meeting then temporarily changed: Lionginas Šepetys insisted that "the present government
of the land of Soviets" would never act as Stalin had
in 1939, and a Catholic priest, Edmundas Atkočiunas,
called on the people to join him in decrying the sins of
the modern world. The juxtaposition in a public meeting of the ideological chief of the party with a Catholic priest was unprecedented, but the priest's message
missed its target in this audience. Landsbergis inter-
vened to say, "We are against any sort of spiritual
dictate; we are for freedom of spirit and mind in all
respects."

History returned to the microphone with the appearance of Gediminas Rudis, who recounted how "Soviet
propaganda called France and England 'imperialists'"
in their war with Hitler's Germany. The events of 1940
in Lithuania, the "revolutionary situation," could not
be understood without reference to the context of Nazi-
Soviet relations: "Enough of acting as if [the protocols]
did not exist! . . . The traditional conception of socialist
revolution in Lithuania in 1940 does not satisfy the public." There had certainly been a crisis in the Lithuanian
government in 1940, but "the crisis at the top was organized from the Kremlin, and not very cleanly at that."

Turning to the contention that Soviet intervention in
Lithuania had saved the land from a plot to turn it over
to the Germans, Rudis declared that this idea was based
on the testimony of one man who had given the information under questioning by the security police. "We
now know well what the methods of interrogation were
at that time. If the interrogating officers had wanted, he
would also have confessed that he was digging a tun-
nel from Kaunas to Vilnius." Historical study, he con-

cluded, should not be produced "in congresses and party committees."

Arvydas Juozaitis took the microphone to give the briefest but at the same time most impassioned statement of the evening: "Today is the day of our great rebirth and cleansing. Therefore I wish that from today we would not see such slander about our people's history as Robertas Žiugžda and his flunkies spread in our periodical and academic press."

Juozaitis's sharp words startled many: "Undiplomatic," I heard some later say of them, "he should not have spoken so." Juozaitis himself later explained to me that he was not on the original roster of speakers. "They were talking about how Lithuania had been occupied, but this was not enough." Before the meeting, in discussing the program with other members of the Initia tive Group, he had declared that this meeting should contribute to the "rehabilitation of historical science." The meeting, however, went a different direction. Juozaitis felt that the "Stalinist historians were just laughing," that something had to be done to pillory at least the man he considered the leader of that camp, Žiugžda. Therefore he sidled up to Landsbergis and announced his intention to address the crowd, assuring him, "'I will now say three sentences.' Landsbergis asked 'Just three?' 'Just three.' And I said just two."

Liudas Truska then undertook to rehabilitiate history and challenged historians' traditional interpretations of the pact of 1939, arguing that signing the pact was in fact not in the best interests even of the Soviet Union. The three Baltic republics, moreover, were the only states to disappear from the map of Europe as a result of World War II, and it was ridiculous to say that any people would willingly give up their independence. It was now time for historians to tell the truth about the costs that Lithuania had had to pay for that pact: "As a historian, I am ashamed that for so long we did not tell the public the entire truth, at times less than half, and that is the biggest lie."

The crowd so enthusiastically received Truska's confession that Landsbergis again had to call on it to keep order. The spectators responded by giving the next speaker, Vladislovas Mikučiauskas, the foreign minister of Soviet Lithuania, so much mock applause that he had to end his speech prematurely.

Sigitas Geda then delivered a history lesson, reading the definition of *annexation* written into the Soviet government's decree on peace in November 1917: "the incorporation of any small or weak nationality by a large and strong state" without the indisputable consent of the small nationality. Conjuring up a biblical parable, he spoke of two strong neighbors' visiting a weak but free man and saying to him: "We will take your roof from above your head, we will take your land, and your woman, your children. . . . We will share your property, everything that here belonged to your ancestors, but you will be happy for it." Lithuania, he concluded, can still recover: "Not to believe today in Lithuania means not to believe in sense, conscience, freedom, and honor."

As darkness settled on the park, the spectators lit candles: according to the printed account of the meeting they represented "the eternal light remembering the senseless victims of Stalinism and Hitlerism."[12] Juzeliunas suggested that the independence the Lithuanians had enjoyed until 1940 had protected their culture from the ravages of Stalinist political and cultural persecution in the 1930s; Kazys Saja, a writer, gave an impassioned defense of the hunger strikers in Gediminas Square and called for "freedom to prisoners of conscience!" After several more speakers, Virgilius Čepaitis, a translator, returned to the theme of history, asserting, "We must know our history. And not just know it, but also remember that each of us is there and participating." The meeting ended with Juzeliunas's conducting the singing of the *National Hymn*.

On television the previous Saturday Landsbergis had spoken of the meeting lasting an hour. In fact it continued for almost three. As rain started to fall, the spectators left in groups as they had come, discussing the speeches, evaluating who had made good points, who had failed. The speakers had raised many issues that in the past people would have feared to mention in public; no one could now dare to suggest that the protocols had not existed.

The speakers had aroused different memories for each listener, recalling personal experiences, family, or friends. Buračas had called for the posthumous restitution of membership in the Academy of Sciences of two emigres who had taught at the University of Lithuania before World War II, Vincas Kreve-Mickevičius and Mykolas Biržiška. Algimantas Liekis of the Institute of History had first voiced this demand in *Komjaunimo tiesa* of August 13. Hearing their names aroused my own private memories.

Vincas Kreve, who had been my Russian professor at the University of Pennsylvania, was a noted writer who had served as dean of the Humanities Faculty of the University of Lithuania. In 1940, when Lithuania was incorporated into the Soviet Union, he had been the country's foreign minister. After the war, he had entered the United States and, as an émigré, had become an "un-person" in Lithuania. When he died in Philadelphia in 1954 a speaker at his funeral declared that when Lithuania was free again the people would take Kreve back there. On October 10 the Presidium of the Academy of Sciences recommended that the Council of Ministers rescind its decision of January 18, 1946, depriving both Kreve and Biržiška of their status as members of the academy. When, on October 17, ELTA announced that the Lithuanian government had approved restoring both men to the status of Academician, I thought to myself that at least Kreve's spirit had returned.

Biržiška had been active in Lithuanian socialism before World War I and had written extensively on Lithuanian culture and folklore. His name was closely associated with Lithuanian efforts to establish their presence in Vilnius under Polish rule in the early 1920s. Like Kreve, he had emigrated after World War II, and he had settled in Los Angeles. In 1956 I interviewed him for the beginning work on my doctoral dissertation; like Kreve he would not have emigrated from Lithuania of his own free will. That evening in August I left Vingis Park with the feeling that the Lithuanian national consciousness had established an important benchmark in its new spurt of growth.

While most of the people went directly home, many made their way to Gediminas Square, some to commune with the hunger strikers, others just to see what might be happening. They found the square closed off by a line of uniformed militia. In the distance, in the middle of the otherwise deserted square, the demonstrators still held their place, although Cidzikas was missing because he had gone to the meeting in Vingis Park and now could not pass through the militia line to rejoin his comrades.

Militia and security officials subsequently gave varying explanations for their action. A week later the head of the security forces, Eduardas Eismuntas, told Sajudis leaders that the militia had moved to block a demonstration in the square by the Freedom League; a more disingenuous explanation spoke of Sajudis leaders' having requested that the militia protect the hunger strikers from "hooligans." At any rate, the militia's actions excited some young demonstrators to the point that they marched in protest up to the nearby headquarters of the Ministry of Internal Affairs. Stasys Lisauskas, minister of internal affairs, came out of the building to demand that they disperse.

The authorities also appealed to Sajudis for help with the situation. They telephoned Landsbergis and Petkevičius, and the two men hastened to the square to help calm the crowd. Although the authorities subsequently insisted that the demonstration had broken up before Landsbergis and Petkevičius arrived, the two men in fact circulated for some time among the youths, urging them to disperse. Sajudis in turn resented the Ministry of Internal Affairs' tactic of first requesting help and then denying that it had been necessary.[13]

Once order had been restored, Lisauskas told the press that one person had been sent to a drying-out station for drunks and sentenced to two months' corrective labor. The militia, he assured *Tiesa*'s correspondent, had employed no force, and it was certainly not true that they had pushed anyone under the wheels of a passing car. The militia had acted wisely but firmly: "Democracy," Lisauskas warned, "is not anarchy. I assure you that in the future too we will vigorously maintain the public order on the basis of Soviet laws."[14]

By the morning of the twenty-fourth, downtown Vilnius was again quiet, the hunger strikers were back in place with a new poster showing a smiling Stalin watching the signing of the Nazi-Soviet pact, and the public now had to consider just what had been accomplished in the hectic events of the last several days. People who had been at both meetings in Vingis Park, on July 9 and on August 23, differed as to which they considered the more impressive. The meeting of July 9 had been more emotional, more spontaneous, and it therefore seemed to have appealed more to the basic national consciousness of Lithuanians. The meeting of August 23, more structured and organized, appealed more to the intellectuals. For many the discussions of the Molotov-Ribbentrop Pact were indeed something new, and several intellectuals indicated to me that the talks by Rudis and Truska had had an especially great impact on them.

The thought that many Lithuanian intellectuals had only recently learned of the existence and the substance of the secret protocols surprised me. When I spoke with Justinas Marcinkevičius about his speech in Vingis Park, he explained that once he had become acquainted with the protocols he had felt the need to speak out. Only later did it occur to me to ask him just when he had first read the protocols, and when I had the opportunity to do so—on October 22 as Marcinkevičius headed toward the stage of the Sports Hall to chair the opening session of Sajudis's convention—he told me "the beginning of July." The command structure in history could claim many successes in controlling the national consciousness of the Lithuanians, but in the summer of 1988 it disintegrated.

On the morning after the meeting the public's interest naturally focused on how the media would treat the event. Since Soviet newspapers normally do not observe any particular obeisance to late-breaking news, the reports in the Vilnius morning papers were understandably short, describing it simply as a commemoration for the victims of Hitlerism and Stalinism and promised an extensive report the next day.

In the afternoon long lines greeted the arrival of *Vakarines naujienos* in the kiosks. "A Day of Searching for Historical Truth," the newspaper labeled its report, which began by referring to Žepkaite's article and to TASS's piece in *Literatura ir menas,* which, it noted, "unfortunately" had been anonymous. The meeting in Vingis Park constituted "the logical continuation of ongoing discussions." Iakovlev, the newspaper reminded its readers, had declared that "open and conscientious historical research is our gain, because it shows society's spiritual strength and maturity."

That evening, as promised, Lithuanian television played a tape of the meeting, but in a considerably abridged version. The tape omitted a number of "sharp moments" in the speeches: most notably, Marcinkevičius's criticism of Moscow's dubious search in its archives for the Nazi-Soviet protocols, Buračas's criticism of the Ignalina power plant, Šepetys's promise to publish the speeches, the foreign minister's problems in communicating with his audience, Saja's angry defense of the "hungerers," and Rudis's ironic comments on the historical image of the events of 1939 and 1940.

Sajudis supporters reacted strongly to the television cuts. The members of the Kapsukas Drama Theater in Kaunas announced that they would no longer cooperate with Lithuanian television.[15] The Sajudis support group in the television station censured the editor of the tape, Juozas Mažeikis, the deputy director of Lithuanian

Television and Radio, and subsequently published their declaration in the media weekly, *Kalba Vilnius*.[16] The complete tape was finally shown on late-night television in the middle of October.

On Thursday morning, August 25, the newspapers carried extensive reports on the meeting. Writing in *Tiesa*, Algimantas Budrys provided the most complete account of the speeches, filling about 15 percent of the newspaper's four large pages. Under the simple title "Three Hours in Vingis Park," he accurately summarized the speeches. Those who still did not want to believe in the protocols, he concluded, might object to the tone of some speakers; those who believed, "left with glistening eyes." For newcomers, the words uttered in Vingis Park may have sounded daring; for veterans of the meetings with the delegates to the Nineteenth Party Conference, the speeches probably seemed repetitious. Nevertheless, "those three hours of recollection, of spiritual repentence and cleansing, constitute a step forward."

Sovetskaia Litva's report, entitled "For the Honest and Frank Study of History" and written by Sergei Lopukhin, followed the pattern set by *Vakarines*, quoting Landsbergis, Marcinkevičius, and Šepetys at length. In *Czerwony sztandar*, Krystyna Marczyk and Jan Sienkiewicz, under the title "Free Association with Their Own History," summarized the comments of a number of speakers and paid special tribute to Sajudis's organizational competence in structuring and controlling the meeting. Significantly, the two Polish writers did not discuss any possible significance that the Molotov-Ribbentrop Pact might have had for Poland.

The meeting in Vingis Park marked the end of the period of grand meetings of the people. Sajudis had made the public aware of its existence; the mythology of Stalinist historiography had crumbled. The meetings had served the purpose of bringing the people together to share long-suppressed thoughts and feelings; they had brought the national symbols out into public view; and they had set public life in Lithuania onto a new course.

7

A New Political Culture

After the meeting in Vingis Park, the public behavior of
the Lithuanians changed radically. No one had been
sure what would happen that evening in August; after
the fact, few seemed to remember how nervous they had
been before the meeting. The public now spoke more
freely of its concerns; it raised new demands. As the
guardians of public memory, the historians joined in
the new spirit, and the opinions of Moscow were rapidly
becoming less and less important.

Sajudis now stood almost as a second government in
Lithuania. Historians spoke among themselves of *dvoev-
lastie*, dual power, a reference to the uneasy balance
between the Petrograd Soviet and the Provisional Government in the first months of the Russian Revolution
of 1917. Sajudis had no official authority, it could pass
no laws, but it had a moral authority to which the population responded. The authorities had themselves given
witness to this by calling Landsbergis and Petkevičius

to come help control the crowd on the night of August 23–24.

Sajudis gave further notice of its power when it negotiated a provisional settlement of the hunger strike on Gediminas Square, although its path into this question was circuitous. After Kazys Saja had spoken in Vingis Park on behalf of the strikers, Vilnius authorities, who hesitated to approach the strikers by themselves, asked him to intervene to end the action. When the authorities had nothing to offer the strikers in exchange for ending the strike, however, the effort collapsed. That evening, August 24, *Vakarines* criticized Saja's speech in Vingis Park (Saja told me that, angered by *Komjaunimo tiesa*'s article on the strikers, he had originally meant to publish his statement in the press but had then adapted it as a speech), and the newspaper declared that the citizens of Vilnius were becoming angry: "Why have the organs of internal affairs not dispersed the demonstrators?" Individuals, the newspaper argued, had no right to go to Gediminas Square and "disturb the calm of the night." *Vakarines*'s outburst appeared to have emanated from the headquarters of the Saugumas. Concerned about possible police action against the strikers, Sajudis set up a committee to mediate between the authorities and the strikers.

On August 26 Sajudis's representatives, including Ozolas, Antanas Bartuševičius, and Arvydas Juozaitis, presented the strikers with the government's offer to review the cases of the political prisoners. The strikers, however, were not of one mind. Freedom League members who had rallied around Cidzikas demanded that the prisoners be released forthwith; otherwise the strike must continue. With the sound of women's voices singing hymns outside the tent in which the group was meeting, Ozolas argued that one must learn the compromise of politics and that the strikers should trust Sajudis's word that it would stay on the case. Some strikers openly expressed distrust of Sajudis, and the three Sajudis representatives showed increasing irritation with the behavior of the strikers.

Over the opposition of his friends, Cidzikas, the original striker, accepted the government's promise and amid harsh words suspended his action. Although Sajudis spokespersons welcomed this victory for "sane thinking" over "the irrationality" of the Freedom League, five dissenters declared they would continue their strike at home. Cidzikas declared that if the government did not act, he would resume his action later. On the twenty-ninth Radio Vilnius announced, "On Friday night the hunger strikers who were on hunger strike for over a week in Gediminas Square in Vilnius have now left the square and ended the strike. . . . We were informed that a working group has been set up at the Lithuanian SSR Procurator's office."[1]

As exemplified by the daring of the strikers who did not want to end their action, the Lithuanian public was shedding its social and cultural fears. In its twenty-fifth issue (August 19), *Sajudžio žinios* published the United Nations Declaration of Human Rights, adopted in 1948, which contained such unequivocal statements as, "No one can be arbitrarily arrested, taken into custody or exiled" (Article 9). This issue long remained posted on Sajudis bulletin boards; one woman muttered as she stood next to me reading it in a theater, "Everything that we haven't had." The Lithuanians were expressing their thoughts more openly.

At the festive opening of the university's academic

year on September 1 welcoming the new students who were now on their way to join Lithuania's intelligentsia, the university's rector, Jonas Kubilius, mentioned both Šapoka and another emigre historian, Zenonas Ivinskis, as standards of historical writing—but he did not mention any Soviet Lithuanians. At the end of the ceremony, after the curtain had already closed, the students on stage began singing the *National Hymn*. The curtain reopened and the crowd stood. When the singing finished, I turned and saw that even Ringaudas Songaila had been standing.

On September 3, a Saturday, Lithuanians flowed to the west coast of the republic to participate in forming a ring around the Baltic, extended from the Scandinavian lands through Poland, as a sign of concern about pollution of the water. Many drove from Vilnius to Kaunas, parked their cars, and then boarded buses for the trip to Palanga, the coastal region. Despite strong winds, the people waved the national tricolor and sang folk songs along the shore. Once again concerns about ecological problems evoked feelings of national solidarity.

New attitudes and initiatives emerged in all apsects of public life. In a meeting of the Artists' Union on September 22, one person after another rose to criticize the work of the director of the Art Institute. No one offered him any support; a few days later he announced his retirement. A week later, on September 28, people filled a school auditorium for a three-hour celebration of the Lithuanian language, replete with presentations in the four regional dialects. At the end of the evening, the featured speaker, Justinas Marcinkevičius, reminded the audience that all this would not have been possible without the efforts of Sajudis and its Initiative Group.

Such activities bespoke new energies that ignored Moscow. Arvydas Šaltenis, secretary of the Artists' Union and a member of the Sajudis Initiative Group, told me that Moscow had been importuning him all summer to provide Russian translations of his union's proceedings; Šaltenis simply did not know when he would find time to comply.

In the midst of this change, the historians faced new demands on their time and resources. Classes in schools, institutes, and the university resumed at the beginning of September, and the question of the day, as one woman defined it, was, "What will the history teachers in school say to children who have been carrying the tricolor in Gediminas Square all summer?" Both the public and the school teachers demanded new material, new interpretations, new textbooks. An enterprising cooperative-publishing venture in Kaunas called the Institute of History offering to publish anything on Lithuanian history, quickly and without censorship, even paying an honorarium to the author, but the historians had little to offer. The delay between writing and publication probably hurt a little more when a factory in Vilnius announced it would award 1,000 rubles to the author of the best new work in Lithuanian history.

The historians were generally unaccustomed to working so fast. A book might normally take two years to publish once the manuscript was completed. Works now in the process of publication were undergoing hasty revision so as to fit the times. In May the Institute of History hastily withdrew plans to publish a one-volume history of Lithuania in English, divided the manuscript in two parts, and urged the authors quickly to rewrite their sections for publication as something new. The first volume, covering the period to 1917, appeared in October 1988;[2] the second volume, the last I heard, was still delayed, in no small part due to problems of how to present the events of 1939–1941.

In planning for the future, no one could be sure what the publishing climate would be like two or three years further ahead. Just how far could Lithuanian historians go in discussing the events of 1939 and 1940? Presumably they still had to consider Lithuania's incorporation into the USSR to be, in Antanas Buračas's words, "a historical reality"[3] with which they had to live, but the younger historians seemed determined to push the limits as quickly and as aggressively as possible "while the climate was still right."

At the beginning of September the threat of reaction still hung heavy in the minds of some. The failure of the Moscow press, namely *Pravda* and *Izvestiia*, to publish any report on the Vingis Park meeting made them nervous. In a remarkable example of "unreconstructed" journalism, Moscow radio's international service on August 23 reported: "Those assembled honored the memory of the victims lost by the Lithuanian people in the years of the Hitlerite occupation. The speeches noted that Hitlerite Germany, by violating the non-aggression treaty, unleashed World War II. . . . The USSR was then the only real force on whose help Lithuania could count. . . . It was emphasized that the mass deportations that were carried out before the Hitlerites' invasion of the USSR did not promote the cohesion of forces in the struggle against the fascist aggressor." The German Press Agency reported that according to several Moscow newspapers speakers had "justified" the Molotov-Ribbentrop Pact, while TASS warned against "destructive nationalist passions."[4] The central press generally ignored the events in the Baltic, although it

published polemical articles both supporting and condemning other aspects of Soviet foreign policy in 1939.[5]

The Lithuanian public, by contrast, gave the historians no rest. Every Saturday the weekly *Literatura ir
menas* challenged the truths of yesterday. On August 27,
Antanas Zabotka, a teacher, declared that he remembered the events of 1940 and that "this schema does not
satisfy me." He suggested simply saying that the Lithuanians in 1940 had had to make a choice: "And it is good
that we came under Soviet and not Fascist protection."
In the same issue, Antanas Marinonis, a lawyer, was not
so interested in compromise, asserting that "the revolutionary situation" of 1940 had developed from external
pressures rather than from internal forces. On behalf of
the editors, Aldona Žemaityte, reviewing readers' letters, noted the "emotions" expressed in them. Subsequent issues almost invariably carried discussions of
Lithuania's past.

A writer in *Komjaunimo tiesa* of September 16, 1988,
found similar trends in the letters that the newspaper
was receiving. The national question seemed the hottest
topic of the day, but the letters also expressed concern
about "the future of the Lithuanian nation, distortion of
the national policy . . . the teaching of Lithuanian history in the schools . . . the legalization of the national
symbols." Writers complained about the "indifference
of our historians" and argued that "only those who are
totally ignorant of our history and of the character of
the nation can accuse all Lithuanians of nationalism."

The letter-writers challenged the competence, if not
the honesty, of the historical establishment, and, to the
distress of the historians, this attitude carried over into
other intellectual camps. In *Komjaunimo tiesa* of August
31, Arnoldas Piročkinas, a specialist in the history of the

Lithuanian language, questioned whether there were any young historians who could write history as well as Šapoka had. Soviet historians, he charged, had distorted Lithuanian history, and dissertations such as "The Work of the Lithuanian Communist Party in Preparing, Distributing and Educating Cattle-Breeding Workers, 1959–1963" scarcely trained their authors for the serious and demanding work of history: "In writing on these themes, the most important thing was to reason independently as little as possible."

Piročkinas had entitled his essay "Let Us Talk About History in a Neighborly Fashion"; he had not meant to include the entire historical profession in his attack, and he had declared that the historians were not alone in their problems. (He agreed to my suggestion that his article might have been called, "Thoughts While Reading Šapoka.") The historians themselves, moreover, were "the least responsible" for the existing situation: "The young men dance to the old men's tune." Nevertheless, he criticized established historians such as Žepkaite, and he said of the public's demand for the reprinting of Šapoka's history: "Let us be thankful to perestroika that we are getting this. It will at least point out the impotence of our historical science."

Historians reacted angrily, although few cared to put their responses into print. Liubomiras Žeimantas, a journalist and the husband of a historian, took up their cause in *Komjaunimo* of September 13, insisting that the historians had accomplished significant things and that the first volume of *The History of the Lithuanian SSR*, published in 1985, was better than anything written in the past. "Such 'a critique,'" he said of Piročkinas's essay, "did and does no honor to any researcher, much less a humanist. It just misleads the reader." Another commentator later criticized Žeimantas's intemperate language as a relic of the unlamented past.[6]

Although Piročkinas's comments had covered the entire course of Lithuanian history, the debates over Lithuania's history from 1918 to 1953 were the most intense. Although the public, after Vingis Park, considered the secret protocols an established fact, historians could not move so quickly; they needed a Russian text. No one, however, seemed to believe that it would be found: "Molotov probably had them destroyed," said one retired historian. "They are certainly not in the archive of the Ministry of Foreign Affairs." Moscow's failure to respond to the Lithuanians' demands for documents only strengthened the common thought that the Soviet government feared the truth.

The interest in the crucial decade of the 1940s was particularly pronounced in the list of topics suggested for research in a notice posted in September by students of the Historical Institute of the Academy of Sciences: (1) Hitlerite fascism and Stalinist foreign policy in respect to Lithuania on the eve of World War II; (2) historical events in Lithuania, 1940–1941; (3) genesis of the 1940 socialist revolution in the works of the republic's historians; (4) resistance to the German occupation, 1941–1944; (5) civil war in Lithuania in the postwar years; (6) forced collectivization in Lithuania; (7) Stalinist crimes in Lithuania; (8) the loss of Lithuania's sovereignty in economic and cultural affairs, 1940–1985. The list was entirely concerned with reexamining questions of Lithuania's history as a part of the Soviet Union.

The authors of the list were not interested in hearing the old explanations. In the popular weekly journal *Švyturys*, Bronius Vaitkevičius and Solomonas Atamukas published a series of three articles on Lithuania in 1940, arguing that a socialist revolution indeed took place. Although Vaitkevičius insisted to me that the articles indirectly proved the existence of the secret protocols, the authors made no direct comment on Lithuania's relations with the Soviet Union at the time. In the Institute of History someone posted a reprint of one page from the series with the word "Disgrace" printed across it. The document soon disappeared from the bulletin board, but the point had been made.

Popular discontent with the official histories emerged clearly in some of the questions one historian received when he addressed a group in one of Lithuania's smaller towns:

> How will February 16 be treated now? Is there really reason to proclaim it a national holiday? One has to explain to the people that we will not again make mistakes, that we will not mislead people.
>
> It is said that the party will give up running the economy but the first secretaries of party organizations will be chosen to head the presidium of local soviets. Isn't this a tactic of party strategy?—as the people say: *ta pati panele, tik kita suknele* [roughly and crudely translatable as "the same maiden, just masqueradin'"—AES].
>
> 1. We often read the words "bourgeois Lithuania." As far as I know, this was the state of Lithuania, not bourgeois, not capitalist, but Lithuania. I suggest that instead of the word *bourgeois*, we use the words *independent Lithuania*. 2. Which historians have least falsified the history of Lithuania?
>
> How do you look at the defeat of Soviet government in Lithuania in 1918? Looking at the history of Belorussia, the "heretical" thought arises that perhaps losing was better than winning.

Shouldn't everyone who knew historical truth but compromised it be retired? How many such opportunities defended dissertations and now are authorities? Will their dissertations be reviewed?

The historical debates and questions were not just academic; they had practical considerations, too. People deported under Soviet rule, adults and children together with any children born in Siberia, were still second-class citizens. Although allowed to return to Lithuania in the late 1950s and early 1960s, they could acquire full citizenship only through application for individual review of their cases, a laborious process. According to *Tiesa* of September 11, the process was proceeding apace: whereas in 1987 just 80 persons had been rehabilitated, in the first half of 1988, 208 had been restored to full citizenship.[7]

On September 22 the government made a major concession: the Council of Ministers annulled the 1949 and 1951 decrees on deportation, "ruling that the deportations carried out in conformity with those decrees were illegal and baseless." All the victims of the mass deportations of 1949 and 1951 were accordingly rehabilitated and restored to the full rights of Soviet citizens. They also became eligible for possible compensation for their losses.[8] The Lithuanian government left standing the earlier deportation orders, most notably those of 1941 and 1948, insisting that the authorities in Moscow should make any decision on annulling them. Nevertheless the people of Lithuania were now beginning to feel that anything was possible.

Even the history of the revolutionary period of 1917–1919 came under challenge and had to change. When,

on September 5, I taped a television interview discussing 1918 and then on September 12 a radio interview,
I was cautious, although I was assured that nothing
would be censored. By the time the television tape was
shown on October 8, my comments seemed conservative. (It had been originally scheduled for October 1; I
presumed it had been postponed so as not to conflict
with the celebration of the seventieth anniversary of the
founding of the Lithuanian Communist Party, October
1–3, 1918.) Just five days earlier, October 3, party historians had appeared on television discussing the reasons for the failure of the Communist government in
1918–1919 and concentrating on its "errors," rather
than shouting its praises as had been the practice on
such occasions in the past.

   In further discussions through the fall, especially a
meeting of the Academy of Sciences on October 20 and
a meeting of the Žinija society on the twenty-sixth, both
commemorating the seventieth anniversary of the formation of Vincas Mickevičius-Kapsukas's Communist
government, more and more historians challenged the
traditional Soviet Lithuanian historiography. One after
another agreed that the proclamation of the Workers'
and Peasants' government had little to do with concepts
of Lithuania's statehood and that established historical
interpretations had little basis in fact and documents.
Conservatives held firm to their established positions:
"But there *was* a socialist revolution!" exclaimed Šarmaitis as he walked out of the meeting at the Žinija
society.[9] In *Literatura ir menas* of November 5 and 12,
Česlovas Laurinavičius, a young historian working in
the Central State Historical Archive, argued that Communist leaders in 1919 had had no interest in support-

ing any principle of Lithuanian national sovereignty. The public challenge to the official historiography had passed from memories and impressions to monographs.

Revisionist historical views were now becoming commonplace in the press, and the historians became bolder. On September 15 *Gimtasis kraštas* exploded a bombshell with an interview between Valatka and Eidintas concerning Eidintas's work on the life of Antanas Smetona, the dictator of Lithuania from 1926 to 1940. Eidintas criticized the practice of identifying national consciousness with "bourgeois nationalism," declared he had dropped the epithet "fascist" in discussing Smetona's "police-bureaucratic" regime, and generally pictured Smetona as a human being rather than as a class devil. The newspaper waited expectantly for complaints from the readers, but apart from a letter from Mitkin about the article—"Who read it to him?" asked one wag—there was no scandal. The public only seemed to want still greater boldness.

The Lithuanians even had a chance to take their new ideas to Moscow. On September 21 representatives of historical studies in the Baltic area gathered in the Soviet capital for a roundtable discussion of the events of 1939–1940; the absence of Šarmaitis and Žiugžda as representatives of Lithuania drew some comment but no explanation. The Latvian historian Vilnis Sipols opened with a standard, orthodox presentation in which he referred to the Estonians' publication of the secret protocols as "falsification of history." Žalys stunned the gathering with his analysis of Molotov's ultimatum of May 14 to the Lithuanians and his conclusion that the Soviet complaints were trumped up; several Russians exclaimed that these seemed to be "new facts." The gathering drew up no conclusions or directives for further study.

Soviet authorities followed up this roundtable discussion by calling for another meeting, this time in Petrozavodsk, near Leningrad, October 19–21. The Lithuanians, seeing no use to the meeting and calculating that they would be essentially lectured to, made no plans to attend, but then at the beginning of October a telephone call from Moscow demanded that they immediately name a delegation. After a call to Tallinn had established that the Estonians had no intention of going to Petrozavodsk, the Lithuanians declared that they too would save their money and stay home. Moscow was losing its power to summon and command.

At the beginning of October Lithuanian historiography took a major step in a new direction with the publication of Juozas Urbšys's memoirs of the events of 1939–1940. Urbšys served as the foreign minister of Lithuania from December 1938 to June 15, 1940, and he was a member of the 1941 class of deportees. He now lived in Kaunas, and the organizers of the rally in Vingis Park on August 23 had played a tape recording of his memoirs of meeting with Molotov in 1939. A manuscript of his memoirs had been circulating for some time, and Vilius Kavaliauskas published a lengthy interview with him in *Tiesa* of September 11. The formal publication of his memoirs now gave them new legitimacy as a source for the study of this period.[10]

Alongside the discussions of the past, the Lithuanians were also deeply engaged in discussing the future, especially the principle of economic autonomy, "economic self-sufficiency," which many thought constituted the secret formula for an independent existence. The debate in the press began with enthusiastic statements about the idea's possibilities, but with time concerns surfaced. Should one realize this idea quickly or cautiously? Writing in *Komjaunimo tiesa* of September 20, Brone Vainauskiene noted that new concerns, such as a fear of inflation, dictated caution. Another journalist, A. Gašuniene, writing in *Sovetskaia Litva* of September 25, questioned Lithuania's need for its own currency and pointed out that the republic could have problems in obtaining needs such as Uzbek cotton under a purely market economy. "We don't want to live worse than now even for one day," she warned. A writer in *Tiesa*, Petras Navikas, concluded, "It is not so simple as it appears."[11]

A conference of representatives of the three Baltic republics, meeting in Riga, September 21 to 23, accepted the Luthuanians' recommendations as a basis for further consideration of the principle of economic self-sufficiency. The three Baltic republics had each sponsored discussions of models for economic self-sufficiency, and the Lithuanian proposal was the work of the Academy of Sciences and the Lithuanian State Planning office. The program as accepted proposed republican control of all resources and taxation within its borders and recognition of private as well as socialist and cooperative property. The economy should be founded on the demands of the market; the government should set prices only in cases where such intervention would serve the private good; and the republics would need a stable, convertible currency to carry out their programs to completion.[12] As Iakovlev had suggested in August, the central government in Moscow would maintain control of foreign policy and defense. At the beginning of October, the Lithuanian government published its own plan for achieving economic autonomy, calling for its enactment by July 1, 1989. The Lithuanians considered Moscow's position at this time to be encouraging.

The question of "economic autonomy" proceeded not just from Gorbachev's program of perestroika and khozraschet but also from the new discussion of the meaning of the USSR constitutional provision that declared, "A Union Republic is a sovereign Soviet socialist state" (Article 76) with "the right freely to secede from the USSR" (Article 72) and the obligation to "ensure comprehensive economic and social development on its territory" (Article 77). Lithuania, moreover, had "the right to enter into relations with other states, conclude treaties with them, exchange diplomatic and consular representatives and take part in the work of international organizations" (Article 80). Although cynics declared that the constitution was hardly worth the paper it was printed on, both Moscow and Lithuanian authorities were preparing revisions of their respective constitutions, and the provisions were the subject of lively debate.

Even the magic word "secession" arose in conversations. The Freedom League had raised *independence* as its fundamental banner, but I myself first heard the word uttered publicly on August 20 at a Lithuanian "Hyde Park" gathering in Vilnius's Old City when a speaker exclaimed, "Give us independence and we need nothing else." As the meeting broke up, I heard another man say, "Independence! That's it in one word." To utter the word in public at that time still seemed a daring act.

Some argued that the prohibition against discussing secession actually hindered rational consideration of the subject. In *Sajudžio žinios* of September 7, Algimantas Rusteika spoke of secession/separatism/independence as the "last goblin"—people did not dare to discuss a right that the constitution guaranteed them. It was unrealistic, he declared, to think seriously of Lithuanian independence within the next ten to fifteen years, but one should not fear "the last goblin of Stalinist chauvinism," the danger of being accused of being a "separatist."

The question actually came up in the Sajudis Initiative Group's meeting on Tuesday evening, September 6. In the middle of a rambling discussion, Romualdas Ozolas rose to declare that the group should draw up policy papers on three questions: (1) the national question, (2) democratic elections, and (3) secession (atsiskyrimas). The group looked at him in some surprise, and Vytautas Landsbergis declared that he preferred to use the word *self-determination* (apsisprendimas). Asked his own position, Landsbergis explained that the future Soviet Union being pictured by Moscow was so promising that the Lithuanians would surely want to be a part of it—but it was good to have the alternative written into the constitution.

Another aspect of the question of "sovereignty" concerned Lithuania's control of its own human resources, and here discussion focused on the tragic fate of a young man named Arturas Sakalauskas. Drafted in the spring of 1986, Sakalauskas had been serving in the Internal Army of the Ministry of Internal Affairs, working mainly as a guard in the transfer of prisoners. The duty was difficult; his gentle nature apparently led his fellow conscripts to persecute him—some said "to terrorize" him—beating him and forcing him to pull extra duty in their place. On February 23, 1987, his supposed comrades attempted to assault him sexually. The young man rebelled and, taking a pistol in each hand, he killed eight fellow soldiers. He immediately fled, but five days later, on the twenty-eighth, he surrendered to authorities.

According to law, Sakalauskas was subject to the death penalty, and after extensive psychological examinations, lasting from June to August 1987, the authorities pronounced him sane and normal. From mid-August to the later part of September 1987 he was in Moscow, and then he sat in solitary confinement in Leningrad until April 20, 1988. In isolation he became ill and autistic, losing the power to speak. He was then sent to Kaliningrad for treatment, and after two months he managed to utter simple sentences such as "How much longer do I have to live?" and "When will they shoot me?" The authorities then returned him to Leningrad, where he again reportedly lost the power of speech.

Leningrad television brought the case to public notice in July 1988, using the occasion to criticize the Soviet military. Several officers, it was claimed, had lost their positions, but military officials refused to cooperate with television's investigation. When they produced a sequel, however, the television team apparently chose to rehabilitate the army: the second program ended with two young, sympathetic Soviet soldiers asserting that they had never had any trouble in fulfilling their military duties.

The Sakalauskas case electrified the Lithuanians. There had already been considerable publicity surrounding the case of Petras Grazulis, who had been sentenced to ten months' imprisonment for his refusal to respond to a call for three months' military reserve duty.[13] *Komjaunimo tiesa* first reported the Sakalauskas case on July 28, and Lithuanian television reran the

Leningrad programs as well as investigating the topic on its own. The Lithuanian public and then the government too demanded that Sakalauskas be returned to Lithuania for treatment.

The case intensified Lithuanian objections to fulfilling compulsory military duty in other parts of the Soviet state, especially when it meant mixing with recruits from the southern and eastern regions of the Soviet Union. Early in October, I heard a priest demand from his pulpit that Sakalauskas be returned to Lithuania and that young Lithuanian men be permitted to complete their military service in the Baltic area. The Lithuanians, moreover, collected complaints from parents of soldiers from other regions and stimulated a campaign against the Soviet military in general. *Sajudžio žinios* no. 51 of November 8 published a list of sixteen Lithuanians who had died while fulfilling their military obligations. Sajudis's program, published on October 12, stated that "the current method of performing military conscription in the armed forces of the USSR is outdated and immoral." Party and military officials, naturally enough, disliked such publicity.[14]

As the end of September approached, there seemed to be no areas of Soviet life immune to public discussion and debate, and carrying the battle were the newspapers and periodic press. Every day the morning television show, "Labas Rytas" (Good Morning), would briefly point out interesting articles in that day's publications. "We don't even talk about meat any more; we just stand in line for newspapers," said a voice behind me one day as we stood waiting at a kiosk. Some people bought three or four copies of their favorite publication, bestowing the extras on less fortunate friends in the course of the day.

The most popular publications were *Komjaunimo tiesa*, the organ of the Communist Youth League, and *Vakarines naujienos*, the organ of the Vilnius party organization and of the city government. Both appeared five times weekly, *Komjaunimo* Tuesday to Saturday mornings, and *Vakarines* Monday to Friday evenings, and both published identical Lithuanian and Russian editions. *Komjaunimo* had a circulation of 500,000; *Vakarines*, which circulated only in Vilnius, published something more than 100,000 issues per day, and the lines waiting for it seemed to grow daily.

The editors of *Tiesa*, the basic organ of the Lithuanian Communist Party, claimed that Sajudis's boycott had had no effect, but this was the newspaper most likely to remain when all others had sold out at a kiosk. It printed some 300,000 copies daily, of which about 75 percent were for subscribers and 25 percent went out on the newsstands. The Initiative Group called off its boycott in mid-September, and by November some conservative party members complained that *Tiesa* at times seemed to be representing Sajudis as much as it was the party. Both *Sovetskaia Litva* (in Russian) and *Czerwony sztandar* (in Polish) printed about 50,000 copies each day, with about half of *Czerwony sztandar*'s run being exported to Poland.

The weeklies *Gimtasis kraštas* and *Literatura ir menas* were always quick to sell out, while *Kalba Vilnius*, the organ of Lithuanian radio and television, which reportedly had for some time been receiving unsold copies back from the kiosks, appeared to gain new popularity in the fall. *Gimtasis kraštas*, which appeared on Thursdays, had prospered since Čekuolis took it over in 1986, and in the fall of 1988 it averaged over 100,000 copies per issue, with 3,000 of them sent to the United States and 10,000 to the rest of the world. Beginning in January 1989, the newspaper expanded its printing to 249,300 copies; its subscriptions were said to be higher than *Tiesa*'s. A standing joke suggested that party leaders spent the first part of every week recovering from the blows dealt by *Gimtasis krastas* every Thursday, *Vakarines*'s special Friday edition, and then those of both *Literatura ir menas* and *Komjaunimo* on Saturday, the latter frequently saving its most controversial material for the end of the week.

The popularity of the press forced changes in editorial practices. In the past, one editor told me, "we used to divide up stories; now we don't tell each other what we are planning." (When Vilius Kavaliauskas learned that *Vakarines* was planning to publish a work by the Russian historian Roy Medvedev, he exerted his considerable influence to win the publication rights for *Tiesa*.) One could not be sure, my acquaintance said, how long the popularity of the newspapers would continue, and therefore each newspaper had to develop as loyal a readership as possible in these halcyon days. Whatever the future, the Lithuanians dedicated themselves with enthusiasm to the study of their past and present.

8

Sajudis Comes of Age

On August 30 Sajudis's Initiative Group took a giant step in regulating its relations with the government when it entertained General Eduardas Eismuntas, the head of the Saugumas, the State Security Committee (the Russian initials would be KGB). Eismuntas, together with an aide, Edmundas Baltinas, attended the group's weekly meeting in the building of the Artists' Union. Cynics had been insisting that Sajudis functioned only by the suffrance of the Saugumas; Sajudis leaders had been complaining about being followed. Now, with Vytautas Petkevičius presiding, the two forces confronted each other directly.

From the start Eismuntas made clear that he took his cues from the party's second secretary: his own view of Sajudis, he explained, was the same as that which "Comrade Mitkin expressed in his talk that was published in *Tiesa.*" Because his office was daily receiving "letters and calls" demanding explanations about Sajudis's activity, he considered this meeting useful for both sides as an opportunity to make their positions clear.

There were no limits as to the topics up for discussion. Julius Juzeliunas began by talking about the deportations. Eismuntas argued that the numbers involved in deportation were exaggerated: "I cannot understand why members of the Sajudis Initiative Group operate with the number 200–300,000, which in fact comes from emigre publications. I can authoritatively assure you that there were no more than we have stated, 120,000." One must, he argued, also remember the victims of the "bandits" and understand the rationale behind the Soviet decision to remove "estate owners" in 1941 and "people connected with the bandits" in 1948–1949.

Eismuntas then launched into a history lecture. Stalinism, he argued, could not be blamed for the "bandits'" activities: "I understand that in each historical truth one can interpret various facts in different ways. History is a matter difficult to master. The basis of history are documents. And the documents show that the *Abwehr* [German counterespionage] created the nationalist underground." After the war, he continued, the Soviet government offered an amnesty to the opposition, "but those whose hands were bloodied saw no way out." Part of the underground fled, part remained to fight Soviet rule. He went on to attack the postwar activities of the Lithuanian emigration.

Sajudis members rose to the challenge. Petkevičius pointed out that if the Abwehr organized a Lithuanian "fifth column," then the "1941 deportations were a fraud, since they did not help to protect the rear of the Soviet army." Stalin's "plan of Sovietization, prepared already in 1938 and 1939," together with the Communist Party's order that party members desist from "any antifascist activity" in that period, meant that the deportations were "absolutely directed against the intelligentsia of Lithuania and against the peasantry." Eismuntas explained that the security forces had had to make do with poorly prepared personnel who did not fully understand their jobs. The two men had then argued over who drew up the lists for deportation in 1941 and who executed the orders.

Bronius Genzelis rejected the argument that the deportations had resulted from "mistakes," pointing out that Marxist philosophy had to seek "the reasons for every phenomenon in objective truth." Why did Eismuntas not want to discuss Stalinism? Eismuntas pleaded for a separation of the concept of "socialism and Soviet power" from the misfortunes of Stalinist "deformations," but Petkevičius leaped in to argue that "there was never any socialism in the years of Stalinism, there was only complete deformation." When Eismuntas insisted that there was no longer any Stalinism in Lithuania, Petkevičius called on higher authorities: "Even Iakovlev, in his speech, said that there is." The refusal "to recognize objective reasons," Genzelis interjected, "is also a characteristic of Stalinism."

Turning to contemporary matters, Eismuntas insisted that at this time there were only four Lithuanian political prisoners and four exiles. To a challenge as to what "anti-Soviet activity" now meant, his assistant, Baltinas, answered, "That is the invitation to change the existing order." There are laws that must be carried out and one must be ready to tolerate varying opinions, Eismuntas immediately added, before anyone could ask what Baltinas's views of perestroika might be. Eismuntas expressed confidence that the eight persons in question would soon be released, not as a result of "the hunger-strikers" but rather "because of democratization generally."

Challenged as to whom he took orders from, Eismuntas explained, "I am a member of the government of Lithuania and the Soviet Union. I am under the Lithuanian–Soviet Union Cabinet of Ministers. We are in a republican-union jurisdiction." In terms of basic questions "concerning my professional work and which do not concern internal problems, I have more to do with the State Security Committee of the Soviet Union. Internal problems are to be resolved in Vilnius in conjunction with the Central Committee, with the Cabinet of Ministers and with the Presidium [of the Supreme Soviet]." Of these various Soviet institutions the party seemed most important: "The party directs the entire process of living. I work for the party."

Eismuntas obviously distrusted Sajudis's unofficial character. Ozolas pointed out Sajudis's positive contribution to ending the hunger strike, but Eismuntas replied that the Saugumas had not requested Sajudis's help, and he warned that the Initiative Group should have nothing to do with people like Cidzikas and Andreika. Genzelis objected, "But your principles are absolutely Stalinist! Why?" Eismuntas replied he was concerned with carrying out the law, and Stalinist practices had nothing to do with law.

Seizing back the initiative, Eismuntas turned on Juozaitis: "Now I want to put a question to comrade Juozaitis. We know you as an Olympian [Juozaitis had won a medal in swimming at the Montreal Olympics in 1976], your family is good. But how could your tongue praise partisans in those demonstrations? What did you mean in using the word 'partisans'?" Juozaitis denied having used the word, but Eismuntas announced, "We have a tape." Juozaitis replied, "I do too," and he denied having used the word or having ever said anything against Russians: "I used the following formula: 'Let us honor the people who died in the forests.'" (Video tapes circulating in the United States indicate that Juozaitis's memory was accurate.) Eismuntas accepted this formulation and dropped his complaint.

Instead the police chief attacked the Lithuanian Freedom League as an anti-Soviet organization: "They want to restore a bourgeois Lithuania, the bourgeois order. What can link Sajudis members with the Freedom League? Why are some of you cooperating with them?" Turning to Arturas Skučas, he asked, "Why do you use the slogan 'We don't need Communists'? How is one to understand this?" Vaišvila responded that most members of the Initiative Group knew nothing of the group, and Eismuntas urged them to read *Tiesa*: "Everything about the Freedom League was clearly said and explained in *Tiesa*."

Sigitas Geda asked why Saugumas so feared the Freedom League. Is every meeting with a member of the Freedom League to be considered a crime? Reportedly all contacts between Initiative Group members and Freedom League members were being "followed and recorded. Is that true? If so, why? It seems to me that the group is rather weak." Eismuntas replied, "I am interested in the ideological, political, and ethical side of Sajudis's relationship with members of the Freedom League." The league's members, he continued, "understand well that their slogan to restore bourgeois Lithuania will be unacceptable and unpopular."

In answer to a question as to how perestroika was affecting Saugumas, Eismuntas explained that his agency engaged in both surveillance and counterespionage: "There is a lot of work here." The committee's building needed repair. There were relatively few employees, and he could not say whether anyone would be released. Lithuanians received priority in being hired, but there were also Russian and Polish employees. The majority spoke Lithuanian; Russians working for the agency could freely discuss Lithuanian history. To assure that illegal practices of the past would not return, "Central Committee control" had to be strengthened. The agency could reform itself even better, he suggested, if Sajudis would just behave itself.

After a reprise of the question whether Stalin could be blamed for the existence of "bandits" in Lithuania after World War II, the discussion turned to Eismuntas's own views on current issues ranging from tapping telephone lines to economic self-sufficiency. Sigitas Geda asked his opinion about "the idea of Lithuania's independence." "If one is seeking to restore the bourgeois order, that is an anti-Soviet, anticonstitutional activity," he answered, but he then denied that he meant to call "the effort to secede from the Soviet Union" as "an anti-Soviet act." His job, however, was just to obey the law. The meeting broke up without having reached any agreements; the two sides had simply participated in a frank and candid exchange of views.[1]

The discussions of the evening made clear that Sajudis owed its existence not to Eismuntas and his agency but rather to the winds that were coming from Moscow. Given his own preferences, Eismuntas stood ready to enforce the laws on the books, and this could well have meant closer surveillance and restriction of Sajudis activities. Complaints that Sajudis leaders were avoiding the Freedom League because of Saugumas's directives,

however, seem misplaced. Saugumas and Sajudis recognized that they had to coexist at this particular moment in Lithuania's history, and they were both, each
for their own reasons, interested in the activity of the
Freedom League.

Initiative Group members came out of the meeting
with a variety of new ideas. Eismuntas's readiness to accept public display of the tricolor stimulated ideas of
raising the tricolor over the Gediminas tower overlooking Gediminas Square, since the tower was not a state
administrative building but rather a museum. When
Sajudžio žinios went on to call for the introduction of
the tricolor into every school room as a means of educating "our children," it was obvious that displaying the
flag was becoming an important albeit delicate issue in
the confrontation of reformers with the old order in
Vilnius.[2]

The details of Eismuntas's conversation with Sajudis
quickly became public. The Sajudis newspaper *Kauno
aidas* published a transcript dated August 31. A few
weeks later Eismuntas told Mindaugas Barysas of *Tiesa*
about the meeting, which he called open and candid,
and he seized the occasion to repeat all his major points.
Again he gave 120,000 as the number of Lithuanians
deported under Stalinist "deformations," repeating his
conviction that the higher figures of 200,000 to 300,000
came from emigre publications. The authorities were
duly reviewing claims of unjustified persecution in the
years 1940–1952—of course one had to remember the
role of the "reactionary emigration" in turning "naive
people" against Soviet rule—and in May of 1988 the
Supreme Soviet had undertaken a review of the cases
of the four men currently imprisoned under Article 68.
Favorable judgments could be expected, and "therefore

not hunger-striking nor any other demonstration but the policy of perestroika" was determining the outcome of the question.

He went on to remind everyone that the Communist Party had originated perestroika and still had to direct it. On the whole, Sajudis's work was positive, but it was still in its "infancy." It should take care that it grows properly; it should work in harmony with the will of the Communist Party. At the same time, he criticized the Initiative Group as having too few representatives of other nationalities of Lithuania—just one Russian and one Jew, by his count. He also expressed concern about Sajudis's contacts with the Lithuanian program of Voice of America and with the Freedom League. The meeting seemed not to have changed any of his views.[3]

After meeting with Eismuntas, the Initiative Group went back to work as usual, developing its contacts throughout the republic. An article in *Sajudžio žinios* had already described a typical meeting: people would be already gathering at 6 P.M., a good hour before the group was to assemble.[4] Visitors would come from all over Lithuania, bringing copies of local publications or bearing petitions that they wanted heard. Sajudis support groups were springing up in factories, clubs, and offices throughout the republic. In some cases they could count on sympathy from factory administrators; in other cases they were meeting only opposition from party, government, and administration.

When the meetings started, visitors would have the first word: a newly organizing support group in Rokiskis needed a speaker. Who could come? A member of the committee volunteered. What can be done about obstinate administrators who opposed the formation of a Sajudis support group? A man from Kapsukas reported that workers in his city were considering petitioning to have the city's name changed back to Mariampole. Eventually the committee asked the visitors to leave so that it could consider some questions privately.

When I attended Initiative Group meetings during the month of September, I found them open to the public; visitors came and went as they pleased. The central working area, marked by tables butted up against one another, obviously belonged to the committee; spectators lined the walls. (Concerning the continuing requests for speakers to come to the "provinces," one Initiative Group member said to me, "They all want to relive the [early mass] meetings. They have to repeat everything. But it can't be the same now.") The committee members seemed unconcerned about keeping any secrets; their working space was dotted with pocket tape recorders.

On September 6, since the auditorium on the second floor of the Artists' Union was occupied by a show, the Initiative Group had to meet in the basement. Here the conditions were not so pleasant. Tables had to be fitted between the four large columns that dominated the center of the room; the resulting geometric contortion, by my calculations, had twelve distinct sides at which people sat. At times committee members could not see speakers because of the awkward arrangement.

As a veteran of decades of American university faculty meetings with their passion for the niceties of Robert's Rules of Order, I found these meetings at first difficult to comprehend. The people were remarkably willing to delegate the actual text of a thought or a proposal to someone else, to be done at another time. General discussions kept breaking down into a cacophony of smaller groups. At times, to the distress of some members of the committee, visitors insisted in joining the discussion, but, in all, the meetings were "brainstorming" sessions that left the details for execution by those most concerned with this or that question.

The questions that dominated Initiative Group discussions during September concerned the group's program and its organization. This seemed to contradict the group's original statements that it was a temporary alignment that would go out of existence as soon as the party fully accepted perestroika. Ozolas had said in June, "Sajudis is not a party, and probably not even an organization, but rather a movement, a wave, which will dissolve when it has achieved its mission."[5] When I raised questions about this in private, members of the group just shrugged their shoulders. In July the committee had also issued a statement that Sajudis "supports and coordinates social initiatives independent of government organs."[6] That statement indicated that there would be work for some time; no one seemed concerned about any contradictions.

The major task in the near future was the organization of a congress of Sajudis support groups. The Initiative Group itself should function only until a congress of support groups could meet and elect a new group with a clear mandate to represent the population of the entire republic, not just Vilnius. As of the beginning of September, there were already Sajudis support groups in thirty-four of the forty-four *rayons*, or districts, of Lithuania, and therefore a congress, or conference, should probably meet as soon as possible.

The group agreed on October as the month for their meeting, but they found the choice of an exact day to be a problem. The congress had to take place as soon as possible, but the Initiative Group still had to draw up a program, distribute it, and then allow two weeks for discussion and reaction before the congress would meet. The group first selected Saturday the fifteenth, but, when they realized that this would conflict with regularly scheduled meetings of party units, they knew they had to find another date. With half of the group's members also party members, participating in party functions had to be a high priority on their agendas.

Besides the question of the date, the group had to consider the size of the congress. Should it plan for a small meeting place or a large one? What arrangements should be made for press coverage? Spectators? Presumably the foreign correspondents in Moscow should be invited, but what about inviting correspondents from the emigre press? Eventually, the group settled on scheduling its congress as a two-day meeting, October 22 and 23, in the largest hall that one could find, the Sports Palace in Vilnius, which could seat 5,000 for a basketball game and, with seats on the main floor, perhaps 7,500 for a concert or a conference.

On September 6 the Initiative Group also considered Sajudis's future organization. The fundamental decision-making body would be the annual congress of representatives from throughout the republic. The congress in turn would elect a *Seimas*, a group of several hundred persons who would meet at least three times a year, and a *Taryba*, or council, a small group analogous to the Initiative Group, that would work continually.

The idea of the seimas disturbed many. *Seimas* had been the name of the legislature in independent Lithuania, and the name suggested a program far beyond what many had thought to be Sajudis's mission. Why not call it taryba (council) and perhaps, further, rename the taryba "collegium"? Advocates of the organizational plan assured the group that they had conferred with specialists, such as the historian Regina Žepkaite, and seimas as a name had an honored tradition in Lithuanian history going back centuries. The group approved the proposed structure in principle with the understanding that it would yet undergo some revision.

Discussing organizational questions meant also, *nolens volens,* opening up the discussion to regional politics. A visitor from Kaunas leaped up to object to what he perceived as underrepresentation of his city. Kaunas, he argued, was the largest purely Lithuanian city in the world; it had more Lithuanians than Vilnius did; the people in Kaunas had had a much more difficult time establishing their Sajudis groups than the Vilnius people had faced; therefore Kaunas deserved a guarantee of far stronger representation in Sajudis's institutions than this first project provided.

The rivalry between Kaunas and Vilnius was a well-established fact of Lithuanian life. Whereas Vilnius had at times taken pride in its multinational population, the people of Kaunas looked at Vilnius with suspicion. "Vilnius is the capital of Lithuania, but Kaunas is the capital of the Lithuanians," goes an old Kaunas saying. Between the two World Wars, when Vilnius/Wilno was a part of Poland, Kaunas had served as independent Lithuania's "provisional" capital, and its residents maintained a fierce local pride. The people of Vilnius, by contrast, tended to regard the people of Kaunas as provincial and materialistic; Kaunas, after all, was second only to Tbilisi among Soviet cities in the number of cars per inhabitant. As one observer said to me, "The Vilniusites are always teaching the Kaunasites, and the Kaunasites—the Vilniusites."

The Initiative Group soberly heard out their visitor's

plaints and responded that it in fact represented all of Lithuania, not just Vilnius. To emphasize this, the Initiative Group endorsed the idea of organizing a separate Sajudis Coordinating Council for Vilnius. When this proposal came up for public discussion in a mass meeting of the Initiative Group with Sajudis supporters on September 13, some questioned its usefulness— didn't this just serve to feed the ego of the people of Vilnius?—but Romualdas Ozolas persuaded everyone to accept it with an impassioned appeal pointing out the committee's heavy work load: "We are all living under heart-attack conditions!" The principle therefore was established: the Initiative Group represented the republic as a whole, and Vilnius soon had its own Sajudis council.

In the first three weeks of September, Sajudis's major public action was to form a "living ring" around the Ignalina nuclear power plant. In July, Brazauskas had announced that the Lithuanian government would no longer finance the construction of the third unit, but when construction continued investigation showed that Moscow had directed new financing through Riga. In Vingis Park, Buračas had spoken of possibly rallying support from the Latvians to organize a massive boycott of the plant. At the beginning of September, acknowledging that public reports about the plant's operation and safety, including one in *Tiesa* of April 1, had been doctored, Lithuanian Prime Minister Vaclovas Sakalauskas succeeded in forcing the central government to agree to "conserve" the third unit, that is, suspend construction so that the issues could be settled rationally.[7] At this point, with the first unit closed for repair, only the second unit was working.

On September 5 news of a fire at the power plant

shocked the Lithuanians. Telephones rang insistently at newspaper offices and at the television station. Why had "Panorama," the nightly television newscast, not shown any film of the accident? On the late news, officials reassured the public that no radioactivity had escaped, but the public had little faith in such unverified statements. When reporters were finally admitted to the site the next day, they found a second fire underway. Again the officials declared that everything was under control and that the security system had shown itself fully adequate in responding to such crises. Ignalina's second unit had to close down because of the fire, and for a while the plant produced no electricity at all. Many Lithuanians wanted it to stay that way.[8]

When the Initiative Group met on the evening of September 6, Vaišvila reported that there were indications that the construction of the third unit, rather than being suspended, was in fact going ahead. After lengthy debate, the group, obviously upset by the news of the fires, decided to appeal to the United Nations and the International Atomic Energy Agency for an investigation of the Ignalina plant,[9] and it called for Lithuanians to gather on Saturday the seventeenth to form a "living ring" around the plant. Demonstrators should plan to stay the weekend, Friday the sixteenth to Sunday the eighteenth, bringing food and shelter for three days. In responding over the next days many people suggested that the demonstrators could even fast for forty-eight hours from Friday to Sunday to emphasize their concerns.

Government and party officials quickly indicated their disapproval of such a demonstration; meeting with Buračas, Landsbergis, Vaišvila, and Skučas, Sakalauskas and Brazauskas pointed out that two commissions were already investigating the accident and that Lithuania now had a deficit of electrical power. At this point, they argued, a demonstration would do no good; it could even be harmful. The authorities were acting and, in any case, Sajudis had not submitted its request for permission to hold a rally ten days in advance as required by law.[10] Brazauskas also announced that the International Atomic Energy Agency had refused to investigate the situation, declaring that this was a domestic issue within the Soviet Union.

The party emphasized its unhappiness with Sajudis by calling in Initiative Group party members for a meeting in the Central Committee building on September 12. Group members who were not party members were excluded. Songaila opened the meeting by reading a litany of complaints about Sajudis's activity, declaring that the party was receiving many letters of complaint from the public. He again reminded the group that the party had originated the idea of perestroika, and he specifically criticized the editorial policies of *Sajudžio žinios.*

The Sajudis representatives responded with complaints of their own, emphasizing their problems in obtaining favorable press coverage, and the two sides went on to discuss problems of "sovereignty" and "economic self-sufficiency" at length. In all, the Sajudis representatives left the meeting feeling that there had been a reasonable exchange of views, and that evening, when the Initiative Group met to consider proposals for its program, the discussions with the party were considered to have been routine—there seemed no reason for special concern.

At Sajudis's meeting with representatives of its support groups on Tuesday, September 13, Ignalina stood first on the agenda. Vaišvila told the group's supporters that officials in Sniečkus had not yet responded to the committee's request for official permission to meet, and he went on to discuss plans for the demonstration. Virgilius Čepaitis suddenly interrupted him with the news that the Sniečkus officials had forbidden holding a rally. Vaišvila calmly turned to the audience and announced that the demonstration would go ahead anyway; Juozaitis added, to strong applause, that a priest would say a mass and that this could not be labeled a rally.

The demonstration would obviously not be able to realize Buračas's ideal of 100,000 people blockading the plant. Speakers at Sajudis's meeting pointed out that schools were under orders not to allow children to leave early so as to accompany their parents for the weekend. Without a rally the demonstration would not have a focal point. Vaišvila insisted that it must go ahead and began pointing out alternatives. When someone in the audience asked how the group could possibly learn of the final plans with only three days intervening before the action, another voice shouted out, "Sakadolskis will tell us!" The suggestion drew laughter, but Vaišvila was in fact to use this alternative.

Romas Sakadolskis, as the Lithuanian voice of the Voice of America, had his own place in the ferment in Lithuania. Conservatives, reformers, and radicals alike listened to his broadcasts and quoted him to make their points in discussions. He actively used his telephone to collect news in Lithuania, and the people he reached sometimes decided to take advantage of this to send out their own information. (In a telephone interview on January 18, 1989, Sakadolskis stated that he called people in Lithuania as a matter of policy.) When Sakadolskis appeared in Vilnius as a correspondent at the Sajudis congress in October, he was a great celebrity, constantly surrounded by people who wanted to speak with him.

In preparing for the demonstration at Ignalina, Vaišvila spoke with Sakadolskis; as he later explained it over Lithuanian television, "I admit that I gave interviews to Voice of America three times, and I want to say that I had to." Although first contacts with the government on the proposed action in Ignalina had been good, he continued, after September 10 Sajudis had no access to the press on this question. The people of Sniečkus were being frightened by rumormongers. "Unfortunately, the only means to publicize this action, apart from our small *Sajudžio žinios*, was the Voice of America. That should be, I would say, a lesson for our mass communications."[11]

Once Vaišvila had completed his presentation at the Initiative Committee's meeting of September 13, the gathering then concentrated on discussing aspects of Sajudis's program. Bronius Kuzmickas, a philosopher, emphasized the need for a clear program on the national question, fully recognizing the rights of the other nationalities of the Soviet Union. Reporting on the group's social program, Buračas, who was chairing the meeting, read its proposals to do away with the privileges of the *nomenklatura*, the political and bureaucratic elite in Soviet society.

Speakers from the floor raised points on all issues, some of them relevant and some of them not. Buračas cut short one man who spoke about the need to "save the nation," saying that the assembly needed concrete proposals, not emotional statements. Amid more serious proposals, another speaker suggested making paganism Lithuania's national religion; the Lithuanians, after all, had been the last pagan people in Europe in the fourteenth century. The Initiative Group took all suggestions under advisement.

The question of Sajudis's relationship with the government arose when Kazimiera Prunskiene spoke about the meeting with the Central Committee the previous day. She read an ELTA news release, to appear in the press the next morning, Wednesday, which basically summarized Songaila's list of complaints and ignored the substantive discussion between the party leaders and Sajudis. "Can we be satisfied with this?" she asked, and the question was opened for discussion.

Responding to complaints about *Sajudžio žinios,* Juozaitis warned that the government's press release only served to intensify the spirit of confrontation. "Without the Central Committee," he declared, "we could long ago have reorganized Lithuania without nationalism." His newspaper, to be sure, was not without its faults, he admitted. This type of endeavor had no precedent in the history of Soviet Lithuania, but he argued that in only one case could the newspaper be accused of "causing" a problem.

Juozaitis already knew of the criticisms of his stewardship. Conservative members of the Initiative Group such as the writer Petkevičius and the academician Buračas had deplored his outburst during the meeting of August 23, and they wished *Sajudžio žinios* could be more cautious. Juozaitis called the assembly's attention to the statement of editorial policy that he had published in the thirty-first issue of *Sajudžio žinios,* and he urged people to let him know of their complaints. The assembly was not about to challenge him. When a woman asked from the floor whether it might not be better to have a professional journalist edit the newspaper, another voice shouted out, "Laurinčiukas"—Albertas Laurinčiukas was still formally the editor of *Tiesa*—and the discussion dissolved into laughter.[12]

Although the Sajudis supporters reacted sternly and determinedly to the tone of the party's press release, the publication of the release in the morning papers of September 14 stimulated strong concerns among the public as a whole. Combined with the refusal to permit a demonstration at Ignalina and with the publication on Friday the sixteenth of Eismuntas's account of his meeting with Sajudis, a new feeling of confrontation grew. Of the people I spoke with privately, only one, a journalist, suggested that the party leadership recognized that it was losing and that it was therefore struggling to save face; otherwise I heard only pessimistic expectations of trouble. Nevertheless, a few days later the Central Committee issued a supplementary statement noting that the meeting with Sajudis members had resulted in agreement to allow the Initiative Committee greater access to the media.

The concerns may well have contributed to keeping down the crowd in the Ignalina demonstration on Saturday, but there was no serious confrontation; both Sajudis and government seemed determined to avoid trouble. About 15,000 people gathered in all, guided into place by Sajudis volunteers who stood with banners along the roadside to direct traffic. The staff at Ignalina gave visitors guided tours of the power plant. The pastor of a neighboring church addressed the demonstrators, welcoming them and praising Vaišvila's work, but instead of saying a mass he chose to lead the group in just two prayers, an Our Father and a Hail Mary.[13]

In the week following the demonstration at Ignalina, Sajudis's power seemed again on the rise. On September 19 the Initiative Group held its first late-night television forum. With the journalist Česlovas Juršenas as moderator, Petkevičius, Landsbergis, Prunskiene, Ozolas, Vaišvila, Juzeliunas, and Marcinkevičius had the opportunity to speak freely on topics telephoned in by viewers. Prunskiene spoke of economic autonomy, Vaišvila admitted his conversation with Voice of America, and Juzeliunas discussed the consequences of Stalinism. Petkevičius repeated his thesis that everything new and valuable in society came from the intelligentsia. The television authority's newspaper, *Kalba Vilnius*, subsequently published a transcript of the forum.

Sajudis's relationship with the government and party took yet another positive step forward with the appearance of its legal publication, *Atgimimas* (Rebirth), formally announced as a weekly but in fact of uncertain frequency. Its editor, Romualdas Ozolas, had told the Initiative Group on September 6 that there would be 8,000 copies printed in Lithuanian, 2,000 in Russian; if need be, more copies could then be photocopied—Sajudis had a lot of paper suitable for photocopying but not for printing. The first issue would reprint the speeches given at Vingis Park on August 23, and the copy would not be submitted to censorship.

Asked how this publication would relate to *Sajudžio žinios*, Ozolas explained that *Atgimimas* would be Sajudis's publication for the Lithuanian republic and *Sajudžio žinios* would become the publication of the Vilnius Sajudis Council. (He allowed the possibility that the two publications might on occasion disagree with each other.) Individual copies would cost forty kopecks. (Ozolas explained that they had calculated the cost per copy and then added 100 percent to establish the price.) Although Ozolas on September 6 insisted that the first issue was ready to go to print, the organizers kept running into problems. On the positive side, however, new sources of printing paper arose, and on September 13 Ozolas announced that the first issue would have a run of at least 30,000 copies. In the final count, the first run of issue no. 1, dated September 16, was 30,000 copies, followed by a second run of another 70,000.

The publication established Sajudis's official status in society. *Atgimimas* was legal, even uncensored; *Sajudžio žinios* maintained its semilegal existence, also uncensored, taking the name "Publication of the Vilnius Council of the Movement for Perestroika in Lithuania" with its thirty-ninth issue on September 20. To be sure, neither publication was available through subscription; that would require registration by the authorities. Sajudis was not yet a legal entity or juridical person, but with the Initiative Group hard at work elaborating its program for the upcoming Constituent Congress, that seemed only a matter of time.

9

Confrontation in
Gediminas Square

Wednesday September 28 was a turning point in Ringaudas Songaila's tenure in office as Lithuanian party
boss and generally in Lithuanian affairs—the government chose to act decisively and it lost. From the beginning of my stay I had heard cynics saying, as they
looked at the signs of dissent, that the authorities could
clean up this entire situation in just five hours if they
wanted to. On September 28, the authorities tried to
reestablish their control over Gediminas Square, and
they failed.[1]

The Lithuanian Freedom League (LFL), interested
in forcing confrontation with the authorities, had announced its intention to meet in Gediminas Square at
6 P.M. on September 28 to mark the anniversary of the
second Nazi–Soviet agreement, signed on September
28, 1939, by which the Germans had traded Lithuania to the Soviet Union. In its announcement, dated
September 8, the LFL proposed to make a series of demands: publication of all secret documents in the cen-

tral press, denunciation of the Nazi-Soviet alliance as a crime "against peace and the freedom of peoples," a statement that Lithuania was incorporated by force, denunciation of Stalin as an international criminal, and the establishment of a date by which "the army sent by Stalin" should withdraw from Lithuania.[2]

The city authorities chose to block this meeting. On September 19 the City Soviet's Executive Committee (Excomm) received notice of the LFL's intentions—the letter to the Soviet bore the date of September 17. The league chose not to request permission to hold its meeting; it simply informed the city of its intentions. On the twenty-third the Excomm sent the notice on to the Excomm of the Lenin *rayon* of the city. The rayon Excomm immediately expressed opposition, declaring that the LFL had not observed the proper procedures in applying for permission. The rayon Excomm notified the secretariat of the city Excomm of its decision by telephone. According to the report of the official commission later named to investigate the events, the Lenin rayon Excomm left no paper trail of its deliberations, but a spokesman of the league reported that the Excomm also sent "a written notice" to the organizers of the proposed meeting.[3]

The city Excomm then notified the LFL that the meeting should not take place, adding the observation that the historical questions surrounding the Nazi-Soviet cooperation of 1939 had been fully discussed in the press and that therefore there was no useful purpose to be served in any public meeting. Disturbed by the proliferation of unauthorized meetings throughout the city, and worried by rumors that the demonstrators planned to raise the tricolor on Gediminas tower, the authorities made plans for enforcing their decision.

League officials in turn made clear their own intention to force a confrontation with the authorities. A spokesperson telephoned the Lithuanian Information Center in Brooklyn to say that "sanctions, including imprisonment, may be imposed against the public rally's organizers. Last Friday and again on Monday, one League member was detained by militia for several hours for posting flyers advertising the event."[4]

On the morning of the twenty-eighth, despite the city fathers' assurance that there was nothing more to be said about any secret protocols in Nazi-Soviet relations of 1939, *Komjaunimo tiesa* carried another article by Henrikas Šadžius, discussing just this question. All the circumstantial evidence, he noted, indicated that there had been just such an agreement, but Soviet historians had nevertheless been unable to find the document in Soviet archives: "If it cannot be found, that means it did not exist," he solemnly concluded. The prospective demonstrators could only be encouraged by such observations from a specialist on the history of socialism in Lithuania.

In anticipation of confrontation, the Vilnius city Administration of Internal Affairs prepared its own special militia forces, adding a special motorized unit of the USSR Ministry of Internal Affairs' internal army as well as other groups and assembling a force totaling over eight hundred men. On September 27 the Lithuanian Ministry of Internal Affairs approved the action and notified appropriate party figures. Songaila and Mitkin were specifically informed, as were the organizers of the proposed meeting. Preparations went ahead throughout the day, but no one made any public announcement that the meeting had been banned—neither the city authorities nor the LFL let the citizens of Vilnius know that both sides expected trouble.

At five o'clock on the afternoon of the twenty-eighth, the security forces, largely military, took possession of Gediminas Square. They carried truncheons, or "bananas." Using loudspeakers to announce prohibition of the meeting, they urged all the people there—at the time mostly protesters against the nuclear power plant at Ignalina—to leave the area; they hoped to cordon it off as they had during the night of August 23–24. The public withdrew, but they jeered the lines of militiamen and chanted insults: "Shame, shame, shame . . . " and "Occupiers, occupiers, occupiers . . . " Individuals drifted through the lines of militiamen, while photographers and video operators documented the scene, even moving in for closeups of the militiamen as they impassively listened to the chanting.

At 5:45 reenforcements for the militia drove up in buses and deployed across the square. Spectators and demonstrators soon collected on the small square to the south in front of the Ministry of Internal Affairs building, where a representative of the Freedom League began to speak through a bullhorn. The military's special units, using their "bananas," moved to disperse the crowd.

Over the next forty-five minutes, the demonstrators flowed in waves, withdrawing in the face of militia and military attacks and returning when the authorities themselves pulled back to the square. The demonstrators threw rocks and bottles at the troops, the troops struck back with their clubs. The major action took place at the beginning of Pilies Street, near the Ministry of Internal Affairs, but there was trouble on other edges of the square, especially in the northeast near the Lower Castle. Traffic on Lenin Prospect was totally stopped.

Each side subsequently blamed the other for the violence. Representatives of the Ministry of the Interior insisted that the demonstrators had brought about the confrontation and that the militia and the military had only used force in self-defense, certainly not against any women or children. Military officers insisted that their forces had not struck anyone. Speaking for the Freedom League, Bogušis naturally enough defended the actions of the demonstrators: "They had no other choice but to defend themselves."[5]

At 7 P.M., after the demonstrators had lustily sung the *National Hymn*, Terleckas called on them to retire to the Dawn Gate, about a mile to the south on the other end of the Old City. Members of the Freedom League obliged, and at the gate, reenforced by students, they agreed to march to the Saugumas headquarters on Lenin Square, about a mile to the west of Gediminas Square. (Located next to the Music Conservatory, the Saugumas was referred to at times as the "Department of Percussion Instruments and Solo Singing.") For the students among the demonstrators, this represented the first opportunity since the beginning of the school year to participate in a public demonstration, and they added their own slogans calling for the resignations of the director of the Pedagogical Institute, the director of the Art Institute, and the prorector of the university. Waving the tricolor, the group surged back into the city and headed for Lenin Square.

Since darkness had by now settled over the city, the authorities considered it prudent to withdraw from Gediminas Square, moving to protect both Gediminas hill and the Saugumas building on Lenin Square. By

8 P.M. the Lithuanian Freedom League, now in control of Gediminas Square, resumed its disrupted meeting. League sources estimated the crowd at 15,000 to 25,000 people, and the demonstration proceeded without any further incident. Speeches, claimed the league, "were often interrupted by applause and chants of 'Lithuania will be free!' The demonstrators dispersed peacefully by 9:15 P.M."[6]

During the night, a group of dissidents, including Algimantas Andreika, one of the two original strikers of August 17, decided to resume the hunger strike that had been broken off a month before; the government, they argued, had not lived up to its promises to review the cases of political prisoners. In the wee hours of the morning they began to assemble by the cathedral. At 4:50 A.M. on the twenty-ninth, three buses full of special forces, fitted out with bananas, helmets, and shields, unexpectedly returned to the square and demanded that the crowd of perhaps fifty people disperse. Those who could quickly fled, but the strikers themselves, surrounded, could not get away. The forces of law and order then fell upon the demonstrators with cries in Russian such as "We'll remind you of Karabakh!" Witnesses insisted that some of the attackers were drunk and that the strikers were beaten before being hauled off in police wagons.

Aroused by telephone calls, Vytautas Landsbergis, Romualdas Ozolas, and other Sajudis representatives hurried to the militia station on Kosciuszko Prospect to counsel the arrested. The authorities allowed the Sajudis representatives to speak with the detained persons, but they did not permit the use of either tape recorders or video cameras to document the prisoners' accounts of how they had been beaten. The militia assured Landsbergis and Ozolas that they had used no force.

The number of injured remained unclear even after the ensuing investigation. The authorities claimed at first that eighteen militiamen had been injured and forty-seven demonstrators had been arrested. Later the number of injured militiamen was reduced to six. Injured demonstrators could not obtain doctors' certification that they had suffered from action by the authorities; the doctors cautiously insisted that the militia itself had to sign the documents confirming the use of force. Three days later, five or six individuals finally obtained certification of their injuries from participants in a founding meeting of a Sajudis doctors' group. Andreika was one of the injured demonstrators.

The authorities had failed to intimidate the population. As regards the authorities' motivation, one Western commentator concluded, "The use of force to break up the planned meeting in Vilnius is one more indication of the party's hostility toward the growing demands for radical reform. . . . The Lithuanian Freedom League, which does not command the same support and official tolerance as the Lithuanian Restructuring Movement, was a convenient target for police action."[7] The authorities may not have chosen the LFL with the degree of calculation suggested here, but they had surely wanted to establish some sort of control over the multiplying public meetings.

One should also note the absence of random violence on the part of protestors. In an age when looting is a standard element of social protest in the West, the protestors in Lithuania were accused of damaging military cars and buses but not of causing any damage to stores or buildings. Sajudis leaders made a point of dissuading

youthful spirits from violence, but in this case the supporters of the LFL also refrained. "Do not yield to provocations," was the slogan—the authorities would only
welcome random violence as an excuse to attack more
enthusiastically.

However much one might regret the personal injuries, the LFL probably welcomed the net results of the
demonstration as a success for their style of confrontation. LFL leaders had wanted to picture Soviet rule in
Lithuania as an outside force imposed on the population. The use of militia as well as of Russian-speaking
troops from Minsk could not have illustrated their argument better if they had orchestrated the events themselves. The government had chosen the battle, but it had
not thought through its strategy.

Controlling the mass media, the government immediately put out its own version of the events. (This being
the Soviet Union, "immediately" meant Thursday evening's issue of *Vakarines naujienos*, the Thursday-evening
television news, and Friday morning's newspapers.) *Vakarines* titled its account "A Rally Without Permission"
and complained that the Freedom League was systematically trying to undermine the work of reform and
even the work of Sajudis. "To keep order and peace
in the city, the militia had to take appropriate action,"
the newspaper reported, adding the observation that
unsanctioned rallies "serve only the opponents of Reform. . . . Democracy is incompatible with anarchy, glasnost is not a means for whatever one wants and opposing the established norms of law and order."

A press release in the name of "The government
of the Lithuanian SSR" complained of the proliferation of "unauthorized" rallies, and it accused the Freedom League of having "provocative goals hostile to

socialism." Despite "repeated calls" for order, league representatives had allegedly provoked impressionable youths to "irresponsible actions." The deputy minister of internal affairs, Marionas Misiukonis, told a press converence that the militia, "polite as always," had done everything possible to avoid violence: "Such is the difficult task of the defenders of law and order." The authorities played a videotape showing police calling on the crowd to leave the square.[8]

Members of the Lithuanian Freedom League telephoned their own version of the events to contacts in the United States, and, aided by the eight-hour difference in time between Vilnius and New York, the Lithuanian Information Center in Brooklyn issued a press release dated the twenty-eighth under the headline "Riot Police Clash with Vilnius Demonstrators." According to Bogušis, "They beat everyone and anyone, even children and old women. . . . People scattered in all directions, but then regrouped and came back shouting 'Fascist occupiers out of Lithuania!'"

Denied access to the mass media, Sajudis protested to the city Soviet and to the party Central Committee, and called a meeting in Gediminas Square at 1 P.M. on the twenty-ninth. As the hour approached, early arrivals had the opportunity to look at photographs of the action the night before. As I stood in a small group with a packet of photographs in my hand, a teenage girl peering past me at a picture of a line of militia with helmets and shields—"spacemen" the Lithuanians called such special forces—exclaimed, "Ooh, neat! Just like abroad!" Conditioned by the media to think of such things as occurring only in other countries, Soviet citizens now had the opportunity to see that they too had such forces. Posters in the crowd proclaimed "The militia—the government's face!" and "Down with the Red Terror!"

The demonstration brought together Sajudis and the Freedom League on the same platform for the first time, and Freedom League members obviously relished the moment. When the appointed hour came, Terleckas stood on the low wall in front of the cathedral and, speaking through a bullhorn, called upon the "men of Sajudis" to come forward. Applause greeted the appearance of Landsbergis, Vaišvila, Gintaras Songaila, and others. As Bogušis told his friends in New York, the "rally was significant because it marked the first time that representatives of the two major nongovernmental groups pressing for reform in Lithuania shared the same stage. Prior to today's rally, the officially tolerated Movement to Support Perestroika had avoided joint public appearances with the more radical Lithuanian Freedom League, which advocates the restoration of Lithuanian independence and has been branded an 'anti-Soviet' organization by Communist authorities."[9] Once the meeting began, Vytautas Landsbergis took control of the bullhorn, but Terleckas had his own opportunity to speak.[10]

Sajudis's representatives did not defend the league as such, concentrating on the attacks on the hunger strikers early in the morning rather than on the demonstrations of the night before. Landsbergis, who recounted his own conversations at the militia station, several times exhorted the crowd, which numbered perhaps 3,000 to 4,000 people, to maintain calm and not to respond to "provocation" by the authorities.[11] Songaila read an account of the militia's assault on the strikers, and Vaišvila, exclaiming, "It is time for us to wake up!" emphasized the theme of seeking political power and urged his listeners to acquaint themselves with their representatives in the Lithuanian Supreme Soviet.

Landsbergis struck yet another note in political agitation when he asked rhetorically how the children of the officer in charge of the attack would look at their father's action. Throughout the fall Lithuanians brought their children to peaceful demonstrations with the intention of educating them, and the involvement of the children obviously had to have an impact on any schoolmates who came from families not sympathizing with the Lithuanians' new self-consciousness.

The crowd frequently interrupted speakers with chants of "Shame!" and "To court!" and occasionally with individual shouts such as "Fascists!" "They lie!" and "Down with the occupation army!" The speakers kept calling for order, however, and after the Sajudis speakers had promised that they would somehow publicize the results of their scheduled meeting with the public procurator Ludvikas Sabutis, the group broke up at 2 P.M. to return to work, taking back with them the news that the militia had stooped to "battling three girls." The rally was itself an unauthorized gathering, but militiamen stood quietly in the distance and made no effort to disrupt it.

The next day, the thirtieth, a crowd of several hundred gathered at the Lithuanian television studio to protest the official news coverage of the events. Many employees of the studio watched from the windows of the building as a spokesman for the station awkwardly observed that he understood all revolutionary movements wanted to seize control of the mass media but insisted that he was just doing his job as an employee of the government. Sajudis leaders knew well that they had support among the employees of the station: for more than a month a bulletin board inside the building had been displaying copies of *Sajudžio žinios*, and workers from the station frequented Sajudis meetings, suggesting ways to obtain more coverage.

By the weekend the official press had its slogan for reporting the event: "The citizens of Vilnius are responsible for their city's honor" (Vilniečiai atsako už savo miesto garbe). The city's Executive Committee issued a public statement declaring that the LFL, known for its past "anti-Soviet statements," had wanted "to split [supriešinti] the interests of Lithuania and the Soviet Union, to slander the policies of the Communist Party, and to incite national discord." Insisting that "the law is the law," the authorities had regrettably had to use force to quell this provocation. The demonstration of the twenty-ninth, moreover, was also unsanctioned, and both Landsbergis and Terleckas had allegedly used "unproven or intentionally distorted facts" to criticize the authorities. The announcement ended with an appeal for calm: "The comfort, spirit, and honor of Vilnius depends on all of us."[12] *Vakarines naujienos* of October 3 and 4 published reports and comments by citizens endorsing the city Executive Committee's stand.

With the population of the city suddenly polarized, the forces of change seemed to enjoy the greater momentum. The authorities' attack on Landsbergis raised some concern for his safety but, when they did not follow through, the public mood grew still more daring. Intellectuals in the city were generally critical of the government. The authorities complained of the way teachers, especially of history and of geography, were answering students' questions about the demonstrations. Photographers complained that soldiers had broken their equipment, and the leaders of the Writers'

Union condemned the use of force in Gediminas Square, calling for the punishment of those responsible.[13]

Compounding the confusion over the events of the twenty-eighth were a collection of other events, the most important being a change in government in Moscow. News of an extraordinary plenum of the Soviet Central Committee the next day circulated on the twenty-ninth, and it was only when people heard that the USSR Supreme Soviet would meet on Saturday that it became clear that Mikhail Gorbachev had succeeded in forcing Andrei Gromyko to retire from the post of president of the Soviet Union. The Lithuanians welcomed Gorbachev's victory, but the changes in Moscow also threatened trouble. Aleksandr Iakovlev now took a new post as a specialist in Soviet foreign relations, and replacing him as specialist in nationality affairs was Vadim Medvedev. The Lithuanians feared that they had lost an important source of support in Moscow.

October 1 also marked the seventieth anniversary of the founding of the Lithuanian Communist Party in 1918. A year earlier, the party had intended to make this a day of great celebrations; the debates about Lithuanian history and the events of the twenty-eighth now made the observance far more modest than anyone would have expected. A report on Lithuanian television on the morning of September 30 told of a delegation's leaving for Siberia to look for traces of Lithuanian exiles or graves of the dead. In a discussion of Baltic affairs on late-night television on Saturday, October 1, Estonians spoke openly of "the Russian empire," "occupation," and "Russification." Few seemed ready to celebrate the party's birthday with any enthusiasm.

By Monday the authorities seemed to be in retreat.

An extraordinary plenum of the Lithuanian Communist Party's Central Committee was called for Tuesday, October 4. The topics of the day would obviously include the developments in Moscow as well as the events of September 28. On Monday evening, "Panorama" carried a statement by Šepetys announcing the formation of a commission, including Sajudis members, to investigate the events surrounding the disorders of the twenty-eighth and to report back in ten days.[14] The official press quickly muted its accounts of the events of the twenty-eighth and twenty-ninth.

Putting additional pressure on the government at this point was the renewal of the hunger strike on the square. At the end of the rally of the twenty-ninth in Gediminas Square, Petras Cidzikas announced that he was resuming his action on behalf of political prisoners. By evening, the demonstrators had established control of the corner of the cathedral outside St. Casimir's chapel, and a hut had appeared to house the striker. Sympathizers placed candles and flowers in a niche of the cathedral wall. Along the side of the cathedral, some thirty-five yards of fence were filled with photographs, posters, and artwork, all denouncing the action of the authorities and representing the ideas of the Lithuanian Freedom League far more than the ideas of Sajudis. Hundreds of people stood around excitedly arguing with one another about what had happened.

This time Cidzikas carried on his strike alone, although he eagerly explained his protest to visitors and well-wishers. In speaking with Sajudis's Initiative Group on August 30, Eismuntas, the chief of the Saugumas, had specified that one hunger striker might be tolerated but a group could not be. Sabutis, the republic's procurator, now told *Vakarines naujienos* that he actually had no legal basis for moving against Cidzikas: "Even the jurists' opinions differ in this question." As long as there was no law against Cidzikas's action, Sabutis continued, it could go ahead.[15] Despite such seeming assurances, Sajudis, now essentially endorsing Cidzikas's action, set up a guard to protect him from arrest by the militia or the Saugumas.

Over the next month the flow of people coming to observe Cidzikas's action was constant. During the day the crowd could number in the hundreds. In the evenings it would swell, through the night it might dwindle to a handful, but there were always some spectators. The people came to see Cidzikas, to gaze at his hut, perhaps to chat with him, to place flowers at his hut or against the wall of the cathedral, to read the notices and look at the posters that "decorated" the cathedral wall, and of course to argue. Against the wall outside St. Casimir's chapel someone put a package with the sign "Earth from the graves of Lithuanians in Siberia."

Jogging past at 7 A.M. on Sunday morning October 2, I counted about twenty people looking at the fence decorations and six or seven young people sitting together quietly singing; at the same time the next day, a Monday, there were only seven or eight people present, including a couple of men wearing green Sajudis armbands. In the evening of October 3, proclaimed youth night, waves of people singing folk songs made their way through the crowded square. On the wall in front of Cidzikas's hut lay five petitions for people to sign: a protest to the Ministry of Internal Affairs, a call for Arturas Sakalauskas's return to Lithuania, a call for the release of Vladas Petkus, a general call for the release of all political prisoners, and a demand to stop construction of the Ignalina nuclear plant.

Cidzikas's action and the popular support it generated embarrassed the authorities. Although Cidzikas now had the support and protection of Sajudis, his action probably benefited the Freedom League even more. Cidzikas was known for his role in demonstrations in the past. His behavior now won the respect of people who had distrusted him before, and it improved the public image of the Freedom League. More people learned of the league's existence and its aspirations; its emotional appeals on behalf of prisoners of conscience and for a new Lithuania found new targets.

The strong public support that the forces of change enjoyed became clear on Tuesday, October 4, when the Central Committee of the Lithuanian Communist Party met in its thirteenth plenum with a number of Sajudis Initiative Group members watching. Several thousand demonstrators gathered in Cherniakhovsky Square facing the Central Committee building, in an unprecedented "picketing" action. The ground rules for this strange situation had been laid in intense negotiations between Vilnius party boss Kestutis Zaleckas and the Vilnius Sajudis council. The city authorities would not interefere with the demonstration, a Sajudis representative would be able to address the plenum, and the party was even ready to hear a demand for Songaila's resignation. Momentum definitely lay with Sajudis.

On Cherniakhovsky Square, Freedom League supporters stood together with Sajudis supporters, and enthusiasts told me that the action had been called by the "Sajudis–Freedom League coordinating committee." Not all Sajudis leaders were happy to be standing so close to the league at this moment, but the government's actions of September 28–29 had forced the two groups together. The demonstrators kept expecting someone to come out to address them. At one point they chanted, "Son-gai-la, Son-gai-la," in the expectation that they might even see the party boss. No speaker, however, came forth, although Sajudis representatives attempted to keep the group informed of developments and thereby to keep them quiet.

Inside the Central Committee building, Songaila opened the meeting with a long speech, admitting that the party had "not always" been "well-disposed" to the "political activism of society, especially of the creative intelligentsia and the youth." Nevertheless he criticized Sajudis members for not recognizing the right of the party leaders to have "differences of opinion." He admitted that the authorities had made mistakes on the twenty-eighth and that these had contributed to the violence, but he placed primary blame on the demonstrators themselves.

Other members of the Central Committee were not so generous toward the government's actions, even suggesting that the government's leniency had encouraged the troublemakers. Rimas Rimaitis, the head of the Kaunas party organization, complained about the authorities' efforts to please people who in turn only criticized local party officials, and he urged the party to show more initiative of its own. The chief of the Ministry of Internal Affairs political section, A. Builis, declared that every good citizen of Vilnius had to resent the mess created in Gediminas Square by the LFL, and he complained that not only were militiamen suffering psychological and moral injury in carrying out their orders, but the militia was also having trouble in recruiting and keeping personnel because of the bad publicity it had been getting. The head of the Party Control Commission, S. Aspinavičius, complained about the behavior of those party members who supported Sajudis, and he pointed to Algimantas Čekuolis as a particularly irresponsible miscreant.[16]

The representatives of Sajudis demanded their turn to speak. Party leaders, complaining about the "picket," declared that they could not work under these conditions; they proposed letting Bronius Genzelis speak if the picketing was called off. Čekuolis insisted that the picketing would be ended only *after* Genzelis had spoken. The party leaders had no choice but to yield.

Genzelis sharply criticized Songaila's opening statement, saying that the speech could have been given twenty or thirty years before, and he asserted that the party, having failed "to understand all the processes going on in our country," lacked the confidence of the people. Speaking of having seen "one provocation after another," he demanded the resignation of several figures, including Songaila and Lisauskas. Occasionally he launched into heated exchange with his listeners, who called out "Demagogy!" "Who empowered you?" Genzelis at one point declared, "I see you don't want to listen." "Nothing to hear!" came the answer.[17] Once Genzelis had finished, a Sajudis spokesperson went out into Cherniakhovsky Square to call off the picket, posting a sign saying in effect: Genzelis has spoken, our demands have been met. The crowd began to break up, but members of the Freedom League stayed on to continue their demonstration.

Apart from the discussion of the troubles of September 28, the Central Committee plenum manifested its own signs of change. This, said one member, was the first meeting in fifty years in which the participants had spoken Lithuanian instead of Russian. In a very tense discussion, moreover, the plenum decided to divest Mitkin of his position in charge of party cadres. "This was a revolution," declared a participant in the meeting.

When Sajudis's Initiative Group gathered that evening for its regular weekly meeting, the session with the Central Committee stood as the major topic on the agenda. Speakers emphasized the opposition of party leaders to change; Prunskiene quoted Vytautas Astrauskas as saying there would be no economic self-dependence, no separate Lithuanian currency, and no separate Lithuanian army. The Initiative Group's members displayed growing impatience with the party's resistance to change.

The discussion also evoked self-criticism. Cekuolis said that Genzelis should have written out his speech in advance; he had allowed himself to be sidetracked by the interjections of his listeners. Vaišvila complained that the people in Cherniakhovsky Square received too little information. Another speaker declared that when he had seen the cryptic sign announcing "All our demands have been met," he thought that Songaila had resigned. Although Sajudis guards had kept good control of the crowd during the day, their removal after Genzelis had spoken had left the square to the Freedom League. Next time, the group agreed, the overall strategy would have to be established clearly in advance.

Sajudis had not achieved its goal of removing Songaila from his party post, but new opportunities lay ahead in the near future. October was a month of local party meetings, and Sajudis's own Constituent Congress loomed just two weeks away. Even closer was Constitution Day, October 7, when the Soviet Union would have a holiday to celebrate the anniversary of the Brezhnev Constitution of 1977. Already some intellectuals were insisting that the constitution was in fact a sham and that the proper way to demonstrate one's scorn for this document would be to go to work in spite of its being a holiday. Party leaders, in retreat, knew that they needed to improve their image.

10

Removal of the Party Secretaries

On October 6 party and government moved to achieve civil harmony. Rumors began to circulate in the afternoon, and in the evening "Panorama" made it official: the next day, Friday, October 7, Constitution Day, the authorities, by decree of the Presidium of the Lithuanian Supreme Soviet, would raise the tricolor over Gediminas tower. For good measure, the Presidium also recommended a constitutional change making the Lithuanian language the official language of the republic.[1]

There could be no doubt that this action stemmed from the Central Committee's reflections on the events of September 28 and 29. Rumors about the tower had been circulating for a month. On Friday September 2 several hundred people had collected in the square because of a report that the tricolor would rise at 7 P.M. Nothing happened, but as an exercise in rumor-mongering, the experience offered lessons to both Sajudis and the party; it seemed just a matter of time before something did happen.[2] In speaking to the Central Committee plenum on October 4, Kestutis Zaleckas insisted, on the one hand, that party leaders had to work at becoming more popular and, on the other hand, that the government should take action quickly on the questions of making Lithuanian the official state language and of accepting the national symbols, such as the flag. Delays and uncertainty, warned Zaleckas, were only stimulating agitation and nationalist feelings.[3] His colleagues agreed, and the public received the news on the evening of the sixth.

The news spread quickly, and at 9 A.M. Friday morning the square was already crowded. According to the Lithuanian Information Center in Brooklyn, which had interviewed Vytautas Landsbergis by telephone, "Landsbergis estimated the crowd at no more than 10,000, though other sources reached in Lithuania put the figure closer to 100,000. . . . According to Landsbergis, the number of participants in Gediminas Square would have been much larger if more advance notice of the public rally had been provided."[4] Landsbergis's estimate of the size of the crowd seemed correct to me.

People came to the square joyfully, individually, in families, in groups, carrying tricolors of all sizes mounted on poles, sticks, and rods. Friends greeted one another and embraced, congratulating each other and crying. Here and there one could see elderly people, even incapacitated ones, surrounded by friends and relatives who had brought them to share the moment. As at other emotional occasions during these months, many wistfully spoke of friends and relatives who had not lived long enough to experience this. Some people later said that they found this event more moving than either July 9 or August 23 in Vingis Park; the receptivity to one ceremony or another was obviously a matter of personal background as well as intellectual and emotional makeup.

At 9:55 a marching brass band, replete with pom-pom girls, appeared on the scene, and promptly at 10 A.M. the ceremony started. Mayor Vileikis presided, and behind him stood Zaleckas. The city authorities wanted full credit for this moment. As the flag rose the crowd chanted "*Lie-tu-va, Lie-tu-va*" (Lithuania, Lithuania), and then, accompanied by the band, it sang the *National Hymn*.

The speeches that followed disappeared into the wind due to an inadequate loudspeaker system, but everyone seemed to agree that this was a significant moment. Landsbergis, Petkevičius, and Marcinkevičius spoke, but Landsbergis's father, Vytautas Landsbergis-Žemkalnis, the architect who had directed the last reconstruction of Gediminas Square almost fifty years earlier, drew special cheers.

I must confess to thoughts of historical irony when a speaker read an account by Kazys Škirpa of how the Lithuanian flag had been raised over the tower in 1919. I recalled the last time I had seen Škirpa—he was then an émigré working at the information desk of the Library of Congress. Over the years Soviet historiography had treated him as a villain, "an enemy of the people"— in 1926 he had been military chief-of-staff in "bourgeois Lithuania," and in 1939 he had been a Lithuanian diplomat in Berlin. Now, posthumously, he held a place of honor at this celebration—another unbelievable example of welcoming émigrés back into Lithuanian history.

After the formal ceremony had ended at 10:50 A.M. and the band had marched off, most of the crowd lingered in smaller or larger groups, singing folk songs, including songs recounting the deportations and resistance to Soviet rule. When I ran into a small group who I knew had planned to work as an act of protest, I asked them why they were on Gediminas Square. They answered laughingly, "This is obviously a diversion by the government to make us take the day off." On Lenin Prospect a river of people flowed around stopped buses, cheering drivers who accepted tricolor flags, and climbed atop their vehicles to mount them.

For the moment, the Lithuanians seemed at peace with themselves; the government, in Vytautas Landsbergis's words, had "provided an emotional boost from the oppressive atmosphere created by the events of September 28–29."[5] Various segments of the Lithuanian public insisted on holding their own observances in honor of "the return of the flag." The Catholic Church celebrated with a special mass at the small chapel in the Dawn Gate on October 16; a flag hung out the open window overlooking the crowd of several hundred people in the street below; a dove sat on the cross above the gate for a good twenty minutes. As a reminder of the realities of Vilnius life, there was some pushing and shoving when worshippers coming out from a Polish mass in the neighboring church tried to pass through the gate.[6]

Voices warned that the Lithuanian people must not not sit back satisfied. Freedom League representatives objected that the people must not allow themselves to be satisfied merely with symbols such as the flag. A sign posted along the wall of the cathedral in Gediminas Square proclaimed, "Lithuania, you cried when they raised the flag of freedom, but why won't you help those brothers who sacrificed their freedom so that they would raise that flag?" The general spirit of the moment was nevertheless one of optimism.

With attention now turning to the Sajudis congress,

scheduled to take place on October 22 and 23, the party leadership recognized that it was entering a time of crisis. Sajudis's criticism of Songaila undermined the authority of the party; Songaila, it was charged, had wanted to convince Moscow that Lithuania represented another Karabakh and that therefore the authorities should have a free hand in suppressing the demonstrations. The party leadership seemed intent on making concessions to Lithuanian national feeling—the Cabinet of Ministers expressed regrets about the events of September 28, the Central Committee promised help to Sajudis in organizing its congress, and the Central Committee even met with Cardinal Sladkevičius to discuss problems of the Catholic Church in Lithuania. On October 20, *Tiesa* came out strongly for making Lithuanian the official language of the republic.

Sajudis, by contrast, expanded its base of support into the ranks of the party itself. The Central Committee of the Communist Youth League endorsed the principle of membership in Sajudis. A report that the party unit of the Lenin district of the city of Vilnius had formed a Sajudis support group sent tremors through the entire party establishment, and Sajudis sources insisted that only the intervention of Stasys Lisauskas himself had blocked the formation of a Sajudis support group in the militia.[7] At the same time, the newspapers, or at least so Landsbergis reported on television on October 19, insisted that the majority of the letters they were receiving were critical of Sajudis.

One issue both the Lithuanian government and Sajudis seemed able to agree on was Ignalina. *Tiesa* warned of possible problems with obtaining enough electrical power in Lithuania should Ignalina not be completed, but the Lithuanians responded angrily when an American specialist visited Ignalina under the guidance of his Russian hosts and assured the public that the plant presented no special dangers; capable personnel could run it without serious problems. Lithuanians objected that he had looked only superficially at the plant, but Moscow cheerfully publicized his comments.[8] On Thursday the twentieth, Vilnius television warned viewers not to eat dried mushrooms that had just appeared on the market and not to buy mushrooms from unknown vendors; the latest shipment of mushrooms in town had proved to be radioactive.

On Monday afternoon, October 10, the Central Committee Bureau, the party's executive organ, summoned Initiative Group members to discuss organizational details of Sajudis's congress, and the next day the Central Committee held a press conference to announce plans for media coverage of the gathering. In order to assure that the work of the congress would proceed in the spirit of the Nineteenth Party Conference, Šepetys announced, the mass media stood ready to help. There would be a series of television forums during the week before the congress, and provisions would be made for simultaneous translation into Russian and Polish as necessary. Landsbergis told the press conference that he was gratified by the spirit of cooperation that the party and government were showing.

Sajudis published its program in the daily press of October 12. The document consisted of nine sections: General Principles, Society and the State, Human and Civil Rights, Social Justice, Nationality, Culture, Religion and Society, Economics, and Ecology. It defined Sajudis as a citizens' movement supporting the principle of perestroika as advanced by the Communist Party of the Soviet Union. Sajudis's purposes were the establishment of the soviets as the "competent and sole organs representing the people's will" and the revival of "a civilly conscious and active society." To these ends, "Sajudis initiates projects for laws and referendums, participates in electoral campaigns, watches over election procedures, and organizes public actions."

Speaking of civil and human rights, the program called for observance of the U.N. Declaration of Human Rights, guarantees of the integrity of mail and telephone communications, freedom of speech and of conscience, revision of the penal code, and assurance that "no citizen of the Lithuanian SSR can be deported outside the boundaries of Lithuania against his will." Émigrés should have the right to return home and, declaring "The current order for fulfilling military service in the Armed Forces of the USSR is outdated and immoral," Sajudis called for the "demilitarization of public life." The document went on to urge improvements in housing, social insurance, family policies, and the structure of wages. Society must intensify the struggle against alcoholism and drug abuse, and there must be an end to the privileges of the nomenklatura.

In its national policy, Sajudis guaranteed the "social, economic, and cultural rights and freedoms" of all minorities in Lithuania, but it added that "national equality can be realized only if the representatives of all peoples recognize the right of the Lithuanian people to self-determination, the sovereignty and territorial integrity of the Lithuanian SSR, and become acquainted with and respect the history, culture and language of the Lithuanians."[9] The Lithuanian SSR should have its own citizenship so as to be able to control immigration into its territory.

The program called national culture "a single whole

that cannot be split up by ideological considerations" and demanded improvements in the teaching of Lithuanian language and history: "Historical memory is necessary for the consciousness of any nation; it helps maintain national identity and continuity. This memory is especially important for the Lithuanian nation, which has a rich and dramatic history." It emphasized both freedom of conscience and freedom of religion, it demanded economic autonomy for Lithuania, and it insisted on a rational program of economic development that would not injure the already-endangered environment of Lithuania.

The program was the product of intense and prolonged debates within the Initiative Group. In discussing the text, the group's members had repeatedly emphasized that cultural freedoms, cultural pluralism, a spirit of renewal, ecological concerns, sovereignty, and the education of the youth were their prime areas of concern. In a meeting on September 12, Petkevičius had insisted that the cultural section of the program should precede the political section: "Without culture there is no politics." At times comments were sharp: when Ozolas, the chairman of the meeting, asked how to formulate Sajudis's political goals, Prunskiene said curtly, "The restoration of the Soviet order"; but Petkevičius interjected, "We can't speak of restoration; we have never experienced a Soviet order." Arguments arose over when and where to use "people," "nation," or "society." Ozolas, as chairman, kept calling on the group to concentrate on general principles, not on details.

Once the program was published, the Initiative Group could turn to other matters while Sajudis support groups studied it, drew up responses, and prepared resolutions to submit to the congress. (Many members of Sajudis, moreover, took time to participate in the founding congress of the Green Movement in Lithuania on the weekend of October 15–16.) Sajudis's congress would undoubtedly consider condemning the government's actions of September 28, expressing no confidence in the party leadership, and this could provoke a crisis. Appearing on television on Saturday, October 15, Čekuolis declared that party leaders would be invited to attend the congress as guests but that he himself could not understand why Songaila would want to come.

Throughout Lithuania the tide seemed to be flowing against the party leadership. Local party units, meeting for their own annual elections, reportedly were demanding Songaila's resignation. In a stunning development within the party, Bronius Genzelis, a member of the Initiative Group, was elected the secretary of the party committee at the University of Vilnius: "The university now has its own autonomous Communist Party," one faculty member said to me. Genzelis announced that the reorganization of the teaching of social sciences at the university constituted the most important issue of the day for the party committee: the party committee would "propose to introduce two social science disciplines, political science and the history of philosophy, and to close the history of scientific communism, atheism, and the party."[10]

Faced by rising opposition, Songaila traveled to Moscow, where he reportedly obtained Gorbachev's backing. When he returned to Vilnius in the company of two Russian advisors, he seemed to consider himself justified and reestablished. At the same time, Moscow sent other observers to Vilnius to investigate the situation and to observe the upcoming Sajudis congress. On Mon-

day, October 17, the visitors interviewed party functionaries at almost all levels of public life.

At this point, the commission investigating the events
of September 28 made its report, specifying that Songaila and Mitkin had approved the use of the militia and
the special forces in Gediminas Square. The party
leadership had attempted to pressure the commission
to omit this point, and it suppressed it in the text published by the government, saying that this concerned
individuals and need not be made public. The Council
of Ministers' version of the report emphasized the point
that the Freedom League had insisted on going ahead
with a forbidden meeting.[11]

Sajudis was not to be silenced. *Gimtasis krastas* published the full text of the report, even preparing an
English translation for the benefit of the foreign journalists expected to be attending the Sajudis congress.
The party organization of the Writers' Union had already, on October 12, declared its "no-confidence" in
Mitkin and in Ceslovas Slyzius, the head of agitation
and propaganda. Now leaders of the creative unions—
writers, artists, musicians—gathered on very short
notice and drafted a telegram to Gorbachev, dated October 18: "We inform you that a decision was taken at
a meeting of party bureaus and administrations of the
creative unions to express no political confidence in
Lithuanian CP Central Committee Secretaries R. Songaila and N. Mitkin. . . . The only solution from the present situation, in our opinion, is quickly to summon a
plenum of the Central Committee of the Lithuanian CP
to consider organizational questions."[12]

Songaila's future suddenly dimmed, and the visitors
from Moscow conferred with Sajudis leaders who were
party members. Who did they think should replace

Songaila? The obvious choice lay between Brazauskas and Šepetys, but some Sajudis representatives, unsure about Moscow's attitudes, reportedly refrained from making any recommendations, calculating that their support for one or another might actually compromise him in the eyes of Moscow. Others spoke their piece: "I never before felt so much like a kingmaker," one said to me. Some Sajudis members subsequently insisted that they had in fact brought Brazauskas to power, protecting him from difficult questions at public meetings and generally grooming his image.

Now struggling for survival, Songaila and Mitkin joined other party leaders before the television cameras on Tuesday evening, the eighteenth, to answer questions from viewers. Songaila reminded viewers that the party had originated perestroika, and he expressed pleasure at the high degree of social activity displayed by the population. Vytautas Astrauskas, president of the Lithuanian Supreme Soviet, called for cooperation between Sajudis and the party; Vytautas Sakalauskas, Lithuania's prime minister, emphasized his own most popular issue, expressing hope that an international commission would investigate Ignalina; Mitkin assured viewers that Lithuania was not in danger of experiencing the fate of Czechoslovakia in 1968; Šepetys declared that he was against extremism anywhere; Brazauskas spoke of the need to reorganize and rationalize the economy.

Neither Songaila nor Mitkin converted many viewers. In a separate effort to save Mitkin, a last-minute public relations offensive arranged publication of an interview with him in *Tiesa* and *Sovetskaia Litva* on just that day. Even so Mitkin refused to give an oral interview; he insisted on answering written questions. Declaring that he had come to Vilnius at the behest of the "Polit-buro of our party" and that the Lithuanians had then "elected" him as their second secretary, he expressed sorrow that his busy schedule had interfered with his learning Lithuanian, and he concluded by warning that "democracy and glasnost do not mean anarchy and permissiveness."

In the television forum Mitkin told the Lithuanians that the Soviet Union needed their agricultural produc-tion: "*You* have to work harder so that *we* have meat," was how Lithuanians summarized his message the next day. He also spoke out sharply against the criticisms of the army. Whereas Astrauskas had spoken hopefully of reforms in the conditions of military service, Mitkin de-clared, "Military service is a sacred duty." The army, he insisted, developed *men*; it constituted "the best school for life." Songaila expressed the hope that such televi-sion appearances could now become a new tradition for party leaders, but the next few days made clear that he and Mitkin would not be around to participate in them.

On Wednesday the nineteenth, Sajudis leaders again received the call to the Central Committee building to meet with the Committee Bureau. This time the debate raged around Songaila's person. He tried to defend him-self, and then he left the meeting, presumably to talk on the telephone with Moscow. He returned crestfallen; he had obviously lost. After the Initiative Group members had left the room, Šepetys formally proposed that Son-gaila step down, and the bureau agreed. Songaila re-signed, and the party leaders, with the approval of their visitors from Moscow, chose Brazauskas as his successor.

As rumors swept through the city, Brazauskas hast-ily departed Vilnius for Moscow, where early in the morning of the twentieth, before breakfast, he met with Gorbachev to receive his approval. (A Lithuanian Communist Party representative later explained that this was a matter of courtesy.) He also met with Georgy Razumovsky, chairman of the Party Organization and Cadres Commission, with whom he discussed party affairs including the work of both Songaila and Šepetys, and with Viktor Chebrikov, chairman of the Party Legal Commission. Presumably he also discussed the work of Comrade Mitkin. This done, he hurried back to Vilnius, where, in the afternoon, the party Central Committee met in its second plenum of the month. Despite all the intense politicking that preceded the meeting, it was far more than just a formality. The decision as to who should be the first secretary was clear; there remained, however, an equally important decision to be made on the fate of the second secretary.

The meeting opened with the announcement of Songaila's request that he be released from the post of first secretary and permitted to retire from public life. The plenum, at which 128 of 145 members of the Central Committee were present, approved and proceeded on to the Central Committee Bureau's recommendation that Brazauskas become the new first secretary. The first discussants, Zaleckas and Rimaitis, noted that the other members of the Central Committee Bureau had to share the blame in the party's shortcomings in responding to the demands of perestroika, and A. Asmonas, from Klaipeda, later suggested that perhaps the Central Committee Bureau should be reorganized. Another member suggested, "Comrade Šepetys is tired. He is sixty years old. Why can't we let him also retire with honor?"

Speaking for the bureau, Astrauskas spoke of his respect for Songaila but added, "In the Central Committee

Bureau we frequently criticized R. Songaila." S. Gied-raitis, a Central Committee secretary, declared, "We all agree that the authority of the party has seriously declined. . . . Our task is to restore it." Šepetys drew support from Kašauskiene of the Institute of Party History and from Antanas Macaitis, the director of the Komjaunimas.

Many spoke of the necessity of republican autonomy in party affairs. Algirdas Žukauskas, vice-president of the Academy of Sciences, warned that the new secretary would have to defend the interests of the republic and avoid blindly responding to orders "from above." Several speakers pointed to shortages in consumer goods produced in Lithuania, ranging from television sets to meat, as examples of Lithuania's being drained on orders from elsewhere. "Our leadership keeps looking to the center," declared S. Šimkus, rector of the Higher Party School of Vilnius, "at what often poorly qualified curators say." V. Statulevičius, another vice-president of the Academy of Sciences, suggested that "one of the First Secretary's errors was that he listened too much to the Second Secretary."

The comments of various speakers made clear that the events of September 28 were the key to Songaila's fall. Zaleckas spoke of the events having "seriously sharpened the situation in the city"; A. Žalys, from Klaipeda, said both Songaila and Mitkin must go: "One cannot send the army against the people." Šimkus declared, "The use of force was a gross mistake, which deepened the crisis in the republic."

Referring to Mitkin directly, several speakers insisted that his presence compromised the people's faith in the party. "We have to end the practice of being shown from above whom we should elect in the republic and how to do that," said Asmonas. A pensioner, J. Januitis, spoke out sharply: "Party organizations accept resolutions concerning the second secretary's inactivity, his incompetence, and nothing is done." Astrauskas and other members of the bureau urged the committee members not to act hastily.

Speaking on his own behalf, Mitkin declared, "I have worked and I work conscientiously; I can look people straight in the eye. I have done nothing, so to speak, really bad, that could harm the party, I have done nothing of the sort and I plan to do nothing." He understood, he declared, the questions raised "about the status of the Second Secretary, and, I will say, I approve of the regulation. Therefore, speaking openly, I do not want to say anything more on the question. . . . Whatever you decide, that will be." He was ready to retire, but he questioned whether this was in fact in the best interests of the party: "Think about that."

The speakers waxed eloquent about Brazauskas's qualifications. "Competent, determined, bold, conscientious and always truthful" were the qualities that P. Noreika wanted in a first secretary, and "Comrade A. Brazauskas is just such a man." "The people know, love, and respect Comrade A. Brazauskas," declaimed another speaker. The new leader would have to be ready to appear among the people and to speak on television and radio, argued V. Kornienko of Širvintai.

After the committee had voted to accept Brazauskas, Songaila thanked the group for past support, and the new first secretary then took the floor, recounting his visit to Moscow and urging his colleagues to learn from their mistakes. Referring to Mitkin, he agreed that the Central Committee had to respond to complaints but, "like it or not, he exists. This is a representative of the Politburo." The Lithuanians did not have the power to decide the question by themselves; they would have to negotiate with Moscow on Mitkin's status. Put into the form of a resolution, Brazauskas's proposal to refer the matter to Moscow passed immediately by a vote of 123 in favor, 2 against, 3 abstentions. With this, the meeting ended.

Mitkin in fact soon left Vilnius on an extended vacation preliminary to his retirement from the post of second secretary. Since a Russian normally occupied the post, the Lithuanians chose a Russian from Lithuania, Vladimir Beriozov, as the new second secretary of the Lithuanian Communist Party.

While awaiting news of the outcome of the party plenum on Thursday evening, Sajudis staged yet another television forum, which opened in a spirit of self-congratulation and announced plans for the congress. Commenting on the commission's report about the events of September 28, Petkevičius reported that both Songaila and Mitkin had tried to soften its conclusions. The party, he insisted, had compromised itself and must change leadership. Sajudis, he declared later in the evening, did not want to take power, but if the party should fail to meet its responsibilities Sajudis stood ready to act. The forum broke off just before midnight so that television could carry a report of the ending of the plenum.

On Friday, Brazauskas, together with other party leaders, held a press conference, which he opened by thanking everyone for their congratulations. There was much work to be done, and he looked forward to working productively with Sajudis. He had gone to Moscow, he explained, simply because tradition dictated that the new party secretary should visit the capital to become acquainted.

Sajudis held its own press conference later in the day; Čekuolis presented a number of Initiative Group members to the journalists who had come to cover the congress. Declaring that Sajudis was not a party, not an organization, not an opposition, he asserted that Sajudis supported the party line of perestroika. Sajudis did not mean to confront the government or the party, declared Petkevičius, it opposed only those "Stalinists" who did not understand the meaning of perestroika. All speakers welcomed Brazauskas's election, although the writer Vitas Tomkus declared that he looked forward to the day that a new party secretary would not have to travel to Moscow as his first task in office. Perestroika had begun three years earlier, declared Landsbergis, but "only yesterday" had it reached the leadership of the Lithuanian Communist Party.

When pressed by Western correspondents as to what kind of political system they considered ideal for Lithuania, Sajudis leaders offered a variety of views. Landsbergis spoke of favoring a "democratic socialism," and one definitely not like North Korea or Romania. Ozolas declared that "sovereignty" involved cultural maturity and that Lithuania had a long road to pass before it would enjoy juridical sovereignty. Buračas spoke of the need to establish a real government of Soviets. Juozaitis declared that Sajudis, building on Lithuania's Catholic traditions, could serve as a healthy opposition without being a party. Ozolas interjected that the Lithuanians were in fact heading into unknown territory, and Čekuolis asserted that he was a Marxist-Leninist who rejected the Stalinist model and supported Gorbachev.

Despite the general relief at Songaila's departure and

feelings of welcome for Brazauskas, Lithuanian activists made clear that much was yet to be done. Landsbergis told a German reporter, "There is a long way to
go before the main street in Vilnius, Lenin Prospect, is
again named for the founder of the city, Gediminas."[13]
Freedom League representatives, by contrast, suggested
that in fact nothing had been done. Terleckas later
argued that there was really no difference between Brazauskas and Songaila—on a still later occasion he declared that there was no difference between Gorbachev
and Stalin—Lithuania, he insisted, would not be free
until it was rid of Communist leadership altogether.[14]

The last flurry of activity in preparation for the Sajudis congress struck out in all directions. The Vilnius
press published commentaries on Sajudis's program,
both adulatory and critical, all week. On Wednesday
night, Gediminas Rudis appeared on the television
show "Vaidrodis" (Mirror) to talk about the "Rainiai" af-
fair, the killing of political prisoners, Lithuanians, by
Soviet authorities in the face of the German advance in
June 1941. The next day, the twentieth, *Gimtasis krastas*
published a long article on the case; *Sovetskaia Litva* reprinted this piece on Friday; and rumor had it that a
group of military veterans who had been planning to
organize a demonstration against Sajudis dropped all
thought of such action in the light of the Rainiai story.[15]

In *Gimtasis krastas* of the twentieth, Čekuolis criticized the widespread use of Lenin's name in society and
asked, "Is there a more idolatrous country in the world
than ours?" Stalin, Čekuolis wrote, had established this
cult; "We destroyed the cult of Stalin and seized the cult
of Lenin. . . . You see if there is no cult we have to think
for ourselves, perhaps even think critically." Calling
Leninism "a method, not a book of recipes," he urged
cessation of building monuments to Lenin, prohibition

of the use of Lenin's name on factories and enterprises, returning the historic names to all streets and squares in Lithuania now bearing Lenin's name, and using the occasion of Sajudis's congress to return the name "Gediminas Street" to the main thoroughfare of Vilnius.

In order to avoid a new cult of personality by over-using Gediminas's name, Čekuolis proposed to rename Gediminas Square "Cathedral Square." The cathedral, to be sure, was currently still an art museum, but it should be returned to the church: "Personally a convinced atheist of long standing, I urge that this be done now. . . . When I pass the Cathedral I want to hear organ music and see the flickering light of candles. It will be good for me, as a Communist, in my heart, to know that things are well with my fellow countrymen."

On Friday the twenty-first, the day before the Sajudis congress, the Lithuanians were almost overwhelmed by the sense of movement and change in their society. Šepetys suggested that priests could say mass in the museum/cathedral. Church officials did not care for this half a loaf, but they welcomed a government announcement that the Museum of the History of Atheism and of Religion, located in the church of St. Casimir in the Old City, would be moved and that the building would be returned to the church. Early Friday morning a crowd gathered at the train station to welcome Julijonas Steponavičius, the bishop of Vilnius whom for twenty-seven years the Communist authorities had blocked from performing his duties, and who was now returning to the city after a visit to Rome. The government also announced plans to declare the deportation orders of 1941 and 1948 null and void, thereby granting another large group of Lithuanians full citizenship rights. At this point anything seemed possible.

11

The Sajudis Congress

The "Second" Great Vilnius Seimas took place on October 22, 23, and 24, 1988. The first, which had taken place in December 1905 in the midst of revolution in Russia, had marked the maturing of Lithuanian self-identity after years of oppression and struggle.[1] The second, born of perestroika, represented no less of a revolution in Lithuanian national self-consciousness. "All of Lithuania" wanted to fit into the Sporto Rumai where the congress of the Movement for Perestroika in Lithuania took place, wrote the *Vakarines Naujienos* of October 24, and the result, in Vytautas Landsbergis's words, was "two days that changed Lithuania."

Sajudis had summoned the congress in order to establish its mandate as the voice of Lithuania; the meeting also presented a great opportunity to win worldwide publicity. Čekuolis headed the press committee, planning to publish a daily bulletin in Lithuanian, Russian, German, and English. Čekuolis also arranged a daily press conference organized around a topic. On

Friday, the day before the congress was to open, Sajudis leaders answered general questions; on Saturday the press conference would focus on the national questions in Lithuania; and the Sunday conference scheduled Lithuanian history as its theme. Čekuolis was in charge of all press conferences, and he participated actively in answering questions. From the first he made clear that he would give preference to questions from foreigners; he wanted the world to become acquainted with Lithuania.

For the people of Lithuania the congress constituted a celebration of their national identity but also a grim reminder of their past. Across the republic those who were unable to be in Vilnius sat glued to their television sets. "I could not eat or drink for two days," a friend from Kaunas told me. Another spoke of her father's refusing to leave the television set in the living room even to go to the kitchen for food lest he miss something. A third declared that his father had taken to his bed, mumbling that nothing good could come of all this. Yet another told me of a neighbor's pounding on the door at 11 A.M.—a former deportee to Siberia, he desperately felt the need of a drink and someone to sit with. No one could remain unaffected by the proceedings.

On Saturday morning, when delegates and spectators gathered in front of the Sports Palace for the congress's ceremonial opening, the atmosphere was festive. Besides carrying the national tricolor, people bore banners with the coats of arms of various regions—Druskininkai, Alytus, Biržai, Varena, Zarasai, Kelme, and others. One sign announced, "Rainiai—Your Blood Is Our Flag"; another declaimed, "Vytautas, Gediminas, Kestutis: We Are with You, You with Us"; and yet another: "Welcome, Guests from the USA!" Later in the morning, after the session had begun inside, sympathizers of the Freedom League took over the plaza with their own signs: "We support the secession of Russia from the USSR," and "Withdraw the Occupation Army." The authorities gave no sign of reacting to these provocative statements.

Party and government officials made every effort to declare their support of the event. Standing in front of the Sports Palace before the opening, Lionginas Šepetys assured me that "we" had looked forward to this event: it was an important moment for Lithuania. Sajudis and government had to work together to resolve delicate social and national questions. He concluded with the hope that the congress would be properly understood elsewhere, especially in other republics.

The meaning of this last statement eluded me until I understood that he must be referring to a critical editorial on the front page of Moscow's *Pravda* on Friday, October 21. On its front page the newspaper had published a letter from a Russian teacher in Šiauliai, objecting to "speculation" with Lithuanian history and "falsification of the past." The paper's editorial spoke of the blood spent in wars and, although granting that the "popular fronts" in the three Baltic republics were correct in principle, it insisted that the Soviet Union had to remain indivisible: "The national nihilism of the recent past must not become nationalism."

As became clear in a press conference later in the day, none of the Sajudis leaders had read that issue of *Pravda*; only the party leaders seemed to be keeping up to date with Moscow's opinion. Once the congress had ended, Lithuanian journalists sought out the teacher, S. Bezrukova, who explained that she refused to learn Lithuanian and that she was horrified by stories that

her pupils, who were Russians, were asking their
fathers whether they were "occupiers." On November 1,
she declared on Lithuanian television, "I don't feel at
home here." At the start of the congress, however, most
Lithuanians seemed cheerfully oblivious to warnings
from Moscow.

Inside the Sports Palace the giant scoreboards on
either end carried the message "For Your Freedom and
Ours," a call originally used in the rising against Russian rule in 1831 in an effort to rally Russians, Poles,
and Lithuanians alike against tsarist oppression. An
enormous yellow-green-red banner began in the center
of the ceiling, ran to the wall behind the stage on the
long side of the building opposite the grandstands, and
then continued down the wall to the floor. Tricolor flags
abounded; I saw no Soviet flags in the hall. The congress
registered 1,021 delegates, 96 percent of them Lithuanians. There were 8 Russians, 6 Jews, and 9 Poles. Most
delegates were men (854). In terms of "social origin,"
299 came from the peasantry, 202 from workers, and
459 were administrators. The 283 "scientists and artists" represented the largest occupational group.

Members of the Initiative Group with whom I spoke
were without exception jubilant about the course of
events. Juzeliunas expressed satisfaction with the government's announced plan to repudiate the deportation
orders of 1941 and 1948; Arunas Žebriunas expressed
his personal gratitude to the Lithuanian emigres who
had preserved Lithuanian culture during the dark days
at home.

Applause greeted the appearance of Justinas Marcinkevičius and Meile Lukšiene on the stage as the official
chairpersons of the opening session. "At last the day has
come," Marcinkevičius began. "The day has come when

we have finally joined our civil and political will, our intellectual and creative means, all the forces of our body and spirit, joined them for the rebirth of Lithuania." Sajudis, he declared, "has formed and worked as a democratic movement of all the nation, of all the people, growing out of our history, out of the distant and not so distant past, out of the best traditions of our national life. We have finally understood: woe to those peoples whose history and memory are silent or tell falsehoods."

As the congress's first order of business, a delegation immediately left to place a bouquet of flowers at the grave of Jonas Basanavičius, the "Patriarch of the Lithuanian National Renaissance." The emotional pitch then rose with the appearance of Vytautas Landsbergis-Žemkalnis, Vytautas Landsbergis's father, who declared that the building was now not a sports hall but "Lithuania's shrine." He enthusiastically joined with the crowd in chanting "*Lie-tu-va, Lie-tu-va,*" and the assembly joined in singing *Ilgiausiu metu* ("Many Years," a song serving as both "Happy Birthday" and "For He's a Jolly Good Fellow") in his honor.

After several speakers had offered greetings, Algirdas Brazauskas came out of the guests' section to address the delegates. He had been taking his own notes, rising when the delegates did but not always joining in the applause. This constituted his first major public appearance, his "speech from the throne," as Čekuolis had put it in English at Friday's press conference. The delegates greeted him with strong applause and cries of "Valio!"

Offering greetings on behalf of party and government, Brazauskas reported that Mikhail Gorbachev "asked me to pass on his most sincere greetings and good wishes to all the creative and industrious people of Lithuania,

whom he highly values and respects. Comrade Gorbachev declared that he sees in Sajudis that positive
force that can well serve the good of perestroika and
even better strengthen the authority of the Soviet system." Sajudis, Brazauskas went on, had done much;
"our creative intelligentsia" had accomplished remarkable things. Few had believed that Sajudis could become such a force, and the party had not properly
appreciated it. Now, he promised, things would be different: the two forces, the party and Sajudis, had to
respect each other and to cooperate. Similarly, the
other nationalities of Lithuania need not fear the "revival of Lithuanian national consciousness."

Developing his theme of reconciliation, Brazauskas
paid homage to the victims of Stalinism, and he called
for the elimination of "all the blank spots" from Lithuania's history. A "commission of competent specialists"
should examine the "tragedy of the Rainiai woods" as
well as other Stalinist misdeeds in Lithuania. Lithuanians, he declared, must join together to honor those
"who have suffered unjustifiably; let us wipe away their
tears and those of their children." He himself joined in
the applause of the delegates at this point.

The secretary then asserted the party's position on
a series of other issues, reminding the delegates that
the Communist Party had originated the program of
perestroika, praising Sajudis's efforts to regain the national symbols, supporting the principle of "economic
self-dependence," and advocating strong action to improve the environment, including stopping construction
of Ignalina's third unit. He concluded by quoting Marcinkevičius: "The Fatherland is difficult work."

For all the sympathy that the delegates showed to
Brazauskas, they constituted a tough audience. Listeners responded restlessly to sentences that sounded like

Songaila's leftovers. When he noted that perestroika had begun with the party, delegates laughed, and they seemed amused at his plaint that it seemed difficult at times to find an avenue of communication with the public: "To be sure, we did much before, but perhaps we publicized it too little." Nevertheless the overall reaction of the public to the speech was positive. Applause accompanied the secretary back to his seat, and the delegates again sang *Ilgiausiu metu.*

The congress's work through the morning consisted of position papers by Sajudis speakers and communications of good will from other parts of the Soviet Union and from emigres. The Russian poet Andrei Voznesensky read a poem written in Marcinkevičius's honor. During the lunch break, the congress's second press conference featured what *Time* magazine's correspondent characterized as "a joint Polish-Russian offensive," challenging the right of Lithuanians to speak for the population of the republic. Čekuolis and his associates easily deflected the verbal blows.

The afternoon session saw speeches becoming more emotional. A representative of Lithuanians still living in Vorkuta, the site of an infamous prison camp, called for a "Lithuanian Lithuania" and asked for help to bring Lithuanians home: "Lithuanians must return to Lithuania." Terleckas warned of the dangers of compromise and declared, "We do not want autonomy, we want independence." Juzeliunas denounced the writings of Šarmaitis and Žiugžda, saying that the vulgarization of history had hurt the Lithuanian people. By late afternoon, the congress had fallen well behind the tight schedule that had been set for it, and the organizers were already telling some delegates who wanted to speak that there was no room for them.

The delegates added to the delays in the program

by repeatedly interupting speakers with applause, and their enthusiasm did not seriously distinguish between them. They had sung for Brazauskas, they cheered Terleckas for thirty seconds when he called for the removal of "foreign armies" from Lithuania, and they cheered Vytautas Bieliauskas, a Lithuanian emigre from Chicago who was head of the World Lithuanian Community, for fifty-one seconds at the end of his speech. Bishop Vytautas Aliulis, speaking for the episcopate, drew twenty-seven seconds of applause for his statement that the bishops would not enter the cathedral/art museum for a mass until the church controlled it, twenty-seven seconds for his announcement that Vincentas Cardinal Sladkevičius would preside at a mass outside the cathedral the next morning, and twenty-two seconds when he finished. Since speakers in any case frequently exceeded their allotted first ten and then eight minutes, the applause contributed to dragging out the proceedings.

Some commentators later complained that Stalin had taught the people to cheer that way, but at least part of the problem lay in the mixed character of the gathering—was it a victory celebration or a business meeting? The cheering expressed the congress's celebration of the Lithuanian national idea, even as it interfered with the task of giving Sajudis a permanent organization. The presiding officers repeatedly asked the delegates to refrain from standing ovations in the middle of speeches, but to no avail. The celebratory mood repeatedly prevailed over the working mood in the delegates' behavior.

At about twenty minutes before eight in the evening, the presiding officer, Antanas Buračas, interrupted the proceedings with a sensational piece of news: the government and party had announced that as of that day, October 22, the cathedral in Gediminas Square had been restored to the Catholic Church. The delegates rose cheering, and their applause ran for more than ninety seconds before Buračas finally stopped it. There was, however, little more that could be done that day. Organizers had planned a procession from the Sports Palace to Gediminas Square at 8 P.M., that ceremony now became the apotheosis of Lithuanian national feeling.

The decision to return the cathedral to the church constituted the most popular action that the leadership could conceivably have taken at this moment. The decision-making coterie of party and government— Brazauskas, Sakalauskas, Astrauskas, and Šepetys— had apparently made their decision after hearing Aliulis speak, and they had obviously not had time to communicate with Moscow. They had sent Justas Paleckis up to the rostrum to deliver their message to Buračas; now they could just enjoy the evening.

When the quadrumvirate left the building to lead the procession, the plaza in front of the Sports Palace was packed with people awaiting them, and everyone already knew of the decision to return the cathedral. The group passed through a double line of women wearing peasant costumes and holding candles. Mayor Vileikis told me the next day that the women had pressed food on them, insisting that they must be hungry after such a hard day's work.

The citizenry fell in behind the leaders, and the procession, carrying banners, torches, and lighted candles, slowly made its way across the Nerys River to Lenin Prospect. As they walked along, passing stopped and deserted buses that had nowhere to go, groups sang folk songs and songs of deportations. Particularly catching my ear was the line, "They put them all into a car, and took them no one knows how far." As we entered Lenin Prospect, or "Gediminas Street" as it was called this evening, a rocket arched over the city and finally extinguished itself just before landing on the roof of the Institute of Party History. At least 20,000 crammed into Gediminas Square; thousands filled the streets around the square; many more could not hope to enter the area and hurried home to watch the festivities on television.

Brazauskas spoke again in Gediminas Square, reminding the crowd of how in June, when Sajudis was first forming, everyone was still speaking hesitantly. Now, he told us, the speakers at the conference had felt free to speak openly. The talks had been of varying quality, he observed, but one theme seemed to predominate: all agreed that "We residents of Lithuania" had to unite. Declaring, "We" had decided, "quickly and firmly," to return the cathedral to the people, he called the walk to the square moving and impressive, and he hoped that this spirit of unity could continue. In response the people chanted *"A-čiu, a-čiu, a-čiu"* (Thank you) and waved their flags.

The celebration extended far into the night. Food services remained open long after their normal hours; euphoria prevailed. Returning to my hotel at 1 A.M., I saw that people had lined the center of Lenin Prospect from Gediminas Square to Soviet Bridge with their candles, which were still burning. Even the weather had been kind to the Lithuanians. On Sunday night, at the end of the conference, it was cold and misty, but on Saturday night and Sunday morning, it was clear.

At 7 A.M. on Sunday morning, Gediminas Square was again full, and the tricolor flag was again prominent.

Cardinal Sladkevičius presided at a celebratory mass in front of the cathedral, and those unable to attend the service could watch the mass on television. Even the woman who introduced the program on television was dressed in national costume. All across the land believers gathered in front of their sets to experience this unprecedented occasion.

The cardinal began his sermon by saying that at noon on Saturday, preparing his text, he had planned to talk of "wrongs," but that now he wanted to "thank our national brothers who have shown such great understanding" in returning the cathedral. The cathedral had now expanded to all of Lithuania, and the people had reason to rejoice. But as they rejoiced, they also "must learn to wait, to be patient." Later in the day even Brazauskas was to quote the cardinal's message of "Rejoice, wait, and grow."

Early arrivals at the Sports Palace could hear the voices of the faithful echoing across from the cathedral. The attitude of the delegates was one of nervous excitement. They had shared the emotional bath of national rebirth; now, they realized, they had considerable power, for better or for worse, to shape the course of Lithuania's future. Inside the hall, the delegates greeted Brazauskas with applause, while spectators nodded and agreed that things would have been very different were Songaila still in office.

At midmorning the delegates finally adopted their organizational rules. There had been conflicting views of what Sajudis should be: one wing had favored making it a dues-paying organization that could amass a treasury to finance its own political candidates; the other wing had favored keeping it a looser organization in which anyone could claim membership. A little before 11 A.M. the congress adopted its rules based on the looser model, and the chairman, Kazimieras Motieka, announced that according to Soviet law Sajudis was now a legal entity. The delegates could proceed to elect the Seimas, a council of 220 members.

Soon thereafter a fundamental difference of views between Vilnius and Kaunas flared up; once again Kaunas balked at following Vilnius's lead. Although the Initiative Group had published its program less than two weeks earlier, the Sajudis organization in Kaunas had drawn up its own program back in September. Differences between the two documents lay mainly in tone and emphasis, rather than in substance, but Kaunas's insistence on offering its own version irritated some members of the Initiative Group.[2]

At the congress, the Kaunas delegates distributed a flyer outlining their recommendations for the section on "General Principles" in the Initiative Group's program. Particularly striking was the second point: "Sajudis asserts that the incorporation of the Lithuanian Republic into the USSR in 1940 was a result of the Ribbentrop-Molotov Pact of 1939, violating treaties between Lithuania and Soviet Russia and Lithuania and the Soviet Union. The act of incorporation annulled the independence of the state of Lithuania."

Kaunas delegates agreed among themselves that they would emphasize the theme of "occupation" in their speeches to the congress, and on Sunday morning Rolandas Paulauskas, one of their number, called on the delegates to make a clear decision on Lithuania's future, suggesting that some members of Sajudis were "flirting" with the government for their own purposes, perhaps seeking administrative positions for themselves. Moscow, he warned, "gives to the Baltic republics that which won't be difficult to take back. . . . The only simple question," he declared, "is whether to belong to the Soviet Union or not." Sajudis, he insisted, must remain an opposition force lest it be coopted by the very authorities it was now opposing.[3]

In essence Paulauskas's speech was no stronger than Terleckas's the previous day, but because of his fame as a popular composer and his role as a member of the Kaunas delegation, his words aroused excitement. Vytautas Petkevičius and Vaclovas Daunoras, the chairmen of this session, both took the podium to denounce this "provocation." Petkevičius angrily denounced the tactics of the Kaunas group, and Daunoras called on the delegates to remember the words of the cardinal. The fact that the delegates successively gave Paulauskas, Petkevičius, and Daunoras standing ovations spoke eloquently to the mixture of emotions and reason that fueled the passions of the congress.

Paulauskas had actually given his speech twice before in preliminary gatherings in Kaunas. Because of time limitations, however, he had to squeeze his presentation, which he had planned for ten minutes, into just three. He also had not used the concept *flirtavimas*, flirting, in his trial runs in Kaunas, but the Kaunas delegates stood with him, criticizing Petkevičius and Daunoras for their heated responses. If Paulauskas had had his full ten minutes, one Kaunasite assured me, the impact of his speech would have been far more favorable. As it was, he had wrenched the delegates' emotional strings—in the words of my friend from Kaunas he had simply said what most already had "on the tips of their tongues"—and the organizers of the congress had to spend considerable time and effort to bring the delegates back into line.[4]

During the congress's luncheon break, Čekuolis presided over the daily press conference, this time devoted to questions of Lithuanian history. As an accredited representative of the Chicago Lithuanian newspaper *Akiračiai*, I took advantage of Čekuolis's concern for letting foreign correspondents speak and posed the first question: "In the past, Soviet Lithuanian historians tried to establish their own interpretation of Lithuanian history, and they officially spoke of foreign 'bourgeois' historians as their enemies. What is the attitude toward foreign historians now? Will there now be a new Lithuanian interpretation of Lithuanian history?"

Alfonsas Eidintas declared that in the past Soviet historians had used even worse epithets to refer to westerners, but he declared that the "years of confrontation have passed." The Lithuanian historians hoped that now they could obtain access to sources held in the West and that they could enter into a dialog with their Western counterparts on as broad a basis as possible. He noted the foundation of a new organization, the Lithuanian Historical Society, in which foreigners could become members, and declared his own hope that in the future Lithuanian readers would recognize their history as written by Lithuanians.

Liudas Truska then listed the topics that historians were currently reevaluating: the role of the Catholic Church in Lithuanian history, the Lithuanian national rebirth, the formation of the Lithuanian state after World War I, evaluation of the accomplishments of the Lithuanian republic between the wars, the fateful years of 1939–1940, the "so-called revolutionary situation and socialist revolution" of 1940, the "so-called class struggle" after World War II, and the collectivization of the Lithuanian peasantry in 1948 and 1949.

Asked how the new history would differ in discussing the events of 1940, Gediminas Rudis framed his response as an example of "the new pluralism," declaring that *he* would say that Lithuania had been "occupied" and that the decision of the "People's Seimas" in 1940 to request incorporation into the Soviet Union constituted "political theater." Truska then pointed out that a Russian historian from Moscow, Yuri Afanasiev, had been the first to call the events of 1940 in the Baltic an "occupation."[5] Delegates from Kaunas had spoken of "occupation," but this was the first occasion that a Lithuanian historian had dared to use the word in public.

In answer to a question from *The London Guardian*'s correspondent, Truska declared that Lithuanians had experienced deportations in each year of Stalin's rule. He could not produce exact figures, but he put the minimal estimate of deportees at 150,000 and the maximum at 350,000. The maximum figure, he noted, would constitute some 12 percent of the population of Lithuania. When Česlovas Juršenas asked why no attention was being paid to the victims of Nazi occupation, Truska explained that research on that topic had been conducted for over forty years, whereas historians had not been able to write a single line on the victims of Stalinism.

Other topics in the press conference ranged from the secret protocols to Sajudis's attitude toward the Freedom League. Romas Sakadolskis asked two questions concerning the historians' attitude toward the resistance to Soviet rule after World War II. The Kaunas influence seemed to lie behind a question as to what place the historians would give Romas Kalanta, the young man who had immolated himself in 1972; Eidintas responded that historians were not yet ready to consider this question. When a correspondent from *Moscow News* asked the panel to discuss the benefits that Lithuania had received from being a part of the Soviet Union, Čekuolis pointed out that although one could of course list many benefits, it was also true that in 1939 Estonia had enjoyed a higher standard of living than Finland—if the correspondent could assert that Estonia now still enjoyed a higher standard of living, "I congratulate you on this discovery."

Although *Czerwony sztandar* published a transcript of the press conference, little of it aroused press comment; historians, however, reacted sharply. Rudis's statements were considered especially controversial. One veteran historian stopped me on the street the next day to say that Rudis had been wise to state that he was offering only his own opinion; he also took the occasion to deride my question about the use of terms like *bourgeois historian*: "You've always been concerned about that," he chuckled. "Don't worry, we'll use those terms again."

When the congress resumed its debates on Sunday afternoon, the excitement of Paulauskas's speech lingered on. Antanas Antanaitis criticized Petkevičius for having used the term *provocation*, but Petkevičius stood by his position. Vitas Tomkus urged Party Secretary Brazauskas to be "worthy of the name Algirdas" in deciding between the interests of Vilnius and Moscow. (The Lithuanian Grand Duke Algirdas warred with Moscow in the fourteenth century.) Sigitas Geda offered an idealistic view of how American Lithuanians could come to the aid of their fellow countrymen if only offered a real opportunity. Petras Cidzikas requested support for his hunger strike and urged Brazauskas to speed up consideration of the political prisoners' cases. (When Cidzikas left the stage, he received nearly a minute of applause.)

Late in the afternoon, with tensions running high, Brazauskas came to the podium for the second time to set the tone for the final phase of the meeting. "Many opinions have been expressed," he began. "We will try to consider all of them together with Sajudis's leaders. . . . I am extremely grateful for . . . these two days and for our walk to Gediminas Square. . . . Some talks from this beautiful white lectern were very depressing. . . . And I turn to the rationally, sensibly, realistically thinking people, and I ask them to think over these talks very carefully. Can one really decide such questions so freely with words? Won't we be returning to our original point of departure, or perhaps even further back?" In conclusion, he too quoted the cardinal: "I truly want to say, dear friends, Let us learn to wait. I support and I ask you to support the words uttered today in Vincentas Cardinal Sladkevičius's sermon: Let us learn to wait and let us not climb on each other's heels." In their established style, the delegates gave Brazauskas a standing ovation.

In the evening, under the direction of Romualdas Ozolas and Vytautas Landsbergis, the delegates considered the thirty-three resolutions that had been submitted to them before the congress opened. Here too differences of opinion arose and, although Ozolas willingly accepted some stylistic suggestions, he constantly urged the delegates to abstain from substantial amendments and to accept the spirit and "principles" of the resolutions that the Sajudis leadership wished to adopt.

Most of the resolutions, ranging from problems of relations with the emigration to ecological questions, passed with at worst only a few abstentions; some, such as one establishing national holidays, were referred to the Seimas; a few, such as one on the question of a Polish consulate and cultural center in Vilnius, registered a few negative votes. Resolutions on the rehabilitation of victims of Stalinism and on the return of the cathedral to the church required significant editorial changes because the conditions in which they had been written had altered in the last few days. Other resolutions included a call for international examination of Ignalina, economic autonomy, and the end of privileges for the nomenklatura, the political and administrative elite of the republic.

The most serious discussion arose over a resolution, written in Songaila's time, expressing no confidence in the party and government leadership. Ozolas and Landsbergis pleaded with the delegates and harangued them to give Brazauskas their support, insisting that the spirit of the resolution had already been realized. Some delegates nevertheless wanted to criticize specific individuals in the government. Ozolas finally ruled that the resolution had been eliminated from the agenda without announcing any vote tally.

Even when the discussion of resolutions had finished, the work was not yet done. An Armenian, who had previously been denied the right to address the meeting, quietly told the delegates the dispute in the Caucasus over Nagorno-Karabakh was their problem too. Then Landsbergis asked the delegates to approve a protest against the Voice of America's Russian program that had called the congress "a Lithuanian nationalist congress." (The Lithuanians objected strongly to the use of the term *nationalist*, which has bad connotations both in Lithuanian and in Russian.)[6] The delegates rose with a chant of "Shame, shame." Čekuolis then read the text of telegrams to Gorbachev and to Iakovlev.

Finally, with almost half the visitors' seats empty and more than half of the press corps gone (foreign correspondents were hurrying back to Moscow to meet German Chancellor Helmut Kohl), at 9:51 P.M. the 220 newly elected members of the Seimas, 202 men and 18 women, 209 of them Lithuanians, came onto the stage to the applause of the delegates, who sang the *National Hymn* and *Ilgiausiu metu*. Members of the Initiative Group came forward to make individual statements before the members of the Seimas, and at 10:10 P.M., finally left the stage, waving their flowers to the crowd.

The members of the Seimas now adjourned to the upper floor of the Sports Palace to elect the Sajudis Council, or Taryba, and the delegates in the hall were treated to songs and films. The Seimas spent six hours in its debates over the election of the Taryba. Once again friction had flared up between representatives of Kaunas and of Vilnius, and two hours passed simply in establishing the delegates' views and positions. The Kaunas delegation had come with their own slate of ten candidates for the council. Daunoras and Petkevičius both expressed disgust with the proceedings; Petkevičius later explained that his action was simply a tactic aimed at bringing the "young" people to their senses. A number of individuals, including Bulavas, Lukšiene, and Marcinkevičius declared that for various reasons they would prefer not to be elected. Some seventy persons had the opportunity to speak for one minute each. The available computer proved to be inadequate for the voting system that the Seimas members decided on; the ballots had to be counted by hand. The members finally resolved that they would take the top thirty-five candidates in the voting, instead of the first twenty-five as had been originally planned, and a majority would not be necessary for election.

At 5 o'clock in the morning of October 24, the Seimas reported the results of its vote to the delegates still remaining in the hall. Ozolas had received the most votes, 193 of 212, while the only Kaunasite elected, Kazimeras Uoka, received just 68. Prunskiene was the only woman elected. Once the congress had approved the election results, Landsbergis, who spoke of "two days that changed Lithuania," led them in singing the *National Hymn,* and the exhausted delegates could finally leave the hall. Outside they found taxi drivers ready to drive them home free of charge.[7]

The members of the Taryba had yet to face one more press conference before they could go home. (Lithuanian journalists proudly noted that all the foreigners had left.) Since Lithuanian television had already gone off the air, the conference was shown on Monday night after the "Vremia" news program. Čekuolis could hardly speak; his voice was raw, but he again presided, declaring that many of the newly elected representatives were only half alive at this point. The members of the Taryba had little to say. The congress had finally ended, and new tasks lay ahead once people had had time to rest up from the exhilarating but exhausting weekend.

12

Into A New Era

In the aftermath of the Sajudis congress Lithuania entered a new era, one with an organized popular movement that stood ready to challenge the party. Sajudis had grown from a discussion club into a mass movement. From an organization struggling for survival and recognition, it had become a force that embodied the hopes and frustrations of the Lithuanian people. It had begun to dictate events to the point that Moscow was reacting to its initiatives. Whereas in past years Lithuania had trembled when Moscow spoke, now the Lithuanians seemed to regard pronouncements from on high as the starting point for further action—Moscow had changed its mind before and it could again. The Lithuanians had made great strides toward establishing that "political culture" for which Arvydas Juozaitis had been searching in April.

The events of September 1988 stand as a major turning point. On August 23, the people of Vilnius had sullenly watched as militia and troops controlled Gedi-

minas Square; on September 28, the crowd resisted the
effort of troops to clear the area. As the ultimate single
point of qualitative change, one is tempted to cite the
dramatic moment on September 13 when Zigmas Vaišvila, interrupted in his discussion of plans for a "Living
Ring" around Ignalina by the news that the government
had forbidden a demonstration, announced that the
demonstration would go ahead anyway. Sajudis was no
longer willing to stay only within the boundaries dictated by the authorities.

Although Aleksandr Iakovlev had endorsed Sajudis in
August, Moscow reacted in horror to the news from the
Baltic. *Pravda* struck the first blow on October 21, publishing its warning to the Sajudis convention about the
necessity of recognizing the Soviet Union "as our common homeland." Iakovlev struck the next blow, telling
Philip Taubman of *The New York Times* that groups in
the Baltic were putting forward "many ideas that are
out of touch with reality." In contrast to his statements
of two months earlier, he dismissed the proposals of
"performers and musicians and people of this sort" as
unrealistic and not worth discussing.[1] Taubman did not
ask him why his views of Sajudis had so changed, but
Iakovlev, who had now shifted his attention to international relations, was presumably clearing the way for
Vadim Medvedev, his successor in handling the national question within the Soviet Union.

The Moscow press emitted a variety of unfavorable
and even threatening rumbles. In its first reports of the
Sajudis congress, TASS complained about "extremist
and provocative" speech.[2] The influential *Moscow News*,
to which foreigners looked for insights into the minds of
Moscow reformers, called Brazauskas "one of the most
popular personalities" in Lithuania, but it also noted

"causes for concern. There were splashes of extremism. Antanas Terleckas . . . suggested that Lithuania be freed of Russians. Delegate Rolandas Paulauskas demanded the secession of the Republic from the USSR."[3] Kaunas delegates to the congress angrily considered whether they could sue *Moscow News* for its charge of "extremism," but they apparently decided to concentrate instead on other issues.

The correspondents of *Izvestiia* and *Pravda* in Lithuania, Leonid Kapelushny and Domas Šniukas, both reported cautiously and critically. In *Pravda* of October 26 Šniukas offered an overall sympathetic summary of the congress and quoted Brazauskas: "The rebirth of Lithuanian national consciousness gives no cause for fear on the part of representatives of other peoples." In conclusion, however, he noted "emotional," "extremist," "provocative and irresponsible" speeches that testified to "political inexperience," and he suggested that "street democracy" may yet be a problem in Lithuania. In *Izvestiia* of November 13, Leonid Kapelushny insisted that Sajudis was not a band of "nationalists." Although Šniukas indicated to me that he saw little difference in their respective views, many Lithuanians considered Kapelushny's article the more favorable.[4]

Moscow's grumbling had echoes in Lithuania. On November 5, marking the anniversary of the Great October Revolution in Russia, the Lithuanian Republican Council of War and Labor Veterans heard its chairman, K. Kairys, complain that the youth were "not always correctly" informed about the past: "There are too many one-sided and unacceptable interpretations." He criticized Sajudis statements for omitting the sacred concepts of "Soviet Lithuania" and "socialism." Romas Šarmaitis called for stricter control of the press: "It has become one-sided. It is irresponsibly publishing material on the history of Soviet Lithuania and of the whole country. The unsuspecting reader could really conclude that the Second World War began only as a result of the agreement between Hitler and Stalin. That is the greatest nonsense and profanation of history."[5]

The Lithuanians' Achilles heel in this new era, however, was located not so much in the disgruntled veterans of the Soviet order as in their own minorities, especially the Poles and the Russians. The Jewish minority seemed basically supportive of Sajudis, but the Lithuanians found themselves in a struggle with the Russians for the loyalty of the Poles.

Stories of national tensions mushroomed. Russians in Kaliningrad had reportedly attacked Lithuanian cooperative businessmen and damaged their cars; Lithuanians reportedly ordered Russians off buses in Vilnius. Anonymous leaflets urged Russians to arm themselves with Kalashnikov rifles; Russians in Vilnius complained about the "swinish language" of the locals; and Lithuanians urged the Russians to "go home." At the beginning of November, fans of the Spartak-Moscow soccer team, picking fights in the streets of Vilnius, denounced the locals as "nationalists" and "fascists."

On November 4 the Russians in Lithuania announced their own "Socialist Movement for Perestroika in Lithuania—*Edinstvo.*" Declaring themselves unswerving Marxist-Leninists despite "criminal distortions of socialist construction in the past," the organizers criticized the "indecisiveness" of the Lithuanian Communist Party and called for strengthening "the union of sovereign republics of the USSR." The group demanded that plans to make Lithuanian the official language of the republic be delayed. It also asserted that "service in the Armed Forces of the USSR" was "the honorable duty of every citizen of the USSR."[6]

Edinstvo (Unity) represented the antithesis of Sajudis. As Šniukas summarized the relationship of the two, "It is no secret to anyone that you rarely meet a Russian in Sajudis or a Lithuanian in Edinstvo."[7] The Lithuanians had treated Sajudis as an organization of renewal; some enthusiasts displayed all the characteristics of religious conversion in joining its ranks. Edinstvo drew on Russians who opposed first of all the use of the Lithuanian language. Sajudis dreamed of a new society; Edinstvo opposed that dream and reasserted traditional values.[8]

Moscow and the Soviet armed forces in particular endorsed Edinstvo. On December 3 *Krasnaia zvezda*, the organ of the Ministry of Defense in Moscow, reported that doctors in a Vilnius hospital could not, or would not, speak Russian and that generally people who did not speak Lithuanian were discriminated against. Edinstvo, the newspaper indicated, provided a healthy balance to the "extremism" of Sajudis. When Lithuanians exposed the story about the doctors as a hoax, *Krasnaia zvezda* simply insisted that its Lithuanian readers had missed the point of the story.[9] The newspaper made its point more clearly on December 20 when it complained about the absence of a strong Russian voice in the Baltic.

In many ways the Polish population posed a more serious problem for the Lithuanians than did the Russians. The Poles formed a community in Lithuania, whereas the Russians did not, and Polish regions in the republic had the potential of becoming another "Karabakh," although up to this point there had been no large-scale violence between the nationalities. Sajudis officials understood the dangerous potential of the situation; on October 25 Vytautas Landsbergis appeared on television to issue an appeal for cordial and understanding relations between the nationalities of Lithuania.

Against this background, Sajudis and Brazauskas enjoyed a brief honeymoon before tensions in their respective camps began to pull them apart. Everyone understood that the enthusiasm of the convention could not last indefinitely. The writer Vytautas Petkevičius complained to me about the unreal and disturbing "euphoria" in the Sports Palace and criticized the activities of "chance persons" who had come into Sajudis without having shared in the struggle to establish it. (He also confirmed a rumor that the windows in his apartment had been broken—"one of the prices of being a public figure"—but he refused to speculate as to who had done it.) Sajudis leaders wanted to move carefully, but they also realized that they stood at the head of an increasingly radical and articulate constituency.

On Brazauskas's side, he had a conservative constituency to which he had to respond. He still had to work with the same Central Committee that had served Songaila; he had no power to change its makeup without the approval of a party congress. At the Central Committee's plenum in February 1989 its members emptied their verbal bile on Sajudis and the current developments in the republic, leading cynics to call this "The Plenum of the Victims of Perestroika." Brazauskas had to tread carefully in finding his way between his own Central Committee, Sajudis, and the instructions, directives, and questions flowing from Moscow.

In his very first days in office, Brazauskas displayed his command of issues together with a feeling for Lithuanian history and the style of a Western politician.

"Brazauskas correctly said that . . . " was a phrase I heard frequently in conversations. Appearing on television on Friday evening, October 28, he announced plans to release the last of the political prisoners. When demonstrators gathered in front of the Central Committee the next day, Petras Cidzikas told the group that he would end his hunger strike that evening. Although foreign reports spoke of "thousands of well-wishers" gathering to see him off,[10] I would estimate the crowd as numbering in the hundreds. Freedom League speakers dominated the brief talks, and the gathering ended after twenty minutes with the singing of the *National Hymn.* The trappings of the hunger strike—Cidzikas's hut and the wall of protests and proclamations—quickly disappeared. Brazauskas could claim a victory.

Brazauskas agreed with Sajudis on Lithuanianizing the republic; he strongly favored the development of economic self-dependency; but he split with Sajudis on political issues involved in constitutional reform. Both the central government and the authorities in Vilnius had endorsed the abstract idea of constitutional reform, but the tendency of Lithuanian reformers ran very much counter to that of Moscow. On the weekend of the Sajudis congress, Moscow had announced its program for reform of the USSR constitution and, in contrast to Gorbachev's avowed intention to decentralize the Soviet system, Moscow's proposals called in fact for greater centralization of the system. Many feared that Moscow in fact wanted to reduce the union republics to the status of units within the large Russian Soviet Federated Socialist Republic.[11]

The Lithuanians' own concept of constitutional reform called for decentralizing the Soviet system. Besides the well-publicized provisions for accepting the national symbols as state symbols and for making Lithuanian the official language of the republic, the Lithuanian Academy of Sciences committee on constitutional reform—the same group that had provided the cradle for the newborn Sajudis—called for republican economic, political, and cultural autonomy and for the establishment of a separate Lithuanian citizenship. A particularly controversial proposal, akin to the principle of "nullification" in American history, demanded that laws adopted in Moscow not be binding in Lithuania unless approved by the Lithuanian Supreme Soviet.[12]

With Moscow and Lithuania on a collision course, Brazauskas advocated caution while Sajudis's Taryba, the council, prepared for the battle that would take place in November when the Lithuanian Supreme Soviet was to consider amending the Lithuanian constitution. Since all but one of its members were from Vilnius, the Taryba could gather at almost any time. "We can contact one another by telephone in the morning and meet in the evening," one member told me. During the week of November 7, the group met three times—"We are working like firemen," another complained. Appearing on television on November 9, Sajudis leaders announced a petition calling for postponement of any consideration of Moscow's proposed changes to the constitution of the USSR; Landsbergis hoped for a million signatures by the weekend. A form of popular referendum ensued, as stands popped up all over Vilnius recruiting signatures. By Monday morning more than 1.5 million people had signed, thereby declaring their opposition to Moscow's efforts at centralization.

Adding to the tension in Vilnius was the visit of an emissary from Moscow, Nikolai Sliunkov, the head of the Politburo's Economic Commission. Brazauskas had been planning to visit Moscow about this time, but he had to put off his visit when Moscow announced it was sending members of the Politburo to each of the three Baltic capitals. (Lithuanians naturally compared this act with the sending of commissars to the same capitals in 1940.) Sliunkov arrived around noon on Friday, November 11, and found the Central Committee being picketed by demonstrators.

All day Friday Lithuanians anxiously discussed what Sliunkov's purpose might be. Rimas Valatka of *Gimtasis kraštas* told me that he was besieged by telephone calls from foreign correspondents in Moscow wanting to know about Sliunkov's activities and intentions. Sliunkov displayed little understanding either of the proposed constitutional changes or of the Lithuanians' ideas of economic autonomy—he in fact insisted that he had not expected to talk about constitutional changes, and he angered his listeners by consistently calling Lithuania a "territory" rather than a "republic." Most people agreed that he was in town to frighten the Lithuanians and to warn local party officials about the dangers of "nationalism" and "separatism."[13]

On Sunday, November 13, while Sliunkov was still in Vilnius, the Sajudis Seimas convened to consider the draft Lithuanian constitution. In opening the session, Arvydas Juozaitis urged the delegates not to fear visitors who insist on "calling our republic a territory." The day's most heated discussion arose over the issue of making the tricolor the official flag of the Lithuanian SSR and the knight the official symbol. Some deputies objected to the thought of allowing the Soviet government to exploit these sacred national symbols,[14] and in the end sixteen delegates voted to deny the government the national heraldry, with seven abstentions, and

about thirty voted to withhold the tricolor, with twenty-
one abstentions. ("The Kaunas group stuck together," a
delegate from Kaunas told me the next day.) In the end
the Seimas endorsed the constitutional draft as presented by the Taryba.

The Seimas deputies went on to condemn the proposed changes of the Soviet constitution as strengthening "centralism and the bureaucratic administrative
system," and Ozolas recommended that if and when the
USSR's Supreme Soviet considered the changes, the
delegates from the Baltic should either vote against
the changes or else walk out of the meeting. The delegates endorsed the idea of nominating candidates for
election in Lithuania and, from a slate of eleven candidates, they chose six to run for seats in the Lithuanian
Supreme Soviet: Ozolas, Juozaitis, Landsbergis, Petkevičius, Vaišvila, and Motieka.[15]

Sliunkov left Lithuania on Monday, November 14,
and at the end of the week, November 17 and 18, Sajudis and Brazauskas faced off in an adversarial situation. Brazauskas hoped to satisfy the Lithuanians by
granting them their symbols and by promising economic self-sufficiency; Sajudis, however, insisted on the
right to nullify laws emanating from the center. The
Estonian Supreme Soviet had adopted just such a constitutional amendment on the sixteenth, and with the
eyes of the Soviet Union and indeed of the world on Vilnius, Brazauskas needed all the persuasive power he
could rally, together with some parliamentary maneu-
vering, to postpone consideration. He succeeded, and
two weeks later, Gorbachev pushed his own constitutional amendments through the Supreme Soviet in
Moscow over the objections of a handful of deputies
from the Baltic area.[16]

Brazauskas's victory threatened to be pyrrhic. The government and party did what they could to rally sympathy and support. The official press featured letters of support from its readers. "The workers of our plant resolutely, and in unison, condemn the actions of certain movement leaders, who seek to destabilize the political and economic situation in Lithuania," said one; "It would seem that much has been accomplished. We should all rejoice in this," added another. According to *Tiesa* of November 23, there were so many letters of support that regrettably the newspaper did not have space for them all.

Brazauskas continued to identify his administration with the fundamental program of economic self-dependence. Astrauskas told the Supreme Soviet in Moscow that people "have grown tired of living according to commands from above that for decades fettered self-government and led to social apathy and indifference."[17] Brazauskas told an interviewer from Radio Vilnius that in respect to economic self-dependency, "We have greatly advanced, even more than some of our neighbors in solving these problems."[18] Speaking on Moscow radio, he struck a balance: "I will not hide the fact that there are strained relations in our public life between the republic's leadership and Sajudis . . . [but] there is no need to claim that you can't even get into the hospital without knowing Lithuanian."[19] *Tiesa* of February 3, 1989, introduced its story about a visit to Moscow by Lithuanian Foreign Minister Vladislovas Mikučiauskas with the headline "We Want to Be More Self-reliant."

The Moscow press devoted more space to criticizing Sajudis than to praising Brazauskas. In *Pravda* of November 22, Šniukas praised what he considered Sajudis's positive accomplishments of the year but criticized what he saw as its one-sided presentation of Lithuanian history. Sajudis, moreover, having opened its ranks to "people of the most varied convictions," was now showing antidemocratic tendencies. In *Izvestiia* of November 24, Kapelushny returned to the theme of "foreign 'voices'" and declared that Sajudis did not represent the Lithuanian people: "Even when it collected up to 100,000 people at its meetings, this was only a small part of Lithuania." Sajudis's day, he suggested, had passed. *Krasnaia zvezda* of November 29 noted, "One cannot fail to see the many negative aspects of [Sajudis's] activity."

The Sajudis Seimas responded to Moscow's attacks by electing Vytautas Landsbergis as its president. After Kapelushny had criticized him by name as one of Sajudis's most radical members, the Seimas gave him its endorsement. In the early days of Sajudis, Landsbergis had represented the absolute center in the group, arguing that matters must be discussed fully and that the group must be ready to sit until midnight if necessary in order to complete its deliberations. He had also served as the wordsmith to whom the group turned when it needed a document carefully prepared. Now he became Sajudis's first elected leader.

In the confrontation with Brazauskas and the government, Sajudis moved to ever stronger demands. At the same time, within its ranks, specific interest groups continued to form and identify themselves. One such, the Democratic Party, organized in November, put out the first issue of its newspaper, *Vasario 16* (February 16), in December. "Sajudis," said a spokesperson, "should play the role more of a political parliament and the Lithuanian political forces should be represented in Sajudis."[20] In the course of 1989 proto-parties multiplied. At a time when Moscow was discussing the meaning of political pluralism and the feasibility of a multiparty system, the Lithuanians were going on ahead.

To the left of Sajudis, demanding Lithuanian independence, stood the Freedom League, which criticized Sajudis's willingness to continue negotiating with the authorities. Although the league's original program, issued in July, had emphasized demands for civil rights, now league representatives opposed any sign of making peace with the Soviet system. Whereas Sajudis decided to participate in the Soviet elections of March 1989 for the new Congress of People's Deputies in Moscow, the Freedom League objected to the idea and called for boycotting the elections: "We are convinced that by participating in the election Sajudis is misleading world public opinion and risks becoming compromised in the eyes of the Lithuanian nation."[21] When more than 80 percent of the population of the republic voted, the Freedom League lost considerable ground in its claims to speak for the Lithuanian public.

The Freedom League's support in the emigration remained a factor with which Sajudis leaders had to reckon. The presence at the congress of figures such as Vytautas Bieliauskas, the head of the Chicago-based World Lithuanian Community, seemed an endorsement of Sajudis, and the head of the Lithuanian Information Center in Washington, Victor Nakas, declared, "I am delighted by the news that the Soviet authorities have returned the cathedral," adding, "I would have been skeptical a month ago, but the more I see, the less I think it's a hoax."[22] The reporting of the Lithuanian Information Center in Brooklyn—and of the *Elta Information Bulletin*, published in Washington—had indeed become more understanding of Sajudis in the course of the

fall, and in 1989 it accepted Sajudis as part of the "Lithuanian patriotic movement" in its news releases.

At the same time, however, many conservative
émigrés harbored doubts about Sajudis and even criticized Bieliauskas. One must be sure one is not "serving the purposes of the occupiers," warned VLIK, the
Supreme Committee for the Liberation of Lithuania.
Sajudis, warned another commentator, is "suspicious
because of the support of Lithuanian Communists,"
and therefore Bieliauskas's participation in the congress "is scarcely justifiable." Sajudis, suggested yet a
third group, constituted just a maneuver by Moscow to
establish more control over Lithuania.[23] Communist
China, curiously enough, seemed to agree: an English-
language broadcast from Beijing on October 23 called
Sajudis "a government-approved movement aimed at
channeling nationalist feelings in the Baltic republic."

Despite such commentaries and despite hostility
from Moscow and resistance in Vilnius the New Year of
1989 brought a stunning series of new victories and
triumphs to Sajudis. The Lithuanians entered 1989 with
a new self-consciousness; as Algimantas Čekuolis wrote
in *Gimtasis kraštas* at the end of 1988, "The greatest
achievement of this year was that we again realized that
we are a people." From this came a new confidence, and
on January 15 Sajudis candidates won all four seats
they had contested in by-elections to the Lithuanian
Supreme Soviet, overwhelming party-endorsed opponents. Most stunning was the defeat of Vytautas Petkevičius, who had broken with the Sajudis leadership.
On all fronts Lithuanian professional organizations—
teachers, writers, artists—were asserting their independence of Moscow. Even party members began seriously

to discuss the possibility of establishing their organizational independence of Moscow.

In something of a contest with the government, Sajudis organized a mammoth February 16 celebration in Kaunas that overshadowed the official observance in Vilnius. Sajudis leaders, moreover, now issued a declaration calling for the full restoration of Lithuania's sovereignty. Challenged on Moscow television as to whether Sajudis was supporting secession, Landsbergis pointed out that the Soviet constitution guaranteed the republics the right of secession, and he declared that Sajudis's intention was simply to assure the Lithuanian people the fullest opportunity freely to decide whether or not they wanted to make use of that right.

In the aftermath of the February 16 festivities, the conservative elements in the party tried vainly to strike back. The Central Committee plenum of "Victims of Perestroika" angrily denounced Sajudis and everything it stood for. Faced, however, by the prospect of being routed in the upcoming elections to the USSR's Congress of People's Deputies, Brazauskas soon moderated his position. He chose to represent Lithuania in Moscow rather than vice versa. Sajudis in turn decided to withdraw its candidates against Brazauskas and the new second secretary, Vladimir Beriozov, calculating that these were the best men available for these positions and that therefore Sajudis should endorse them vis-à-vis Moscow.

The elections to the Congress of People's Deputies ended in a stunning victory for Sajudis. In the first round of voting, Sajudis captured thirty-one of the thirty-nine seats that it contested. In the second round, it won five more for a total of thirty-six of the forty-two seats allotted to Lithuania. Brazauskas and Beriozov were the only two Communist Party candidates to win election in the first round, and Kestutis Zaleckas won a seat in the second round. Prime Minister Vytautas Sakalauskas and President Vytautas Astrauskas were both eliminated in the first round of voting.

In the succeeding months, Sajudis and the Lithuanian Communist Party leadership cooperated. The party endorsed the campaign to condemn the Molotov-Ribbentrop Pact, and in May the Lithuanian Supreme Soviet not only condemned the pact but also proclaimed Lithuania's sovereignty, including the right to nullify Muscovite legislation of which the Lithuanians disapproved.[24] Together, party and Sajudis in the summer won Gorbachev's endorsement of the introduction of economic self-sufficiency in the Baltic as of January 1, 1990. In August, when the Lithuanians, on the fiftieth anniversary of the Molotov-Ribbentrop Pact, declared that the incorporation of Lithuania into the Soviet Union in 1940 had been an illegal act, Moscow objected, but again Sajudis and party stood together, the party of course tending to be the more conservative, Sajudis the more demanding.

At the same time the Lithuanians understood that they could not determine their future by themselves. They sympathized strongly with the Armenians, they invited Belorussian activists to meet in Vilnius, and they published works in Latin characters for the Moldavians. On April 23, 20,000 persons marched along Lenin Prospect in a demonstration of sympathy for Georgians killed in demonstrations in Tbilisi, and on May 17 Sajudis hosted the Crimean Tatars' observance of their national day of mourning, commemorating their mass deportation on the night of May 18–19, 1944.

The three Baltic republics took special steps to

confirm, and demonstrate, their own solidarity. In May Estonia hosted a Baltic Assembly, a meeting of representatives of the popular fronts of all three republics.[25] In July the three republics together celebrated Moscow's approval of their ventures into economic autonomy as of 1990, and in August they marked the fiftieth anniversary of the Molotov-Ribbentrop Pact by forming a human chain extending from Tallinn to Vilnius. In the two years since August 23, 1987, the day of isolated demonstrations, the Baltic peoples had made stunning changes in their lives.

Even the historians could claim progress on their path of atonement and redemption, taking charge of the new image of Lithuania's past. They provided the documentation and argumentation for forcing Moscow to discuss the Molotov-Ribbentrop Pact and eventually to admit that a secret protocol dividing up Eastern Europe had in fact been a part of that agreement. To be sure, Aleksandr Iakovlev publicly insisted that the pact with its protocol had no relationship to Lithuania's incorporation into the Soviet Union,[26] but here, as elsewhere, the Lithuanians looked forward to the next round of arguments.

The Lithuanians had experienced a spiritual revolution. They had ended the schism between their private convictions and their public lives, and in the end they had rather surprised themselves with the result. Their new consciousness as a people, their confidence about their own culture and its place in history, would prove highly resistant to any future external repression. At the same time, however, although thoughts of independence were growing, they had yet fully to develop their own internal political life, to achieve the transition from opposition to responsibility.

No one could be sure of the effect of the changes in

Lithuania on the economic life of the republic, other than the thought that it had not suffered. (Sajudis had not resorted to strikes or violence; it had not had to.) The Lithuanians were still collecting information about their own existence, and although preliminary and incomplete figures indicated a modest rise in the republic's production, much of this probably reflected inflation. The economic test lay ahead in the future.

In the midst of the growing independence movement, Sajudis itself experienced growing pains. In its birth, Sajudis had welcomed the participation of party members; when, in December 1989, the Lithuanian Communist Party elected a new Central Committee, in which over half of the members were "of Sajudis orientation" and such Sajudis stalwarts as Ozolas, Genzelis, and Prunskiene entered the party bureau, the question arose, as Bronius Kuzmickas put it to me, "Is the party 'sajudicizing' or is Sajudis 'partifying'?" Sajudis formally declared itself the "opposition to the Communist Party," and Freedom League members denounced them both as collaborators. Just what combination of concessions, compromises, and new symbols might eventually stabilize the situation remained for the future to decide.

Afterword

Books must end, but life goes on. In the winter and spring of 1990 the confrontation between Lithuania and Moscow exploded into the world's headlines, and with the benevolent tolerance of the publisher, I decided to add a few words.

When I visited Vilnius in January 1990—at the same time Mikhail Gorbachev was there—I found hope and determination but also apprehension about what might happen in the future. The Lithuanian Communist party had just declared its independence of Moscow, and Justas Paleckis, ideological secretary of the LCP, told me, "Lithuania must obtain full independence. . . . Perhaps, after some time, Lithuania, by the will of the majority, will choose some sort of union or confederation. What that will be, no one knows." Paleckis warned, however, that a sharp break with Moscow could be disastrous: "If, let us say, the Soviet Union should proclaim an economic blockade, that would undoubtedly be a complete catastrophe. Neither America nor Western Europe could offer any significant aid."

When I asked Romualdas Ozolas, now a member of the Bureau of the LCP Central Committee, his view of Lithuania's future, he declared that Lithuania must be "a completely independent state, maintaining ties with all states on the Baltic Sea." Lithuania would need to keep economic links with the Soviet Union, but it could in no way live under the roof of the Soviet order. "We have no other course!" he asserted. "Either we will be independent or we will not be."

Vytautas Landsbergis proclaimed that Lithuania was already independent at least in spirit, insisting that whereas the visiting Muscovites thought "they are traveling in their own state," in fact they were visiting a foreign land. He declined to offer a specific vision of the future, declaring that "events have outstripped ideas" and that the Communist way of life had already shown the dangers of living by some "abstract plan." He said he had no model of his own: "Lithuania will find its own path."

On the right of the political spectrum stood the LCP (CPSU), a rump group that had broken away form the LCP over the issue of independence and had declared its loyalty to Moscow. Juozas Jermalavičius, a member of the group's Provisional Central Committee, told me that he saw great danger for Lithuania in the present situation, and he emphasized that above all he wanted to avoid bloodshed of the sort that had beset Lithuania immediately after World War II.

On the left wing of this spectrum, Antanas Terleckas argued that Lithuania could not expect to achieve independence by parliamentary means; the left seemed to consider conflict with Moscow inevitable and declared its readiness to forge ahead whatever the cost.[1]

On February 24, 1990, Lithuanian voters elected a new republican legislature, the Supreme Soviet of the Lithuanian SSR, and rewarded Sajudis with an overwhelming victory. On March 11, Sajudis led the deputies in voting to restore the Republic of Lithuania: "The Supreme Council of Lithuania, expressing the will of the Nation, resolves and solemnly proclaims that the execution of the sovereign power of the Lithuanian State, heretofore constrained by alien forces in 1940, is restored, and henceforth Lithuania is once again an independent state." It went on to "suspend" the Lithuanian Constitution of May 12, 1938, and to ratify the text of the constitution of the Lithuanian SSR as the "Provisional Fundamental Law of the Republic of Lithuania."[2]

The Lithuanians used the resolution of December 24, 1989, passed by the USSR Congress of People's Deputies, which denounced the Molotov-Ribbertrop pact as the justification for their move. Landsbergis said of this resolution, "It is true enough that the Soviet people, as it said in this document, were not responsible. It is clear that it was ruled by dictators, who did not consider the opinions of that people. But that avoids the fundamental question about the responsibility of the state. The state is the same, and it cannot push responsibility off onto one or two people. And it will carry that responsibility in the future . . . and therefore there is a certain nervousness and a disinclination to answer the fundamental question." Whatever its justification, the Lithuanians' declaration of independence unleashed a storm.

The legislature elected Vytautas Landsbergis the president of Sajudis as its chairman, and thereby the president of the republic. Sajudis was still not a party; the mandate commission of the Lithuanian Supreme Soviet did not list Sajudis as a political group in the legislature. But even before the legislature convened, Sajudis organized a "deputies' club" for those supporting its platform. "The club was established to help form a tradition of parliamentary work," explained Lands-

bergis. Its purpose was to determine "a common position"; Sajudis, Landsbergis insisted, "must survive," it
must continue to function.[3] In the ensuing confrontation
with Moscow, Landsbergis, as president of both Sajudis
and the republic, overshadowed Kazimiera Prunskiene,
the new prime minister.

Gorbachev immediately denounced Lithuania's declaration of independence as illegal. Concerned about
Soviet military and naval installations in Kaliningrad,
Klaipeda, and elsewhere in the Baltic and distressed
by the number of Lithuanians who were deserting Soviet army units, military authorities sent Soviet armor
to rumble through the streets of Vilnius. Gorbachev
warned the Lithuanians not to set up their own defense
forces and their own customs offices.

Although Soviet spokesmen insisted that they were
intervening in Lithuania to preserve law and order, constitutional contradictions prevailed. The constitution
guaranteed the right of secession, the councillor of the
Soviet embassy in Washington declared on the McNeil-
Lehrer television news hour and that Lithuania was
"pushing an open door," and yet on March 31, Gorbachev threatened "dire consequences" if the Lithuanians
persisted in their demand for independence. Soviet
Foreign Minister Eduard Shevardnadze announced in
Washington that his government wanted only "honest
dialog" (*chestnyi dialog*) with the Lithuanians, but the
Lithuanians could find no one with whom to speak. Gorbachev himself said little publicly; he seemed to prefer
to give statements to others who in turn made them
public.

Soviet troops roamed Vilnius and complained that
the Lithuanians were showing little respect. Senator
Edward Kennedy announced Gorbachev's promise "not

to use force unless lives are in danger," at the same time that troops seized buildings in Vilnius. Soldiers broke into a psychiatric ward and forcefully arrested army deserters. They went on to seize the Lithuanian prosecutor's office. Moscow encouraged Russians to demonstrate and to strike against the Lithuanian government. Reiterating their concern for law and order, Soviet officials demanded that the Lithuanians retract their declaration of independence before substantive negotiations could begin.

Most curious was the fact that the first buildings seized by the Soviet troops belonged to the Communist party of Lithuania. The troops expelled the leaders of the independent Communist party and turned the buildings over to the rump Lithuanian Communist party (CPSU). According to the new Article 6 of the USSR Constitution, as designed by Gorbachev himself, the Soviet Union now had a multiparty system. The Communist party no longer constituted the fons and origo of authority in Soviet society, and yet Soviet troops in Lithuania put themselves at the service of a local Communist party.

As of this writing, an uncertain calm prevailed in Vilnius. Troops and tanks roamed the streets. Although Moscow denied having imposed an economic blockade, the stores were bare. A growing chorus of voices in Moscow demanded that Gorbachev exercise his "presidential powers," but Moscow has as yet made no move to unseat the Sajudis administration. On April 8, however, when Soviet troop units moved on the major printing establishment in Vilnius, Lithuanians surrounded the building and established a twenty-four-hour cordon of unarmed citizens to protect their freedom of the press. It was unclear how long such a standoff could continue.

Whatever the settlement that might come out of the crisis of March and April 1990, Lithuania cannot return to its docile status before 1988. After two generations of repression, the Lithuanians had awakened and their memory had returned. With the passage of time, Sajudis' leaders have gone separate paths, and the organization itself has experienced problems of growth. The Initiative Group, however, had changed the nation, had given it a new self-consciousness, and had raised hopes for a happier, more productive future.

On Moscow's side of the scale, however one might define "perestroika," those favoring it should not want the Lithuanians to revert to their previous condition. If the Soviet government has only force as an argument against secession, the future has to loom threatening not just for the Lithuanians but for the Soviet Union itself. Repression in the Baltic would have to have repercussions in Moscow. In any case, the Lithuanians will not soon forget the events of the spring of 1990.

April 12, 1990   A. E. S.

Notes

Introduction

1. See Romas Šarmaitis, *Kai kurie XIX a. antrosios pusės lietuvių nacionalinio išsivadavimo judėjimo istorijos klausimai* (Vilnius, 1953); Truska's comment in *Komjaunimo tiesa*, May 31, 1988.

2. Ignas Muldaris, "Istorijos pamokos," *Tiesa*, October 2, 1988.

3. *Sąjūdžio žinios*, no. 28, August 23, 1988.

4. See ibid., which was distributed at the meeting. On the history of the *National Hymn*, also known by its first line *Lietuva tėvynė mūsų*, see *Gimtasis kraštas*, September 22, 1988, and Gediminas Rudis's article in *Komjaunimo tiesa*, June 25, 1988. Balys Dvarionas, who wrote the Soviet state hymn was also a member of the commission that drew up the official arrangement of the *National Hymn* in 1938.

5. *Lithuania: An Encyclopedic Survey* (Vilnius, 1986), p. 45.

6. For a Lithuanian American's account of having visited Ignalina, see Zenonas Rekašius, "Ignalinos Atominėje Jėgainėje," *Akiračiai* 10 (1987): 6–7.

7. See Česlovas Laurinavičius, "Dėl valstybingumo Lietuvoje 1918–1919," *Literatūra ir menas*, October 29, 1988.

8. February 16 became an official holiday in Lithuania in 1920. On February 6, 1920, the government in Kaunas decided to celebrate the upcoming anniversary, and on the

tenth it issued a decree to that effect. On February 16, 1920, therefore, the date became the official anniversary date of Lithuanian statehood. On the events of 1917–1918 see Petras Klimas, *Der Werdegang des litauischen Staates* (Berlin, 1919).

9. See Bronius Vaitkevičius, *Pirmoji darbininkų ir valstiečių ciu valdžia Lietuvoje* (Vilnius, 1988); Povilas Vitkauskas, *Lietuvos Tarybų Respublikos sukūrimas 1918–1919 metais* (Vilnius, 1988).

10. Cf. the repeated emphasis in *ELTA Information Bulletin* (hereinafter referred to as *EIB*), Washington, D.C., especially nos. 1–3 (1987).

11. On emigre debates concerning contacts with Soviet Lithuania, see Liūtas Mockūnas, "The Dynamics of Lithuanian Emigre-Homeland Relations," *Baltic Forum* 2, 1: 50–69. On the "sister-cities" controversy, see Alfred Erich Senn, "Apie Vilniaus-Madisono susigiminiavimą," *Akiračiai* 7 (1987): 2–3.

12. "Gorbachev-supported," in *Eastern European Newsletter,* July 13, 1988; "officially tolerated," in Lithuanian Information Center, Brooklyn (hereinafter referred to as LIC), news release of August 19, 1988; fear of cooptation reported in *The Christian Science Monitor,* October 7, 1988.

1. New Winds

1. On Kudirka, whose story was also the subject of a made-for-TV movie in the United States, see his *For Those Still at Sea,* with Larry Eichel (New York, 1978); and U.S. Congress, House Committee on Foreign Affairs, Subcommittee on State Department Organization and Foreign Operations, *Attempted Defection by Lithuanian Seaman Simas Kudirka: Hearings* (Washington, D.C., 1971); on Kalanta, see Alfred Erich Senn, "Pokalbis su Romo Kalantos šeima," *Akiračiai* 5 (1989): 8–9. *The Chronicle of the Catholic Church in Lithuania* has been translated into English by Lithuanian Catholic Religious Aid, Brooklyn, New York.

2. On that same day, August 23, some 5,000 persons gathered in to lay flowers at Freedom monument in Riga, Latvia, and 2,000 demonstrated in the Estonian capital of Tallinn.

3. Cf. Sadūnaitės' memoir, *KGB akiratyje* (Chicago, 1985); English translation: Nijolė Sadūnaitė, *A Radiance in the Gulag* (Manassas, Va., 1987). See also Vytautas Skuodis's series on the dissent movement in *Nepriklausomoji Lietuva*, December 8, 1988, to February 2, 1989, and especially his "Lietuvos pogrindžio spaudos žingsniai: 15 metų bendroji apžvalga," *Aidai* 4 (1988): 266–272. On Skuodis himself, see my "Nuotykis traukiniui riedant," *Akiračiai* 5 (1983): 1.

4. See *EIB* 2 (1988); LIC press release, August 10, 1987.

5. Tape recording circulating in West, excerpts in *EIB* 12 (1987). The modern technologies of tape and video recording have deeply affected the study of contemporary history; tape recordings of the events of 1988–1989 abound. For a dissenter's account of police repressions at this point, see A. Žemaitis, in *Glasnost* (in English), nos. 13–15 (1989).

6. TASS, quoted in *EIB* 3 (1988): 13.

7. *EIB* 3 (1988).

8. *Pravda*, March 18, 1987; Deutsche Presseagentur Archive, Hamburg, BRD (hereinafter: DPA), dispatch of March 19, 1987; Aleksandras Shtromas, "On the Current Political Situation in Lithuania," in *Occasional Papers on Baltic Political Action*, nos. 2/3, September 1988 (hereinafter referred to as *OPBPA*), 16–17; V. Stanley Vardys, "Lithuanian National Politics," *Problems of Communism*, July-August 1989: 55.

9. Paul Goble, "Gorbachev and the Soviet Nationality Problem," in *Soviet Society Under Gorbachev*, ed. Maurice Friedberg and Heyward Isham (Armonk, N.Y., 1987), 97. On Mitkin's pressure, cf. *Tiesa*, March 14, 1987.

10. For an account of the meeting, see *Akiračiai* 4 (1988): 1.

11. *Literatūra ir menas*, January 9, 1988.

12. Ibid., June 18, 1988.

13. *Komjaunimo tiesa*, July 13, 1988.

14. A television commentator spoke of Romas Šarmaitis's

Lietuvos revoliucionieriai (Vilnius, 1988) as a welcome effort to fill a "blank spot."

15. Cf. the interview with Albertas Laurinčiukas, published as "'Ne vmeshivaites' v nashi dela!'" *Ogonek* (Moscow) 7 (1988): 6–7.

16. On Šarmaitis, b. 1909, see *Romas Šarmaitis. Biobibliografinė rodyklė*, ed. E. Mertinienė (Vilnius, 1986). On Žiugžda, A. Bacys, et al., *Robertas Žiugžda. Bibliografija* (Vilnius, 1980). In *Bibliotekų darbas* 12 (1989): 19–21, Juozas Čaplikas praised Šarmaitis for having saved books "from destruction," but cf. the views of the spetsfonds expressed by Silvia Vėlavičienė, in the same book, p. 21, and by V. Pšibilskis, "Bibliocidas Lietuvoje," *Kultūros barai*, 12 (1989): 33–37.

17. *Tiesa*, June 21, 1988.

18. Konstantinas Navickas, "Ko reikia objektyviai istorinei tiesai," *Vakarinės naujienos*, October 5, 1988.

19. See J. Žiugžda, *Rinktiniai raštai*, 2 vols. (Vilnius, 1986).

20. See M. Stoškienė, ed., *Bronius Vaitkevičius. Bibliografinė rodyklė (1958–1986)* (Vilnius, 1987).

21. See *Lietuvių nacionalinio išsivadavimo judėjimas (ligi 1904 metų)*, ed. Vytautas Merkys, et al. (Vilnius, 1987), approved for typesetting, January 22, 1987, and for printing on April 7, 1987; *"Aušra" ir lietuvių visuomeninis judėjimas XIX a. pabaigoje*, ed. Jonas Kubilius, et al. (Vilnius, 1988), approved for typesetting November 2, 1987, and for printing on January 18, 1988. Note that the book about *Auszra* did not have the word "national" in its title.

22. *Literatūra ir menas*, April 4 and 25, 1987.

23. Ibid., December 12, 1987. See also *Gimtasis kraštas*, January 1, 1988.

24. Vytautas Merkys, "Istorijos mokslo ir istorikų uždaviniai," *Komunistas* 1 (1988): 53–58.

25. *Tiesa*, February 9, 1988; *Gimtasis kraštas*, February 11, 1988.

26. *Literatūra ir menas*, January 30, 1988.

27. *Pravda*, February 6, 1988.

28. R. Songaila, et al., *Mintys apie Lietuvos valstybingumą* (Vilnius, 1988).

29. K. Navickas, *Lietuvių tautos ir valstybingumo atkūrimas ir įtvirtinimas* (Vilnius, 1988). Calling me a "bourgeois historian," he cited my position on the declaration of February but not on the declaration of December. See also his article "The 1918–1919 Proletarian Revolution in Lithuania," in *Lithuania Today* 1 (1988): 8: "It is a matter of record that the rebirth of Lithuanian statehood took place on December 16, 1918, but not February 16, because it was not the Lithuanian bourgeoisie but the proletarian revolution which put an end to the rule of the German invaders in Lithuania and laid down the foundation of Lithuanian statehood." On Navickas, see Daiva Varžinskaitė, ed., *Konstantinas Navickas. Bibliografinė rodiklė, 1953–1987* (Vilnius, 1987).

30. LIC, January 26, February 3, February 10, February 11, 1988.

31. *Tiesa*, February 14, 16, 1988.

32. LIC, February 12, 1988; *New York Times*, February 17, 1988. See also the report by Paul Quinn-Judge, *The Christian Science Monitor*, February 17, 1988.

33. See DPA, February 18, 1988; Moscow radio, domestic and international, February 18, 1988; *Tiesa*, May 6, 1988.

34. LIC, February 15, 1988; *EIB* 3 (1988).

35. TASS dispatch, February 23, 1988; see also *Sotsialisticheskaia industriia* (Moscow), March 3, 1988.

36. LIC, February 24, 1988.

2. The Debate Erupts

1. On the Lithuanian associations, see Judita Sedaitis and Rimvydas Glinskis, "Nuo Gorbačiovo iki Persitvarkymo Sąjūdžio," *Akiračiai* 9 (1988): 12–14. On such associations generally, see Vera Tolz, "Informal Groups in the USSR in 1988," *Radio Liberty Research*, RL 487/88, October 30, 1988; Mike

Niban, "Popular Fronts and 'Informals,'" *Detente* 14 (1989): 3–
8, 27. In the fall, Vladimir Shcherbitsky, a member of the
Politburo, complained that "the leadership" of some unofficial associations "has been penetrated by extremists" and
that "the social danger of such manifestations is underesti-
mated." Radio Kiev, domestic service, October 16, 1988.

2. Published in *Akiračiai* 7 and 8 (1988); summarized in
EIB 8–II (1988). See also the short memoir by Virgilijus
Čepaitis, published in *Litva literaturnaia* 1 (1989): 163.

3. Interview in Sodus, Michigan, September 10, 1989.

4. Antanas Augus, "Iliuzijų kvaitulys," *Komjaunimo tiesa*,
April 14, 1988; Saulius Pečiulis, "Akla praeities nostalgija,"
Komjaunimo tiesa, April 21, 1988.

5. Leonid Mlechin, "The Popular Front," *New Times* 43
(1988): 25.

6. Juozas Jermalavičius, "Vienpusiškai, be atsakomybės,"
Tiesa, April 30, 1988. See also Jermalavičius's *Socialistinė
ideologija Lietuvoje* (Vilnius, 1987).

7. See *Tiesa*, May 7, 1988; V. Bubnys's letter to the editor
by V. Bubnys, *Tiesa*, May 14, 1988; Bražėnas's article in
Pravda, August 20, 1988.

8. *Gimtasis kraštas*, October 14, 1988.

9. See Nijolė Maslauskienė, "Mūsų istorinė atmintis," *Vakarinės naujienos*, October 10, 1988; *Tiesa*, October 17, 1988.

10. Cf. "Regime Poet Condemns 'Criminal' Deportations,"
EIB 7 (1988); but see also Lionginas Šepetys's comments on
how Marcinkevičius's interest in Lithuanian history had
upset the authorities in the past, *Komjaunimo tiesa*, February
9, 1989.

11. Grinkevičiūtė's memoir had first appeared in Russian,
and the Lithuanian Information Center in Brooklyn, N.Y.,
had published an English translation in 1981: Dalia Grin-
kevicius, *Frozen Inferno* (Brooklyn, 1981).

12. "Skausmingi istorijos puslapiai," *Tiesa*, May 21,
1988. Emigres have published a list of 19,285 names of persons deported in 1940–1941, and they usually estimate the

total at 30,000 to 35,000 persons. See *Išvežtųjų lietuvių sąrašas. Stalino teroras*, ed. Leonardas Kerulis (Chicago, 1981). Dalia Grinkevičiūtė is no. 5,004 on Kerulis's list.

13. LIC, May 9, 1988.

14. On Angarietis, see Alfred Erich Senn, *The Emergence of Modern Lithuania* (New York, 1959), passim; *Zigmas Angarietis. Straipsniai ir atsiminimai*, ed. R. Šarmaitis (Vilnius, 1982).

15. On the demonstration of May 22, see Aleksandras Shtromas, "On the Current Situation in Lithuania," in *OPBPA*, 18; *The New York Times*, May 23, 1988: "Authorities in Vilnius Break Up Rally"; LIC, May 15 and 23, 1988.

16. See Alfonsas Eidintas, "Juodas darbas apie 'baltas dėmes," *Komjaunimo tiesa*, June 15, 1988; *Regina Žepkaitė. Bibliografinė rodyklė* (Vilnius, 1985); Alfred Erich Senn, "Struggle and Impasse: Polish-Lithuanian Relations Between the Wars, *Lituanus* 2 (1983): 72–76.

17. *Moscow News* 16 (April 24, 1988).

18. Šepetys's speech was published in *Literatūra ir menas*, July 21, 1988.

19. See J. Žiugžda, *Tarybų Sąjungos pagalba lietuvių tautai apginant savo laisvę ir nepriklausomybę 1939 ir 1940 metais* (Vilnius, 1949); Kazys Sideravičius, *Sotsialisticheskaia revoliutsiia 1940 goda* (Vilnius, 1965); V. Kancevičius, "'Viršūnės' ir 'apačios' 1940 metu socialistinės revoliucijos Lietuvoje iš-vakarėse," *Už socializmo sukūrimą Lietuvoje* (Vilnius, 1969), 199–207; H. Sadžius, et al., *Pribaltiiskim sovetskim respublikam tridtsat' let* (Vilnius, 1970); *O kharaktere revoliutsii 1940 goda v Pribaltike* (Tallin, 1970); *Lietuvos TSR istorija*, vol. 4 (Vilnius, 1975); I. I. Mints, et al., *Sotsialisticheskaia revoliutsiia v Litve, Latvii, i Estonii* (Moscow, 1978); I. I. Mints, et al., *40 let pribaltiiskim respublikam Soiuza SSR* (Vilnius, 1980); I. I. Mints, ed., *Pobeda sotsialisticheskoi revoliutsii 1940 g. v Litve, Latvii i Estonii* (Vilnius, 1983).

20. See Gediminas Rudis, "Ar Lietuvoje 1940m. buvo grobiami raudonarmiečiai?" *Kultūros barai* 10 (1988): 61–64.;

also his article in *Gimtasis kraštas,* September 15, 1988; Vytautas Žalys, "Ar rengėsi kariauti su TSRS Pabaltijo valstybės?" *Kultūros barai* 8 (1988): 57–60.

21. Strumskis's essay appeared in *Vakarinės naujienos,* August 3, 1988, and Burokevičius's in *Komjaunimo tiesa,* August 12, 1988. *Komjaunimo tiesa* of August 19 reported on the telephone calls. See also the attack on Burokevičius by a former student of his in Rimvydas Valatka, "Išsivadavimas iš mitų," *Gimtasis kraštas,* September 8, 1988. On Burokevičius's work see *Mykolas Burokevičius. Bibliografinė rodyklė,* ed. Jūratė Kapčiuvienė (Vilnius, 1987).

3. Birth of Sajudis

1. See *Literatūra ir menas,* March 12 and 19, April 23, and May 28, 1988, *EIB* 4 (1988): 3–7; and 7 (1988): 12.

2. "More conservative style" in *Eastern European Newsletter,* July 13, 1988; "cautiousness" in Shtromas, "On the Current Political Situation in Lithuania," *OPBPA,* 16. On Estonia at this time, see Rein Taagepara, "Estonia Under Gorbachev: Stalinists, Autonomists, and Nationalists," *OPBPA,* 2–15.

3. *Sąjūdžio žinios* 2 (June 13, 1988). Cf. Zigmas Vaišvila's account of the founding of Sąjūdis in *Respublika* (Vilnius), January 6, 1990. On Vilkas's role, cf. Antanas Buračas's comments in *Respublika,* January 12, 1990.

4. See B. Balikienė's summary of the organizational meeting, *Sąjūdžio žinios* 4 (July 3, 1988); open letter from Vaišvila and S. Lapienis, June 13, 1988, *Sąjūdžio žinios* 2 (June 13, 1988).

5. *Sąjūdžio žinios* 5 (July 4, 1988), 8 (July 11, 1988), 10 (July 19, 1988).

6. See also "Ignalinos atominė ekektrinė: gandai ir tikrovė," *Tiesa,* April 1, 1988.

7. Summary of the meeting by J. Malinauskas and A. Medalinskas, *Sąjūdžio žinios* 1 (June 13, 1988).

8. Cf. Saulius Girnius, "The Catholic Church in 1988,"

Radio Free Europe Research (hereinafter: *RFE*), Baltic Area/ 11, October 5, 1988, pp. 39–42; Stanislovas Balčiūnas's interview with Cardinal Sladkevičius, "'Trokštu vieno—pateisinti savo tautos viltis,'" *Švyturys* 19 (1988): 4–9.

9. Cf. "There Is No Freedom Without Freedom of Conscience" [in Lithuanian], *Sąjūdžio žinios* 14 (July 27, 1988).

10. *EIB* 6 (1988): 16. Emigre publications referred to the "proto"-league as "the Lithuanian patriotic movement." Cf. Kestutis Girnius, "Lithuanian Dissent: Proud Past, Uncertain Future," *RFE*, Baltic Area/11, October 5, 1988, pp. 33–37.

11. Program distributed in mimeographed form; see also *EIB* 8 (1988): 12–13; LIC, July 22, 1988.

12. *Tiesa*, June 9, 1988; *EIB* 7 (1988): 17–19. Cf. Terleckas's talk at Vilnius University, December 1988, reported in *Mažoji Lietuva* (Klaipėda), January 6, 1989.

13. Marius Valevičius, "Zyzimas palei herostrato ausį," *Tiesa*, August 6, 1988. On the league's efforts to stand close to Sąjūdis, see also Shtromas, "On the Current Political Situation in Lithuania," *OPBPA*, 21–22.

14. Sąjūdis spokespersons also complained publicly about their telephones' not working properly. See *Sąjūdžio žinios*, passim.

15. *EIB* 8 (1988): 7.

16. LIC, June 13, 1988.

17. Cf. "Religion Is Gorbachev's Enemy—Nijolė Sadūnaitė," *EIB* 4–II (1987), also 5 (1987).

18. See the interview with Sladkevičius published in *Sovetskaia Litva*, July 29, 1988. Some sympathizers of the league were in fact shocked by a public letter league leaders addressed to Sladkevičius insisting that he endorse the league denunciation of the Molotov-Ribbentrop Pact.

19. Statement at a press conference, Vilnius, October 21, 1988, *Suvažiavimo biuletenis* 2: 4.

20. Cf. the adulatory "Truth in Motion," *Moscow News*, September 18, 1988.

21. See *Komjaunimo tiesa*, September 3, 1988.

4. The Period of Mass Rallies

1. See LIC, June 8 and 14, 1988; *Vakarinès naujienos*, June 15, 1988; *Izvestiia*, June 16, 1988. Juozaitis reminisced about the events of June 13 to 24 in an interview in Sodus, Michigan, September 10, 1989.

2. Meeting reported in *Sąjūdžio žinios* 3 (June 28, 1988).

3. Ibid.

4. *Sąjūdžio žinios* 4 (July 3, 1988) and 7 (July 7, 1988).

5. *Vakarinès naujienos*, June 23, 1988.

6. See *Atgimimas* 1 (September 16, 1988).

7. *Tiesa*, October 27, 1988.

8. *Sąjūdžio žinios* 4 (July 3, 1988).

9. *The New York Times*, June 27, 1988, reported, "Lithuanian intellectuals rally for greater autonomy."

10. See V. Petkevičius, "Didysis anonimas. Kaip gimė Lietuvos Persitvarkymo Sąjūdis," *Švyturys* 2 (1989): 8–10; LIC, July 7, 1988. Cf. Lionginas Šepetys's comment on how, in 1988, one could deal differently with the Russian second secretaries. *Komjaunimo tiesa*, February 9, 1989.

11. *Gimtasis kraštas*, June 16, 1988; LIC, June 24, 1988; *EIB* 8 (1988): 6–7.

12. The Lithuanian Information Center in Brooklyn gave Landsbergis even shorter shrift, reporting that 50,000 people attended a rally demanding "a sovereign Lithuania" and noting that Landsbergis "also addressed the crowd." LIC, June 25, 1988.

13. *Sąjūdžio žinios* 5 (July 4, 1988); LIC, July 27, 1988.

14. *Gimtasis kraštas*, June 30, 1988; *Vakarinès naujienos*, June 23, 1988. See the favorable portrait of *Gimtasis kraštas* offered in *Izvestiia*, October 9, 1988.

15. *Materialy XIX vsesoiuznoi konferentsii Kommunisticheskoi partii Sovetskogo Soiuza* (Moscow, 1988), 61.

16. Ibid., pp. 134–140.

17. *Gimtasis kraštas*, July 7, 1988.

18. Cf. "National Question in the XIX Conference—Under the Rug," *EIB* 8 (1988).

19. *Tiesa,* July 9, 1988.

20. Edmundas Rimša, Gediminas Rudis, "Tautinės vėliavos spalvos," *Komjaunimo tiesa,* July 9, 1988. This article, together with a number of other articles from the periodic press about national heroes and symbols, was republished in *Iš kur atėjome,* ed. A. Nekrošienė (Kaunas, 1988).

21. *Komjaunimo tiesa,* July 12, 1988.

22. An article in *Sąjūdžio žinios* 14 (July 27, 1988) blamed conservatives who wanted to prevent Sąjūdis banners from being flown.

23. The group had trouble getting their report published in the central press: *Sovetskaia Litva* had it set in type and then rejected it; *Vakarinės naujienos* gave a preliminary report, July 13, 1988, but delayed and then called a full report too dated. *Sąjūdžio žinios* 30 (August 29, 1988). The report finally made its way into the public press on October 4, 1988, published by *Komjaunimo tiesa.* See also *Sąjūdžio žinios* 9 (July 16, 1988).

24. *Sąjūdžio žinios* 30 (August 29, 1988).

25. Cf. Čekuolis's comments in *Gimtasis kraštas,* December 29, 1988.

26. Geda's speech reprinted in *Sąjūdžio žinios* 10 (July 19, 1988).

27. See *Vakarinės naujienos,* July 11, 1988.

28. *Sąjūdžio žinios* 9 (July 16, 1988). See also Remigijus Auškelis's article, *Sąjūdžio žinios* 5 (July 4, 1988).

29. Ibid. 9 (July 16, 1988).

30. See *Tiesa,* July 17, 1988; *Sąjūdžio žinios* 19 (August 10, 1988).

31. See *Vakarinės naujienos,* July 11, 1988.

32. Cf. Aleksandras Shtromas, "On the Current Political Situation in Lithuania," *OPBPA,* 21–22.

33. LIC, July 12, 1988.

34. Ibid.; *Vakarinės naujienos,* July 11, 1988; *Sąjūdžio žinios* 9 (July 16, 1988).

35. See *Vakarinės naujienos,* July 16, 1988; letter published in *Sąjūdžio žinios* 20 (August 11, 1988); LIC, July 12, 1988;

Sąjūdžio žinios 9 (July 16, 1988); *Vakarinės naujienos,* July 13, 1988.

36. See *Vakarinės naujienos,* July 16, 1988; report in *Sąjūdžio žinios* 38 (September 14, 1988).

37. Quoted in J. Ivanauskaitė, "Ir šviesa ir tiesa mus žingsnius telydi," *Nemunas* 12 (1988): 23. Videotapes of the Rock March are available in the United States. See also *Sąjūdžio žinios* 24 (August 18, 1988). On Antis see Peter Riggs, "Lithuania: Outrageous Acts of Music," *Whole Earth Review* (Winter 1989), 64–66.

38. Interview in Sodus, Michigan, September 10, 1989.

39. *EIB* 8–II (1988): 9, reported 7,000 participants. See also *Vakarinės naujienos,* July 28, 1988; *Sąjūdžio žinios* 16 (July 28, 1988).

40. *Sovetskaia Litva,* July 29, 1988, carried the decision of the USSR Supreme Soviet. The Lithuanian decree, dated August 2, was published on August 4.

41. *Sąjūdžio žinios* 16 (August 2, 1988).

5. The Visitation

1. *Vakarinės naujienos,* July 20, 1988; Arnoldas Piročkinas, "Valstybinės kalbos problema," *Komjaunimo tiesa,* July 20, 1988; *Literatūra ir menas,* July 30, 1988; see also *Sovetskaia Litva,* June 15, 1988.

2. English service of Radio Vilnius, July 25, 1988. See also the comments of Juras Požela, president of the Academy of Sciences, *Vakarinės naujienos,* July 25, 1988; and the comments of Eduardas Vilkas in *Vakarinės naujienos,* September 16, 1988.

3. TASS dispatch, August 1, 1988.

4. *Gimtasis kraštas,* September 8, 1988.

5. For an account of demographic trends, see S. Vaitekūnas, et al., *Karta keičia kartą* (Vilnius, 1986); K. Surblys, *Tarybų Lietuvos gyventojai* (Kaunas 1987).

6. See DPA, June 7 and 16, 1988; Stanislaw Kadziewicz, "The Lost Tribe: Poles in the USSR," *Studium Papers* 1 (13): 13–15.

7. *Sovetskaia Litva*, July 22, 1988; *Sąjūdžio žinios* 11 (July 22, 1988).

8. *Sovetskaia Litva*, July 17, 1988.

9. *Sąjūdžio žinios* 12 (July 23, 1988); cf. Petras Bražėnas's comments in *Pravda*, August 20, 1988.

10. *Czerwony sztandar*, September 4, 1988; cf. the letter to the editor from Henryk Gaigalas, *Czerwony sztandar*, September 7, 1988.

11. Meeting recounted in *Sąjūdžio žinios* 23 (August 17, 1988).

12. Transcripts of both meetings in *Tiesa*, August 14, 1988.

13. Cf. Vytautas Landsbergis's comments in *Sąjūdžio žinios* 27 (August 22, 1988). On the activity of Čekuolis and other Sąjūdis figures in America in September, see *Akiračiai* 9 and 10 (1988).

14. Transcript of meeting in *Tiesa*, August 16, 1988.

15. E. Tadevosian, in *Politicheskoe obrazovanie* 13 (1988).

16. See the interview with Bishop Vaclovas Aliulis, *Tiesa*, December 4, 1988.

17. *Vakarinės naujienos*, August 17, 1988.

18. *Tiesa, Sovetskaia Litva*, and *Czerwony sztandar*, August 23, 1988.

19. *Sąjūdžio žinios* 26 (August 20, 1988) and 31 (August 31, 1988).

6. Exposing the Secret

1. See *Falsifiers of History: An Historical Document on the Origins of World War II* (New York, 1948), introduction by Frederick L. Schuman.

2. *Sąjūdžio žinios* 17 (August 5, 1988).

3. Ibid., 21 (August 13, 1988).

4. See *EIB* 10 (1988) 8.

5. Ibid., 8–II (1988): 8.

6. *Sąjūdžio žinios* 28 (August 23, 1988). *Vakarinės naujienos* carried a brief notice on the meeting, signed by Landsbergis, on August 22. See also LIC, May 19 and 23, 1988.

7. Arvydas Juozaitis and Arūnas Degutis in *Sąjūdžio žinios* 29 (August 26, 1988).

8. Reprinted in *Sovetskaia Litva*, August 19, 1988.

9. *Vakarinės naujienos*, August 17, 1988.

10. Cf. "Apologias for Pact in Lithuanian Official Press: Traditional Excuses and Minor Admissions," *EIB* 10 (1988): 9.

11. *Komjaunimo tiesa*, August 23, 1988.

12. The proceedings were published in full in *Atgimimas* 1 (September 16, 1988) and in its Russian version, *Vozrozhdenie*.

13. Cf. Landsbergis's statement in *Komjaunimo tiesa*, August 15, 1988; statements by Sąjūdis representatives meeting with Eismuntas, *Kauno Aidas* 8 (August 31, 1988); *Sąjūdžio žinios* 30 (August 29, 1988).

14. *Tiesa*, August 25, 1988.

15. *Sąjūdžio žinios* 31 (August 31, 1988).

16. *Kalba Vilnius*, September 2, 1988; *Sąjūdžio žinios* 32 (September 2, 1988).

7. A New Political Culture

1. The discussions in the tent are recorded on an unlabeled videotape circulating in the United States. See also the letter from Cidzikas, *Sąjūdžio žinios* 31 (August 31, 1988); report in *Sąjūdžio žinios* 33 (September 5, 1988); Bartosevičius's criticism of Article 68, *Sąjūdžio žinios* 32 (September 2, 1988).

2. Mečislovas Jučas, Ingė Lukšaitė, Vytautas Merkys, *Lietuvos istorija. Nuo seniausių laikų iki 1917 metų* (Vilnius, 1988).

3. *Sąjūdžio žinios* 24 (August 18, 1988).

4. DPA, August 24, 1988.

5. See *Komsomol'skaia pravda*, August 24, 1988; *Pravda*, September 1, 1988.

6. Donatas Sauka, "Polemikos pamokos," *Komjaunimo tiesa*, October 1, 1988.

7. Cf. Rimvydas Valatka's tough but correct interview with the procurator of the Lithuanian republic, Liudvikas Sabutis, in *Švyturys*, September 27, 1988.

8. Radio Vilnius, English program, September 22, 1988; *Current Digest of the Soviet Press* 43 (40): 7–8.

9. There was no press account of the meeting in the Academy of Sciences; on the meeting in the Žinija society, see *Vakarinės naujienos*, November 15, 1988.

10. Juozas Urbšys, *Lietuva lemtingaisiais 1939–1940 metais* (Vilnius, 1988), approved for typesetting September 15 and for printing September 26. The memoirs were published earlier in the United States in Juozas Urbšys, *Atsiminimai* (Chicago, 1988).

11. *Tiesa*, September 25, 1988. Cf. R. Rajeckas, "Ekonominiai tikslai ir terminologinė kazuistika," *Tiesa*, September 21, 1988.

12. See the Žinija society's handbook for lecturers, co-sponsored by Sąjūdis and published in October: *Lietuvos ekonominio savarankiškumo koncepcija* (Vilnius, 1988). The agreement was written in Russian. When readers criticized the Lithuanian text, comparing it to the Russian as published in *Sovetskaia Litva*, Emelianov, the editor of *Sovetskaia Litva*, expressed delight that his newspaper still had so many readers.

13. DPA, February 3, 1988. On the general criticism at this time of life in the Soviet army, see "USSR: The Army's Stariki Factor," *Eastern European Newsletter*, January 27, 1988.

14. See Kęstutis Girnius, "No Love Lost Between the Military and the Lithuanian Restructuring Movement," *RFE*, Baltic Area/1, January 5, 1989.

8. Sąjūdis Comes of Age

1. Stenogram of meeting published in *Kauno aidas* 8 (August 31, 1988).
2. Artūras Andrušaitis, "Tautos vėliava—į mokyklą," *Sąjūdžio žinios* 32 (September 2, 1988).
3. *Tiesa*, September 16, 1988.
4. *Sąjūdžio žinios* 23 (August 17, 1988).
5. *Vakarinės naujienos*, June 23, 1988.
6. *Sąjūdžio žinios* 11 (July 22, 1988).
7. The discussions with officials from Moscow were shown on Lithuanian television on September 1. See also *Sąjūdžio žinios* 34 (September 7, 1988).
8. See *Tiesa*, September 7 and 9, 1988.
9. *Sąjūdžio žinios* 35 (September 8, 1988). LIC, September 6 and 7, 1988, gave the Freedom League credit for first calling for international supervision.
10. *Komjaunimo tiesa*, September 10, 1988; LIC, September 14, 1988.
11. *Kalba Vilnius*, September 30, 1988.
12. A summary of the meeting of September 13 can be found in *Akiračiai* 9 (1988). On the meeting's call for action at Ignalina, see Paul Quinn-Judge, "Lithuanians Say No to Nuclear Power," *Christian Science Monitor*, September 14, 1988.
13. *Vakarinės naujienos*, September 19, 1988; LIC, September 18, 1988; Saulius Girnius, "A Protest at the Ignalina Atomic Power Plant," *RFE*, Baltic Area/11 (October 1, 1988): 19–22.

9. Confrontation in Gediminas Square

1. The account of the events on Gediminas Square is based on information I received from eyewitnesses and also on vid-

eotapes as well as on information to be found in the press. See especially *Atgimimas* 3. The most complete report in the official Lithuanian press appeared in *Czerwony sztandar*, October 1, 1988.

2. Mimeographed copy of the Freedom League's announcement of the rally.

3. LIC, September 27, 1988.

4. Ibid.

5. Ibid., September 28, 1988. On government claims that the troops did not use force, see *Sovetskaia Litva*, November 6, 1988.

6. LIC, September 28, 1988. On videotapes, which show little in the darkness, one can also hear shouts of "To the tower!"

7. Saulius Girnius, "Police Disperse Demonstrations," *RFE*, Baltic Area/11: 24.

8. "Panorama," September 29, 1988; *Sovetskaia Litva*, September 30, 1988; *Czerwony sztandar*, October 1, 1988; *Tiesa*, October 1, 1988; *Current Digest of the Soviet Press* 43 (40): 1.

9. LIC, September 29, 1988.

10. Speaking on television on September 19, Landsbergis declared that he knew little about the Freedom League. Immediately after the meeting in Gediminas Square on the twenty- ninth, he indicated to me that he had not even known Terleckas by sight before that afternoon.

11. Bogušis estimated the crowd at 5,000, LIC, September 29, 1988. I claim no expertise, but Rimvydas Valatka of *Gimtasis kraštas* and I both estimated the crowd to be smaller.

12. *Tiesa*, October 2, 1988.

13. *Literatūra ir menas*, October 7, 1988.

14. *Tiesa*, October 6, 1988.

15. *Vakarinės naujienos*, October 14, 1988.

16. *Tiesa*, October 9, 1988.

17. Cf. the versions of his speech published in *Tiesa*, October 7, 1988, and in *Sąjūdžio žinios* 45 (October 14, 1988).

10. Removal of the Party Secretaries

1. *Tiesa*, October 7, 1988; *Current Digest of the Soviet Press* 43 (40): 1.

2. In *Sąjūdžio žinios* 38 (September 14, 1988), Dainius Juozėnas suggested October 28, the anniversary of the Lithuanian march into Vilnius in 1939, as a good date to raise the flag.

3. *Tiesa*, October 7, 1988.

4. LIC, October 7, 1988.

5. Ibid.

6. On the history of the Dawn Gate, *Aušros vartai* in Lithuanian, see Juozas Jurginis, *Aušros vartai* (Vilnius, 1987).

7. Petkevičius on television, reprinted in *Kalba Vilnius,* October 14, 1988.

8. See *Moscow News* 44 (1988).

9. On Saturday, October 15, Sąjūdis sponsored a meeting of representatives of the minority nationalities of Lithuania with the aim of organizing their representation at the congress. See *Komjaunimo tiesa*, October 18, 1988; Marytė Kontrimaitė, "Konferencija, bet ne konfrontacija!" *Literatūra ir menas*, October 22, 1988.

10. *Komjaunimo tiesa*, October 22, 1988.

11. *Tiesa*, October 18, 1988.

12. *Literatūra ir menas*, October 22, 1988.

13. DPA, October 21, 1988.

14. Lecture at Vilnius University, transcribed in *Mažoji Lietuva* (Klaipėda), January 6, 1989; see also *Akiračiai* 1 (1989): 3.

15. Rumor also had it that no Russian newspapers from the Baltic were available in Moscow on Friday the twenty-first. On subsequent decisions to investigate killings in June 1941, see *Sovetskaia Litva*, November 6 and 24, 1988.

11. The Sąjūdis Congress

1. On the Great Vilnius Seimas of 1905 see Michal Römer, *Litwa. Studyum o odrodzeniu narodu litewskiego* (Lwow, 1908),

382–436; Pranas Čepėnas, *Naujųjų laikų Lietuvos istorija*, 2 vols. (Chicago, 1977–1986), 1: 339–349.

2. Both programs were published in *Atgimimas* 3 (October 15, 1988). Subsequently criticized for having formed a "bloc," Kaunasites blandly explained that they had only appeared to have formed a bloc because they had met beforehand and formed "common opinions." Antanas Antanaitis on Lithuanian television, November 6, 1988.

3. See *EIB* 1 (1989): 10–11.

4. *Komjaunimo tiesa*, October 25, 1988, spoke of this as an "examination" for "our democracy."

5. Afanasiev was undoubtedly the Russian historian most quoted in Vilnius in the fall of 1988. On his public pronouncements, see *Literaturnaia Rossiia*, June 17, 1988, and *Pravda*, June 25, July 26, and July 31, 1988.

6. Cf. the critique of foreign reporting in Vidas Rachlevičius, "'Nacionalinis katarsis' spaudos karuselėje," *Komjaunimo tiesa*, January 11, 1989.

7. I have published a more personal account of the congress and its aftermath in *Akiračiai* 1, 2, and 3 (1989).

12. Into a New Era

1. See *The New York Times*, October 28, 1988. Moscow did not care for the thought that perestroika and glasnost had encouraged the Lithuanians. Vadim Medvedev insisted that "the exacerbation of interethnic relations in some regions cannot be perceived as a consequence of restructuring." The new conditions simply opened discussion of "problems which had gradually built up over decades." *Pravda*, December 20, 1988.

2. DPA, October 23, 1988.

3. *Moscow News* 44 (1988).

4. Cf. how Kapelushny was praised in *Vakarinės naujienos* of November 14, 1988.

5. *Tiesa*, November 7, 1989.

6. *Sovetskaia Litva*, November 11, 1988; *Komjaunimo tiesa*,

November 12, 1988. On complaints about attacks on Russians in Vilnius, see *Sovetskaia Litva,* November 5, 1988.

7. *Pravda,* November 22, 1988.

8. Edinstvo held its own conference in Vilnius in January 1989. Radio Vilnius, English Program, January 23, 1989. For the thoughts of a Pole, Jan Ciechanowicz, who supported *Edinstvo,* see the interview with him published in *Lad* (Warsaw) 42 (1989), and also his speech reprinted in *Gimtasis kraštas,* January 12, 1990.

9. *Tiesa,* December 11, 1988; *Krasnaia zvezda,* January 17, 1989; *EIB* 12 (1988): 10. During my own experience as an outpatient in a trauma center in Vilnius, I met several doctors, both Russians and Lithuanians, who all spoke both languages.

10. LIC, October 31, 1988.

11. Cf. the comments by Vytautas Martinkus in *Tiesa,* December 4, 1988.

12. Copies of the Academy of Sciences' draft for constitutional reform were circulated in mimeographed form in September and October 1988. The academy's call for a separate citizenship so reminded me of the Swiss laws of cantonal and federal citizenship that I asked Juozas Bulavas whether the committee had examined the Swiss model. He told me it had not.

13. *Tiesa,* November 16, 1988. On Sliunkov's background, see Michael E. Urban and Russell B. Reed, "Regionalism in a Systems Perspective: Explaining Elite Circulation in a Soviet Republic," *Slavic Review* 3 (48): 413–431.

14. See DPA, November 14 and 15, 1988; *Pravda,* November 16, 1988.

15. Cf. the Freedom League's declaration: "The League protests against the Soviet administration's appropriation of the symbols of the Lithuanian nation's freedom and independence—the tricolor, the national anthem, and the emblem of *Vytis.*" *EIB* 1 (1989): 10.

16. According to *The New York Times* of December 2 and

4, 1988, after the Soviets had given "fair hearing" to Baltic protests, five deputies had voted against the constitutional change and twenty-seven had abstained, all coming from the Baltic. In *Moscow News* 49 (1988) Leonid Kapelushny noted that Lithuanians in Vilnius did not protest the vote in Moscow: "The Monday-morning papers carried no sensational news." Kapelushny's report has an odd ring to it in that normally there are no Monday-morning Lithuanian newspapers.

17. Moscow radio, domestic service, November 29, 1988.

18. Vilnius radio, December 2, 1988.

19. Moscow radio, domestic service, December 15, 1988.

20. Radio Vilnius, January 26, 1989.

21. Cf. Saulius Girnius, Baltic Area/12 (October 28, 1988): 24: "The Lithuanian Restructuring Movement is being forced into taking more radical measures by the actions of the Lithuanian freedom League, an organization of Lithuanian dissidents . . . grown rapidly in a few months." See also V. Stanley Vardys, "Lithuanian National Politics," *Problems of Communism*, July-August 1989, p. 58: "The League's main achievement has been to radicalize Sąjūdis and even certain elements in the CPL." See also the reports in *EIB* 1 (1989).

22. Bieliauskas's speech was reprinted in *Gimtasis kraštas*, October 27, 1988; on Nakas, see *The New York Times*, October 27, 1988.

23. Cited in *Akiračiai* 1 (1989): 2.

24. As a sign of the spirit of this session of the Supreme Soviet, the first item on the agenda was the resignation of Jonas Gureckas as the secretary of the Presidium of the Supreme Soviet. In November Gureckas had come under heavy attack for his role in the parliamentary maneuverings that had postponed discussion of the "nullification" proposal, and in February he had given one of the most impassioned speeches denouncing Sąjūdis.

25. The Lithuanians, who had the largest treasury of the three groups, made a large financial contribution to the meeting. For an account of the Lithuanians' participation in the

Baltic Assembly, see Liūtas Mockūnas, "Svečiuose Pabaltijo Asamblėjoj," *Akiračiai* 7 (1989): 6–10.

26. Interview in *Pravda*, August 18, 1989.

Afterword

1. For more detail, see my articles in *Akiračiai*, nos. 2 and 3 (1990).

2. Texts printed in *The Lithuanian Review* (Vilnius) 3 (March 23, 1990).

3. See Ruta Grinevičiutė, "Mirė karalius—tegyvuoja karalius," *Gimtasis kraštas*, March 8, 1990.

Biographical Note

**Members of the Sajudis Initiative Group
Elected, June 3, 1988**

Adomaitis, Regimantas, actor, chairman of the theater society.
Bulavas, Juozas, lawyer, corresponding member of the Lithuanian Academy of Sciences.
Bubnys, Vytautas, writer.
Buračas, Antanas, economist, member of the Lithuanian Academy of Sciences.
Čekuolis, Algimantas, editor *Gimtasis kraštas.*
Čepaitis, Virgilijus, writer, translator.
Daunoras, Vaclovas, opera singer.
Geda, Sigitas, poet.
Genzelis, Bronius, philosopher, professor.
Juozaitis, Arvydas, philosopher.
Juzeliunas, Julius, composer.
Kaušpedas, Algirdas, architect, leader of rock group Antis.
Kudaba, Česlovas, geographer, chairman of the Cultural Fund.
Kuzmickas, Bronius, philosopher.
Landsbergis, Vytautas, musicologist.
Leonavičius, Bronius, artist, chairman artists' union.
Lukšaite, Inge, historian (resigned).

Lukšiene, Meile, pedagogue.
Maldonis, Alfonsas, writer.
Marcinkevičius, Justinas, writer.
Medalinskas, Alvydas, economist.
Minkevičius, Jokubas, philosopher.
Nasvytis, Algimantas, architect.
Ozolas, Romualdas, philosopher.
Pakalnis, Romas, forester, ecologist.
Pečiulis, Saulius, economist.
Petkevičius, Vytautas, writer.
Prunskiene, Kazimiera, economist.
Radžvilas, Vytautas, philosopher.
Rajeckas, Raimundas, economist, member of the Lithuanian
    Academy of Sciences.
Skučas, Arturas, architect.
Songaila, Gintaras, physician.
Šaltenis, Arvydas, artist.
Tomkus, Vitas, journalist.
Vaišvila, Zigmas, physicist.
Žebriunas, Arunas, film director.

**Other Persons Mentioned Prominently
in This Study:**

Andreika, Algimantas, hunger striker.
Astrauskas, Vytautas, chairman of the Presidium of the
    Supreme Soviet.
Barysas, Mindaugas, editor of *Tiesa*.
Beriozov, Vladimir, party secretary, replaced Mitkin as head
    of party organization October 4.
Bogušis, Vytautas, leader Lithuanian Freedom League.
Brazauskas, Algirdas, party secretary, elected first secretary
    October 20.
Cidzikas, Petras, hunger striker.
Ciechanowicz, Jan, prominent Pole in Vilnius.

Eidintas, Alfonsas, deputy director of the Institute of History, Lithuanian Academy of Sciences.

Eismuntas, Eduardas, chief of Saugumas (Committee of State Security).

Imbrasas, Stasys, party Central Committee specialist for Education.

Jurginis, Juozas, historian, member of the Lithuanian Academy of Sciences.

Kašauskiene, Vanda, director, Institute of Party History, Party Central Committee.

Kavaliauskas, Vilius, journalist for *Tiesa*.

Laurinčiukas, Albertas, editor of *Tiesa*.

Lisauskas, Stasys, minister of Internal Affairs.

Martinkus, Vytautas, president of Writers' Union, delegate to Nineteenth Party Conference.

Merkys, Vytautas, director, Institute of History, Lithuanian Academy of Sciences.

Mitkin, Nikolai, party second secretary, went on vacation, October 20.

Navickas, Konstantinas, historian, Vilnius State University.

Paleckis, Justas, party Central Committee specialist for cultural affairs, chosen party secretary for ideology by the Twentieth Congress of the Lithuanian Communist Party.

Požela, Juras, president of the Lithuanian Academy of Sciences.

Rudis, Gediminas, Institute of History, Academy of Sciences.

Sakalauskas, Vytautas, chairman of the Council of Ministers.

Šarmaitis, Romas, former director of Institute of Party History.

Šepetys, Lionginas, party secretary in charge of ideology.

Slyžius, Česlovas, party Central Committee specialist for propaganda and agitation.

Songaila, Ringaudas, party first secretary, resigned October 19, 1988.

Terleckas, Antanas, leader Lithuanian Freedom League.

Truska, Liudas, docent, Vilnius Pedagogical Institute.

Vaitkevičius, Bronius, former director, Institute of History, Academy of Sciences.

Vileikis, Algirdas, mayor of Vilnius.

Vilkas, Eduardas, secretary of the presidium of the Lithuanian Academy of Sciences.

Zaleckas, Kestutis, head of the Vilnius city party organization.

Žepkaite, Regina, Institute of History, Academy of Sciences.

Chronology of Major Events

1987

Aug. 23   Demonstration in Vilnius in commemoration of Molotov-Ribbentrop Pact.

1988

Feb. 16   Demonstrations in Vilnius commemorating Declaration of Independence of 1918.

Apr. 20   Talk by Arvydas Juozaitis on "Political Culture."

Apr. 21   Article by Saulius Pečiulis in *Komjaunimo tiesa*.

Apr. 30   Article by Juozas Jermalavičius in *Tiesa*.

May 21–22   Demonstrations commemorating Stalinist purges and deportations.

May 28   Party announces delegates to Nineteenth Party Conference.

June 3   Formation of Sajudis.

June 14   Demonstration in Gediminas Square. Raising of tricolor flag.

June 24	Departure of delegates for Nineteenth Party Conference.
July 9	Demonstration in Vingis Park greeting delegates to Nineteenth Party Conference.
Aug. 11–14	Aleksandr Iakovlev's visit to Vilnius.
Aug. 17	Legalization of *National Hymn* and tricolor flag. Beginning of hunger strike.
Aug. 23	Demonstration in Vingis Park, commemorating Molotov-Ribbentrop Pact.
Aug. 30	Eismuntas's meeting with Sajudis.
Sept. 3	Ring around the Baltic.
Sept. 5	Fire at Ignalina.
Sept. 17	Living Ring around Ignalina.
Sept. 28	Government action against demonstrators in Gediminas Square.
Oct. 4	Central Committee Plenum.
Oct. 7	Tricolor raised over Gediminas Castle.
Oct. 19	Songaila's resignation.
Oct. 20	Central Committee Plenum. Brazauskas becomes party first secretary.
Oct. 22–24	Sajudis Congress.

Index

Society and Culture in East-Central Europe

General Editors: Irena Grudzinska-Gross and Jan T. Gross

Jan Jozef Lipski, *KOR: A History of the Workers' Defense Committee in Poland, 1976–1981,* translated by Olga Amsterdamska and Gene M. Moore

Adam Michnik, *Letters from Prison and Other Essays,* translated by Maya Latynski

Maciej Lopinski, Marcin Moskit, and Mariusz Wilk, *Konspira: Solidarity Underground,* translated by Jane Cave

Alfred Erich Senn, *Lithuania Awakening*

Designer:	U.C. Press Staff
Compositor:	Prestige Typography
Text:	11/14 Aster
Display:	Aster
Printer:	Edwards Brothers, Inc.
Binder:	Edwards Brothers, Inc.